Atlas of
Stateless Nations
in Europe

Atlas of
Stateless Nations
in Europe

Minority peoples
in search of recognition

Edited by
Mikael Bodlore-Penlaez

Translated by
Sarah Finn and Ciaran Finn

Contents

Lexicon:

Identity card:
• the superscript numbers (^{12345}) indicate the language used.
• the notes ($^{note\,123...}$) refer to the explanatory list of notes at the end of the work, page 158.

Maps:
The towns are indicated by the different signs according to their population and their status:

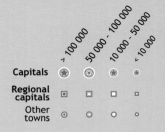

Work edited by:
Mikael Bodlore-Penlaez
bodlore@eurominority.eu
www.eurominority.eu

in collaboration with:
Constantin Andrusceac, Jakez an Touz, Kári á Rógvi, Grégory Aymé, Yannick Bauthière, Estève Castan, Ghjuvà di Cirnu, José Francisco Figueiro Vicente, David Forniès, Øyvind Heitmann, Philip Hosking, Wolter Jetten, Sullõv Jüvä, Hannes Kell, Mari Kerpuñs, Divi Kervella, Alban Lavy, Dídac López, Bareld Nijboer, Michôł Òstrowsczi, Perdu Perra, Pablo Orduna Portús, Dewi Prysor, Andrea Rassel, Sjúrður Skaale, Bartłomiej Świderek, Jean-Georges Trouillet, Filip van Laenen

Y Lolfa Cyf.
Talybont, Ceredigion, Cymru/*Wales* SY24 5HE
www.ylolfa.com • +44(0) 1970 832 304

Layout and maps: **Mikael Bodlore-Penlaez**

ISBN 978-1-84771-379-7
First French edition: Éditions Yoran Embanner, Breizh, 2010
This English language edition: © Y Lolfa Cyf., 2011
Printed and bound in Wales by Y Lolfa Cyf.

Preface

Bernat JOAN I MARÍ
Former member of European Parliament
Secretary for Linguistic Policy of the Generality of Catalonia
Member of the European Free Alliance (EFA) and the Republican Left of
Catalonia (Esquerra Republicana de Catalunya)

The image we have of the European Union and its diversity varies according to
observers. For pro-Europeans who do not challenge the state-nations as they have
been shaped since the eighteenth century, the European Union is simply the sum
of its member states. To be visible in Europe, it is necessary to have one's own
state. Without this condition, it is difficult for people to find their place.

The structure of Europe involves another level to that of states: citizens, who
take part in the intrinsic process of realizing the European ideal, since Europe is
not only a political entity but defines itself by common cultural elements. Moreover, the Copenhagen Criteria lays the foundations of what can be our shared val-
ues on the basis of future common citizenship.

This European citizenship, in other words a Europe of the citizens, is jointly built
with a Europe of the cities, to which so much is contributed by the emblematic
mayors of the big European metropolises.

However, the Europe of the states – European Union as it was configured politically – just like its citizens and cities, would be unsound without all the elements
constituting the variety and diversity of our continent and its unique wealth.

Europe cannot only be a Europe of states, even relying on federalism, as some
people reasonably suggest. Equally, it cannot be exclusively a Europe of the citizens. It would risk diluting us in a kind of cosmopolitan facade or in an artificial
"melting pot", which does not translate into our point of view the true spirit of
the European Union.

It is also necessary to take into account the stateless nations, regions and national
minorities. Without these, the European structure would be imperfect, and Europe could see itself criticised for the difficulties met by minorities, which would
constitute a real disaster. Europe is certainly not responsible for the subordination
of people by states that appear foreign. Also, one cannot make it responsible for
the way certain states treat their national minorities. However, the lack of action
by Europe on the subject could end up engineering less desire for the building of
a United Europe. Ultimately, Europe must embrace its diversity.

Unfortunately, that which makes our continent diverse seems to be unknown by
a large part of European citizens, notably those who have the ability to take deci-
sions in Brussels or Strasbourg. Essentially, it is about the "underground" or "sat-
ellite" diversity formed by the numerous stateless nations and national minorities
who populate Europe. Being interested in this situation contributes to awareness

of the internal wealth of Europe and to the debate on the model that we wish to build, to know a Europe fully and completely at ease.

In this sense, the *Atlas of Stateless Nations* edited by Mikael Bodlore-Penlaez is of great interest. In basing it on his experience, notably on the site eurominority.eu (Internet site of stateless nations), he has produced an exhaustive work on stateless nations and national minorities, compiling a complete panorama of this little-known part of national European variety.

It is, by consequence, a useful work for all of those who wish to know about the "complex" national situations in Europe. It equally facilitiates discovery of the political processes currently in motion, the foreseeable changes and those who are sometimes less in the different regions of Europe. Ultimately, this atlas allows a glimpse at the new national "enthusiasms", that are emerging on our continent, going well beyond the narrow spectrum of stateless nations.

The numerous years of research carried out by Mikael Bodlore-Penlaez on this subject are now available to the general public by means of this atlas. It will be an invaluable aid to actors on the political stage, who serve European interests, national or regional. This work will equally be useful for all those wishing to better know the underlying national multiplicity of Europe of the states and, obviously, for open spirits who know that the nation is not always fulfilled by being subject to a state.

It is highly possible that in a couple of years from now the correlation between nations and states will be different from what it is today, as much as it is now compared to the period before the fall of the Berlin Wall and, earlier still, before the Treaty of Versailles. Nations have a tendency to want to set up sovereign states or contrarily to let them die slowly. It is by no means about an excess of determination, but ultimately the will of the citizens to know what they want, having the ability (or not) to stand up to the pressures inevitably felt by stateless nations. The ultimate value of this atlas is in drawing a complete panorama of the reality of stateless nations at this the start of the 21st century, in being aware that everything evolves, that lines move and that in all logic, the conditions to establish a sovereign state (or not) equally evolve.

Introduction

The news shows us so vividly that so many people worldwide have been struggling for recognition. Whether it is Tibet, Kurdistan or the Basque Country, claims are similar despite strongly contrasting political situations. These claims, which are often expressed violently, can be summed up in three points: greater desire for recognition, expression of a particular strength and the right to self-determination. These aspirations appear legitimate in more and more democratic societies. However, minority peoples encounter a number of difficulties in making their voice heard. Their basic rights are often violated or else secretly abused regardless of international texts, which nonetheless encourage states to recognise minorities, their languages and to respect the integrity of their territory. Contrary to some prejudices, these hopes have nothing to do with ultra-nationalist one-upmanship. On the contrary, it is an expression of a similar feeling of unease experienced on all continents by nations in search of freedom.

Stateless nations, people and national minorities

Europe has a large number of people who aspire for more freedom. They are sometimes called national or "ethnic minorities", "nationalities", "minority peoples" or "stateless nations". These four terms deal with the same thing, but are often perceived in a different way. While the term "national minority" characterises a situation of guardianship with regards to that of a majority, the term "stateless nation" is more neutral. It simply means the people who have lost or never acquired their sovereignty. Thus, in Europe, there are roughly thirty cases corresponding to the definition of "stateless nations", which are distinguished by their political status, vitality of their language and their desire for emancipation. Whether it is the Basques, Catalans, Scottish, Frisians or the more anonymous Ladins or Sorbs, one constant allows them to be grouped together under this term. Even if some groups sometimes have specific rights, essentially that of using their language, others are simply denied the right to exist. In response to simple questions, this work allows a better understanding of the situation of these people of Europe.

The Europe of diversity

Europe is a model of diversity, which perfectly illustrates its motto *United in diversity*. Respecting differences has become a given, history having shown that hate and intolerence only lead to chaos. Encouraged to accept others, to enter into their world, to listen to their language so as to savour the melody is sometimes so rewarding. Unfortunately the reflexes of rejection or ignorance remain, notably concerning stateless nations and minority peoples who must permanently struggle to survive. However, the European Council advises, at a minimum, respect of minority cultures and linguistics. Protecting diversity allows preservation of the original identity of our continent. To ignore minority peoples is to drive them into decline and to lose a little bit of the soul of our continent. In an ever increasing globalised world, they represent an indisputable cultural richness.

Eastern Europe: minorities yesterday, free today

Since the middle of the 19th century the tendency to ignore the minority phenomenon has had grave consequences in history. For example, the fall of the Berlin Wall in 1989 and the revolutions that marked the end of the 20th century brought back onto the international scene people who had up until then been forgotten. A moribund Europe haunted by the Cold War, we spent a few years liberating a number of minorities oppressed by authoritarian regimes. These events were sometimes painful but, by definition, allowed many people to find their legitimacy in the ranks of nations. These movements were marked by the independence of the Republics of the Soviet Union, the split of Czechoslovakia and the conflict in Yugoslavia. Rare for European history, events progressed very quickly. Also rare, the minorities achieved their independence quite suddenly. Who could imagine a few years beforehand that eleven nations (Latvia, Lithuania, Estonia, Belarussia, Ukrainia, Moldovia, Slovakia, Slovenia, Bosnia, Serbia and Croatia) would be independent 15 years after the fall of the Berlin Wall?

Western Europe: what fate for the stateless nations?

But history does not stop there! After this frenzy of independence, Western Europe was touched by another revolutionary phenomenon. It concerns the face of devolution, autonomy and decentralisation which has been emerging for 15 years. The status of Southern Catalonia is reinforced today by its greater autonomy. The countries of Wales and Scotland are already passing legislation in their own parliaments. Italy finally became a federal state and has a proposed programme of autonomy "à la carte". And tomorrow, what will happen? Montenegro has recently gained its independence, like Kosovo, as a result of strong international pressure. Scotland and the Basque Country are getting ready to organise referenda on self-determination. These few examples show that history is in perpetual motion. Europe is not a static continent and its people are alive. They are certainly guided, most often in protest, by a strong desire for freedom. Actually, minority peoples struggle to obtain the position that they believe can hold them in independent or autonomous regard in Europe or at least allow them to express their particularisms without the decree of an oppressive majority. Without doubt, it is that which one calls the freedom of thought, the freedom of acting and, more simply, the freedom to be oneself!

Minority peoples in the world

A number of people live in minority situations around the world, notably in Europe. But perhaps the most emblematic cases are certainly those of Tibet, Kurdistan and Chechnya, which demonstrate the diversity of the minority phenomenon on our planet. Actually, even if it is easy to draw a parallel between these three territories a priori, their history, their position with regards to the central state and their means for recognition are very different in all aspects.

Tibet

For a start, according to the Tibetans, Tibet is made up of a homogenous linguistic territory, which the government call "great historic Tibet". Indeed, even if Tibetans have their own territory within the Republic of China, it is divided. Two other regions (Qinghai and part of Xixhuan) make up part of historic Tibet, where a little more than 6 million inhabitants live. More than 150,000 Tibetans currently live in exile, mainly in India, in the same manner as the Dalai Lama, the spiritual leader, who fled in 1959 at the time of the revolts, which claimed many tens of thousands of victims. Before the invasion of the country at this time by China, Tibet alternated between many regimes classified as feudal by the opposition. Currently, the slightest opposition to the Chinese regime or autonomist or separatist demonstrations are repressed, often violently.

Kurdistan

Since the Middle Ages Kursdistan (Kurdewarî) is a vast divided territory between which Turkey, Iran, Iraq and Syria presently lie. The Kurds are arranged in these different countries according to totally different statuses. In Iraq in 1987, the Kurds obtained considerable autonomy which allowed them to express their culture, their language and to benefit from the natural resources of their territory. This status was obtained following considerable repression by the Baathist regime of Saddam Hussein, which was hidden from the outside world under the guise of granting rights to the Kurds. This repression resulted in the death of more than 200,000 people. After the First World War and the dissolution of the Ottoman Empire, the creation of a Kurdish state was forecast, a project that was quickly aborted. The Western states, dominating the region at the time, crushed every revolt. In Turkey, the situation has not been much better. Indeed, since the 1920s it led a policy of repression while carrying out massive deportation and the "Turkishisation" of the region. Opposition political movements were formed, notably the creation of the PPK (The Kurdistan Workers' Party) in 1978, which leads guerilla warfare operations. This situation rouses anti-Kurd sentiment on the Turkish side, leading the government to arrest and abuse representatives (deputies, mayors of big towns) for simply having used the Kurdish language in public. These dealings tarnish the image of Turkey and have been denounced many times by international organisations including the European Union. Indeed, by overwhelming the Kurdish people, aggressively assimilating them and giving them no place in public debate, Turkey does not grow in stature by such practices. Unfortunately, the Kurds are the main victims.

Chechnya

Of the three examples of minority peoples in the world, much has been written about Chechnya. Equally, many lives have been lost. The Chechen Republic, named Ichkeria by the independents, is a territory under Russian administration in the Caucasus. This part of the world gathers a great number of people of very diverse origin (Caucasians, Indo-Europeans, Turks and Mongols). This mosaic places a number of conflicts in the glare of the world's media: Abkhazia and Southern Ossetia formally under Georgian rule, Nagorno-Karabakh in Azerbaijan and Chechnya in Russia. Although the region was only independent for a short time in 1995, the Chechens have been fighting against Russian rule since the 18th century. The autonomous region was founded in 1922, changing status over the course of decades of political upheaval in Russia and the USSR. Culturally and linguistically Chechnya is very close to neighbouring Ingushetia, a region with which its fate has often been linked. Its Muslim culture and clans are the basis of society. Indeed, clan alliances (*Tieps*) punctuate political and social life. The two conflicts that marked the end of the 1990s commenced with the unilateral declaration of independence by Chechen authorities setting up a sharia regime (Islamic law) and an alliance with the Taliban power in Afghanistan. There were many tens of thousands of deaths and 350,000 people were displaced.

The autonomy of Chechnya was not called into question after the conflict and the ability of the local authorities is very strong despite the vassalage with regards to the regime in Moscow. Chechen fighters continue to fight against Russia and also against the Chechen authorities currently in place, i.e. the Kadyrov clan.

Protest for the independence of Tibet

What is a minority?

The term "minority" refers to many concepts often related and difficult to comprehend. If it is so that this term precludes those of the majority, its definition often becomes delicate when associated with humanity. The complexity of human relations and the multiplicity of situations makes researching a universally accepted definition difficult. Even in international law, no definition of "minority" exists. There are different definitions depending on whether they are texts of the United Nations or the Council of Europe. The UN more readily uses the terms "ethnic, religious or linguistics minorities", while the European texts uses the term "national minorities". It should be noted that despite the absence of a legally binding definition of the term "minority", many agree that a minority must meet objective characteristics (such as language, traditions and cultural patriotism) and a subjective factor, namely the will of its members to assert themselves as such, and assert their commitment to that which makes their identity specific. In developing European texts to defend the rights of minorities, one of the failings was requiring minorities to define the word itself, to find the minimum criteria that enable a group of individuals to be classified as a national minority.

National minority

A "national minority" commonly refers to a population living in a minority situation within a state. There are two types: the people of eponymous states like the Danish in Germany or the Hungarians in Romania. By extension, it also applies to non-sovereign people who do not have their own state structures. The latter are "stateless nations". Brittany, the Basque Country and Friesland are examples of this.

Ethnic minority

By ethnic minorities one means both national minorities as well as allogenic minorities, that is groups of non-indigenous people and foreign communities. The Maghrebis in France or the Turks in Germany are even considered ethnic minorities. Canadian legislation defines them as "visible minorities". The term "ethnicity", derived from the ancient Greek εθνος, meaning "people" or "nation".

Linguistic minority

National and ethnic minorities are often linguistic minorities. The Welsh or the Catalans are linguistic minorities in the state on which they depend, but they can hardly be described as such, their respective languages being spoken by the majority in the whole or in part of their territory. In rare cases, certain groups are able to speak a maternal language other than the state majority without being qualified as national or ethnic minorities. This is the case for the French population of Switzerland.

Religious and sexual minorities

Religious or sexual minorities, even if they fall outside the scope of this work, are often cited when discussing the question of minorities. Among the most famous minorities are the Irish Catholics, the Jews of Morocco and the Muslims of Belgium. Gender minorities correspond to sociological groups in terms of sexual orientation. Homosexuals and lesbians are the most characteristic example.

National minority

According to the definition given in Recommendation 1201 of the European Council on national minorities, national minority is defined as a group of people in a state who:

- **reside in the territory of that state** and are citizens there,
- maintain **longstanding, firm and lasting ties with that state,**
- display **distinctive ethnic, cultural, religious or linguistic characteristics,**
- are sufficiently **representative**, while being fewer in number than the rest of the population of that state or a region of that state,
- are motivated by **a desire to preserve their culture, their traditions, their religion or their language**.

This definition completely obscures the differences which can exist with other minority groups.
Indeed, the term "minority" can refer to three major groups:
– national, ethnical, linguistic and cultural minorities,
– religious minorities,
– sexual or gender minorities.

World, major nations involved in strong claims

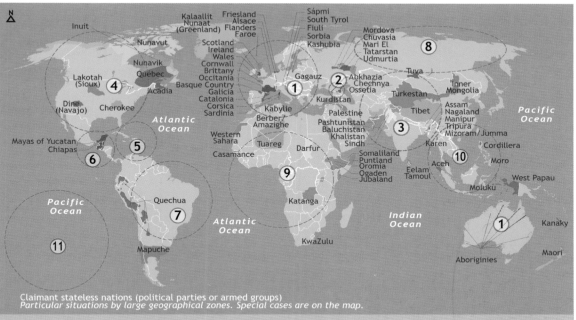

Claimant stateless nations (political parties or armed groups)
Particular situations by large geographical zones. Special cases are on the map.

1/ Western Europe: *Stateless nations fighting for more recognition*
2/ Caucasus: *high concentration of people, many of which are in conflict*
3/ Central Asia: *numerous conflicts for the creation of new states*
4/ North America: *Indian people reduced to occupying reservations*

5/ Caribbean: *highly mixed population without dominant people*
6/ Central America: *numerous Indian people (Maya, Aztec, Mixtec, Zapotec, Kakchikel, K'iche...)*
7/ South America: *Indian people very poorly represented in the general population*

8/ Siberia: *large areas populated by minorities in small numbers*
9/ Africa: *multi-ethnic States with low minority claim*
10/ South-East Asia: *strong presence of undemanding minority*
11/ Pacific Ocean: *many sparsely populated islands, some fighting for independence*

Demonstration of Kurdish Peshmerga in Northern Iraq

Nations, states and stateless nations

Why talk of "stateless nations" rather than "national minority"? The term "stateless nations" largely transcends that of "minority" which is often very restrictive and perceived in a derogatory manner. The term "minority" defines a state relative to a majority. However, it does not refer specifically to what it aspires to be, that is to say a minority people with the characteristics of a nation without having the attributes of a sovereign state. Accordingly, defining the terms "nation" and "stateless nation" seems essential.

In the beginning, the tribe?

"Minority" refers to many terms which often have political overtones. Whenever one speaks of "minority", one often thinks of tribes and ethnicities. In fact tribe is a type of minority, more specifically qualified as indigenous or first people. Also, these minorities can be native or foreign.

The nation, a dual concept

The nation, for its part, is a human community having the belief of belonging to the same group. It falls within defined geographical boundaries. Thus, numerous minorities are defined as people or nations. The distinctive characteristics of a nation are language, culture, religion, history… In contrast, certain nations recognise themselves without being homogenous. In fact, even if language constitutes one of the corner stones of nations, some are multilingual (and respect this fact) or they are comprised of distinct religious communities.

The Council of Europe tried to find a consensus definition of the concept of nation. This exercise is complicated where, according to the languages and the states, this word is perceived differently. Certain countries use it to define their citizenship, i.e. the legal relationship between citizens and the state. Others use it in the sense of a united ethnolinguistic community.

In Latin, however, the word "natio" is derived from "nascere" (to be born). It was used in the Middle Ages to describe membership of a community. In the 18th century, this concept evolved into being related to a community of individuals enjoying equal rights independent of ethnic origin. This concept is very close to the definition of the State-nation or civic nation. In contrast, the notion of the cultural nation is, for its part, a concept defining the nation as a homogenous ethno-linguistic entity.

In its conclusions concerning the definition of the term "nation", the Council of Europe considers that these two definitions are "once again valid today". True, but can we compel a community to accept these two definitions? In fact, the text of the Council of Europe quotes from Ernest Renan, a Breton author considered to be one of the theoreticians of the nation. "'The Nation' is a daily plebiscite". This sentence sums up the situation. We cannot force people to live in a state without their consent and, worse, make them deny their own identity in order to be a citizen of that state, such as the Kurds in Turkey.

How are the minority peoples of Europe classed? An attempt to classify them into four categories: stateless nations, national minorities, indigenous people and nomadic people as well as regions with strong identities that may have similar characteristics to minority peoples.

The state and state-nation

The state is a form of political organisation, based by nature on the sovereignty of the nation. The state is the setting in which the people or the nations can legislate and vote for their own territorial laws. The state-nation characterises a sovereign state constituted objectively or artificially by a desire to live together. We can distinguish between the state-nation and the nation-state. The state-nation can enforce a national feeling. France, Greece and Turkey correspond to the archetypeal state-nation. Conversely, a group can be recognised as a nation and manifest its desire to live together in establishing a state, which we would call a nation-state.

Stateless nations

A stateless nation is a non-sovereign nation with no state structures. Its people often live in varying degrees of attachment to their original nation. Thus there exists in all the stateless nations feelings of identity that can be qualified as contradictory.

Stateless nations

- Alsace
- Arpitania (Aosta & Savoy)
- Basque Country
- Brittany
- Catalan Countries
- Cornwall
- Corsica
- Faroe (Islands)
- Flanders
- Frisia
- Friuli
- Ireland (province of Ulster)
- Isle of Man
- Gagauzia
- Galicia
- Kashubia
- Ladinia
- Occitania
- Romansh
- Sápmi (Laponia)
- Sardinia
- Scotland
- Sorabia
- South Tyrol
- Wales
- Wallonia

National minorities

Community member of an eponymous state
- Åland (Islands)
- Albanians
- Arabs
- Armenians
- Belarussians
- Bosnians
- Bulgarians
- Croats
- Czechs
- Danes
- Estonians
- Finnish
- Germans
- Greeks
- Hungarians
- Irish
- Italians
- Latvians
- Lithuanians
- Luxembourgians
- Macedonians
- Montenegrins
- Poles
- Romanians
- Russians (even Transnistria)
- Serbs
- Slovaks
- Slovenians
- Swedish
- Tatars
- Turks
- Ukrainians

Native people

People sharing their territory with other communities
- Aromanians
- Bunjevci (Bunyevtsi)
- Cimbre
- Csángó
- Ingres
- Lipoviens
- Livonians
- Ludian
- Miranda
- Mocheno
- Pomaks
- Vepsians
- Votes
- Walser

People with a strong identity

- Azores
- Aragon
- Asturias
- Canary (Islands)
- Low Germans
- Madeira
- Moravia
- Ruthenians
- Scania
- Seto
- Silesia
- Voro

Nomadic people

- Roma
- Yeniche

Nations, states and stateless nations

Europe, the nations and the people

Barents Sea

Reykjavik
ICELAND

Karasjok
Enare

Kiruna

Norwegian Sea

SAAMI COUNTRY

FAROE
Torshavn

Karelia

FINLAND

NORWAY

Olso

Helsinki

Stockholm

Tallinn

SCOTLAND

Edinburgh

North Sea

SWEDEN

ESTONIA

RUSSIA

LIVONIA

Moscow

DENMARK

Riga

LATVIA

IRELAND **MAN**

Dublin

Scania
Copenhagen

LITHUANIA

Vilnius

Minsk

WALES

ENGLAND

FRIESLAND

Leeuwarden

Gdansk

KASHUBIA

BELARUS

Cardiff

Amsterdam

Berlin

Varsovia

Truro
CORNWALL

London

NETHERLANDS

FLANDERS

POLAND

Kiev

*Atlantic
Ocean*

Brussels

WALLONIA

Namur
LUX.

GERMANY

SORBIA

Silesia

BRITTANY

Nantes

Paris

Prague

UKRAINE

FRANCE

Strasbourg

CZECH REP.

Moravia

ALSACE

Vienna

SLOVAKIA

Bratislava

MOLDOVA

LIECHT.

AUSTRIA

TRANSNISTRIA

SWITZ. Chur *South
Tyrol*

Budapest

Chișinău

Santiago

Asturias

SAVOY

ROMANSH
LADINS

SLOVENIA

HUNGARY

GAGAUZIA

GALICIA

**BASQUE
COUNTRY**

OCCITANIA

AOSTA

Udine

Ljubljana

Zagreb

CRIMEA

Pamplona

Toulouse

Lombardy

FRIULI

Venice

CROATIA

ROMANIA

PORTUGAL

Aragon

Monaco

San Marino

BOSNIA-
HERZEGOVINA

Belgrade

Bucharest

Black Sea

Lisbon

Madrid

Barcelona

CORSICA

ITALY

Sarajevo

SERBIA

SPAIN

Corte

Rome

MONTENEGRO

Podgorica

Sofia

BULGARIA

CATALAN COUNTRIES

VATICAN

Skopje

ALBANIA

MACEDONIA

Ankara

Andalucia

SARDINIA

Tirana

Cagliari

AROMANIA

Mediterranean Sea

TURKEY

GREECE

Athens

Sicily

Nicosia

MALTA

CYPRUS

HISTORIC NATIONS
Other regions with a strong identity
● Capitals

0   500   1 000 km

Map of "Europe of the people". On this map the people of Europe are represented in their most objective configuration possible if we count the notion of "stateless nations". This map is not the map of official states but more a prospective map of what could be, tomorrow, the Federal Europe of the people.

- Certain people do not exclusively feel part of their nation of origin.
- Others, on the contrary, exclusively feel they are members of the state of which they are citizens
- Finally, a fraction of the population is often divided by two identities, the citizenship acquired by the state and the nationality which attaches it to the nation of origin. Indeed, strictly speaking, citizenship is the link which heightens the authority of the state, contrary to nationality, which is relative to the feeling of belonging to a community in a nation (without necessarily being a constituted state).

From nation to nationalism

Nationalism is the expression which consists of imposing one's view of the world. It is expressed either by the desire to impose one vision of the nation, the so-called negative nationalism, or it can be characterised by the desire to assert one's existence as a nation. This is positive nationalism. These claims may lead to two scenarios: the introduction of a regional autonomy system or the desire for self-determination.

Autonomy

Autonomy allows people to have their own powers and to legislate. Autonomy is characterised by devolution, i.e. the transfer of powers from central state to a more local level. Thus Catalonia, the Basque Country, Scotland or, to a lesser degree, Friesland and Sardinia are today autonomous regions. Unfortunately, many people do not have any status to express their individuality. This is particularly the case of the stateless nations present in France, such as Brittany, Alsace and Corsica, or Kashubia in Poland.

Self-determination

More radical forms of demands can be expressed, such as the quest for independence, i.e. the total detachment from the central state. This is separatism or secessionism. Despite its often sustained character, this is recognised by international law. The right to self-determination is written in the UN Charter, whose objective is "to develop friendly relations among nations based on the principle of equal rights of people and their right to self-determination". In the English version, the term "self-determination" is more explicit.

Ethnocentrism, no to dialogue!

Others consider that this right corresponds to communitarianism or ethocentricism, i.e. the desire to live closed in on oneself and to refuse the dogma of the indivisible state. Denying the existence of minorities, identities and regional languages tends to impose a sectarian and imperial vision of the nation.

Conflicts and claims

Numerous demonstrations are regularly organised by the members of minority communities to claim more rights, notably language. When they gather 10,000 people, as is often the case in Brittany, they are ignored by the mainstream media. However, how can we forget the tens of thousands of Catalans marching through the streets of Barcelona at the start of 2006 in order to urge their leaders to reform the statute of autonomy of the Autonomous Community and thus register Catalonia as a nation? They marched under the banner *som una nació* (We are a nation). These peaceful demonstrations of cultural or political players often have a positive impact but the changes are slow to be put in place.

There are three main types of claims ranging from seeking more recognition to the desire to self-administer, or to benefit from an autonomous status, be that by seceding. It largely depends on the capacity of the state to respect differences and to assign individual powers to minorities. When the attitude of the central state is highly sectarian, irritations arise and this creates tensions leading to conflicts, latent or totally open.

Armed struggle

Forms of radical actions emerge regularly in territories populated with minorities. The most significant examples are the armed conflicts which were particularly prevalent in Ireland or in the Basque Country, where two clandestine organisations operate. Since the War of Independence in Ireland (1919–21), the IRA (Irish Republican Army) was opposed to British power and particularly the Ulster Unionists. In the Basque Country, ETA (Euskadi ta Askatasuna) led a national liberation struggle against the Franco dictatorship until its end (1959), but soon drifted into the organisation of attacks individually targeting civilians. Other territories are or have been marked over the last fifty years by the actions of clandestine armed struggles, such as Corsica, Brittany, South Tyrol or Wales. Finally, Kosovo had to face this type of conflict before the unilateral declaration of independence. In 1997, the Kosovo Liberation Army (UÇK) led an organised guerilla war against the Serbian army. This led to the suppression of autonomous status which existed there a few years previously. These "paramilitary" actions, classified as "terrorists", opposing members of the local organisations of the central power, are most often brutal and reflect a complex situation, the result of misunderstanding, a lack of dialogue and systematic blockages to all claims.

Political struggle

The struggle on "peaceful" political ground is certainly the most used means of expression. These benefits are less profiled than violent actions but enable significant progress. The majority of people fighting in Europe, disapproving of terrorism elsewhere, use this democratic path when the means is given to them. Moreover, in consultation with the central states, the stateless nations may decide upon their status, decentralised, autonomous or independent. Most world conflicts could be resolved if the states accepted the right to self-management and to self-determination.

Europe, waves of independence since the 1990s and current activities

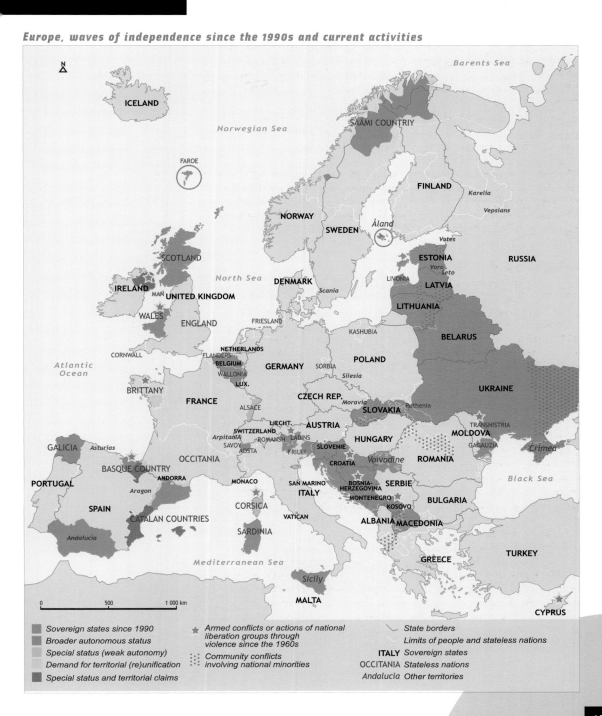

N

ICELAND

Barents Sea

Norwegian Sea

SAAMI COUNTRIY

FAROE

FINLAND

Karelia

Vepsians

NORWAY

SWEDEN

Åland

Votes

RUSSIA

ESTONIA

Voro *Seto*

SCOTLAND

North Sea

DENMARK

Scania

LIVONIA

LATVIA

IRELAND

MAN UNITED KINGDOM

LITHUANIA

WALES

ENGLAND

FRIESLAND

KASHUBIA

BELARUS

CORNWALL

Atlantic Ocean

NETHERLANDS

FLANDERS

BELGIUM

GERMANY

SORBIA

POLAND

WALLONIA

Silesia

UKRAINE

LUX.

BRITTANY

FRANCE

CZECH REP.

Moravia

Ruthenia

ALSACE

SLOVAKIA

LIECHT.

AUSTRIA

TRANSNISTRIA

SWITZERLAND

Arpitania

LADINS

MOLDOVA

SAVOY

ROMANSH

HUNGARY

GAGAUZIA

Crimea

AOSTA

FRIULI

SLOVENIE

GALICIA

Asturias

OCCITANIA

CROATIA

Voivodine

ROMANIA

Black Sea

BASQUE COUNTRY

ANDORRA

MONACO

SAN MARINO

BOSNIA-HERZEGOVINA

SERBIE

PORTUGAL

Aragon

ITALY

MONTENEGRO

SPAIN

CORSICA

KOSOVO

BULGARIA

VATICAN

CATALAN COUNTRIES

SARDINIA

ALBANIA

MACEDONIA

Andalucia

Mediterranean Sea

GREECE

TURKEY

Sicily

MALTA

CYPRUS

0   500   1 000 km

Sovereign states since 1990

Broader autonomous status

Special status (weak autonomy)

Demand for territorial (re)unification

Special status and territorial claims

Armed conflicts or actions of national liberation groups through violence since the 1960s

Community conflicts involving national minorities

State borders

Limits of people and stateless nations

ITALY Sovereign states

OCCITANIA Stateless nations

Andalucia Other territories

Legislation protecting minorities

Two international texts protecting the minorities and their languages are now drawing the attention of minority peoples. These are the European Charter for Regional or Minority Languages and the Framework Convention for the Protection of National Minorities dating from 1992 and 1995 respectively.

Thanks to these two texts, a legislative framework for minorities is able to protect people, often in a position of weakness in the face of overwhelming majorities. Obviously these are not the only international instruments to defend the rights of minorities. State laws sometimes take minority directly into consideration, not least by entering into their constitutions the existence of national minorities and the multilingual nature of society.

European Charter for Regional or Minority Languages

In practical terms, the European charter is the first real enterprise of Europe in favour of multilingualism, that is to say all the states that are members of the European council. This charter provides a variety of actions that the signatories agree to undertake to protect and promote historical regional languages. They must choose "à la carte" at least thirty-five of these acts. The following domains are involved and correspond to sensitive sectors in terms of multilingual policy: education, justice, public services, media, cultural activities, economic and social life. These different sectors correspond to areas of linguistic dissemination and transmission important to the survival of language.

Many states have now signed and ratified this document. It is valid only upon ratification. The first states to apply the charter were Norway, Finland,

Framework Convention for the Protection of National Minorities

0   500   1 000 km

■ Model States: signed and ratified
■ Late States: signed but not yet ratified
■ Refractory States: neither signed nor ratified

Europe, Framework Convention for the Protection of National Minorities

Hungary and the Netherlands from 1993 to 1996. They were the states that had already taken minorities into account in their legislation. It is true that certain states are particularly proactive in this area. This is true in the case of Hungary, which has the most complete arsenal to defend the thirteen minorities living on its soil. This policy in favour of minorities also has the stated aim of encouraging states to respect the Hungarian minorities present (Slovakia and Romania in particular).

Framework Convention for the Protection of National Minorities

The framework convention is a document composing of 34 articles largely defining the rights of minorities, not only in terms of language but for participating in public debate and political life.

Today, whether in respect of one or the other of these two texts, a few member states of the Council of Europe put forward a strong preference to neither sign nor ratify it, namely France, Turkey and Greece. Portugal is a particular case: there is no established minority. The three others are evidence of a pathological blindness regarding the question of minorities. This negative attitude can have serious consequences, in particular the decline of regional languages, considered a universal cultural wealth.

Other texts...

Also, all the international organisations (UN, UNESCO, OSCE) make extensive reference to national minorities in the texts of Protection of Human Rights and Dignity of the Human Being. Examples include the Bill of Rights of Persons Belonging to National or Ethnic, Religious or Linguistic Minorities, passed by the UN on 18 December 1992, the Convention for the Protection and Promotion of

European Charter for Regional or Minority Languages
- Model States: signed and ratified
- Late States: signed but not yet ratified
- Refractory States: neither signed nor ratified

0   500   1 000 km

Europe, European Charter for Regional or Minority Languages

the Diversity of Cultural Expressions by UNESCO, widely promoted in 2005 by France seeking to defend its cultural exception or the final Helsinki Act of 1975, which refers to national minorities and regional cultures.

Languages

Europe, historic linguistic domains

Languages of Europe

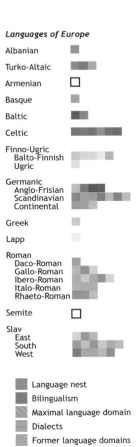

Albanian

Turko-Altaic

Armenian

Basque

Baltic

Celtic

Finno-Ugric
  Balto-Finnish
  Ugric

Germanic
  Anglo-Frisian
  Scandinavian
  Continental

Greek

Lapp

Roman
  Daco-Roman
  Gallo-Roman
  Ibero-Roman
  Italo-Roman
  Rhaeto-Roman

Semite

Slav
  East
  South
  West

Language nest

Bilingualism

Maximal language domain

Dialects

Former language domains

Language isolates

People often forge their specificity from the languages spoken in their territory. However, this is not the only element of their identity. Thus, Europe has over two hundred languages and language varieties that are practised today. However, the European Union acknowledges only twenty-three of these while the states which comprise it often concentrate on only a single language, granting some rights to other languages to a degree. Indeed, language discrimination is a major issue in recent years.

The Europeans speak languages of all origins, the most represented groups being Germanic, Romance and Slavic. These are Indo-European languages, i.e. with common characteristics in linguistic terms (original vocabulary, syntax, grammatical traits etc.), although they are sometimes difficult to detect. Other Indo-European language groups are made up of Celtic and Baltic languages. Other groups exist in Europe, notably the Finno-Ugric language (Hungarian and Finnish are the two most spoken in the group). Similarly, a few isolated languages are also present on the continent. Thus, the Turko-Altaic languages are used in a few regions of Eastern Europe. Finally, the Basque region, whose origin will be discussed, closes this simplified table on the diversity of European languages.

State-nations have used linguistic assimilation as a means to integrate people and have usually imposed a single language to the detriment of others spoken in captured territories. Most states have behaved in this way, including Germany, the Netherlands, France, Spain and Italy.

However nowadays, multiculturalism and tolerance have become international norms, with many states recognising native languages. Driven by local populations and supra-national institutions like the Council of Europe, they have no other choice but to allow their citizens to use their languages freely and also to recognise them officially in order to enable their dissemination and their survival. This new European order has encouraged specific legislation on regional languages.

For example, the European Charter for Regional or Minority Languages provides a better account of languages. It defines a regional language as one being traditionally spoken in a region without it being the language of all the citizens of the state, but prasticed by a group that is numerically inferior to the rest of the population of the same state. However, this language may be a majority in this region.

Languages

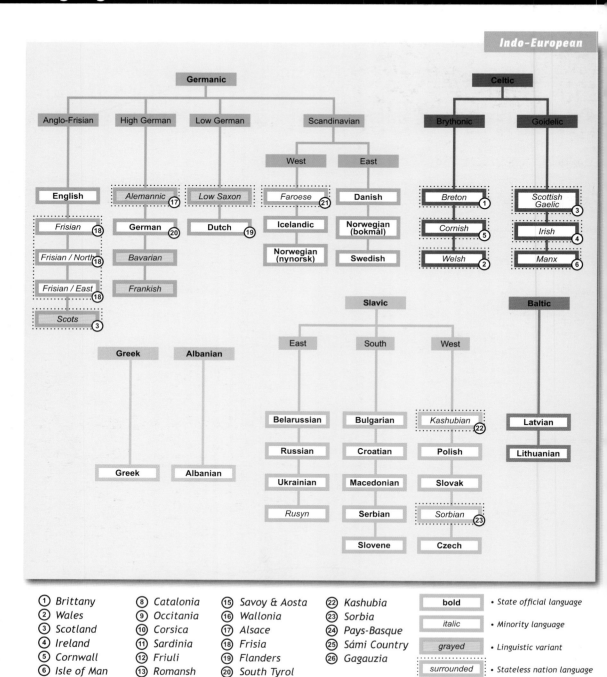

	bold	• State official language
	italic	• Minority language
	grayed	• Linguistic variant
	surrounded	• Stateless nation language

① Brittany   ⑧ Catalonia   ⑮ Savoy & Aosta   ㉒ Kashubia
② Wales   ⑨ Occitania   ⑯ Wallonia   ㉓ Sorbia
③ Scotland   ⑩ Corsica   ⑰ Alsace   ㉔ Pays-Basque
④ Ireland   ⑪ Sardinia   ⑱ Frisia   ㉕ Sámi Country
⑤ Cornwall   ⑫ Friuli   ⑲ Flanders   ㉖ Gagauzia
⑥ Isle of Man   ⑬ Romansh   ⑳ South Tyrol
⑦ Galicia   ⑭ Ladins   ㉑ Faroe

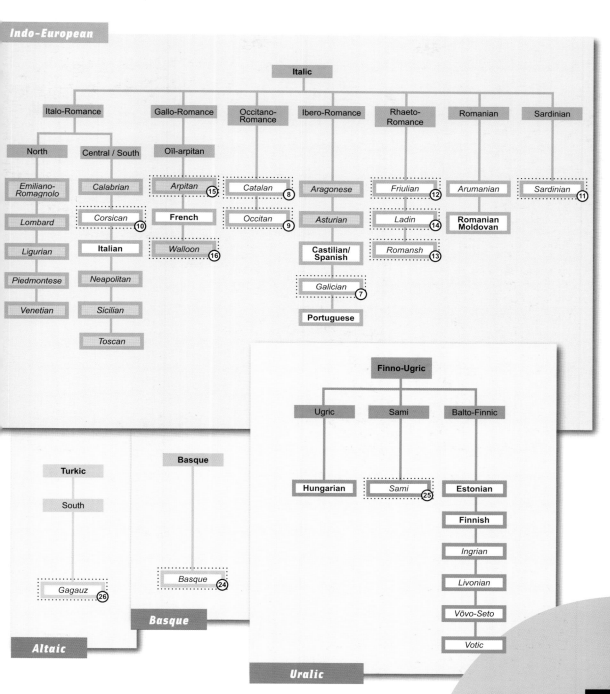

Indo-European

Italic
- Italo-Romance
  - North
    - *Emiliano-Romagnolo*
    - *Lombard*
    - *Ligurian*
    - *Piedmontese*
    - *Venetian*
  - Central / South
    - *Calabrian*
    - *Corsican* ⑩
    - **Italian**
    - *Neapolitan*
    - *Sicilian*
    - *Toscan*
- Gallo-Romance
  - Oïl-arpitan
    - *Arpitan* ⑮
    - **French**
    - *Walloon* ⑯
- Occitano-Romance
  - *Catalan* ⑧
  - *Occitan* ⑨
- Ibero-Romance
  - *Aragonese*
  - *Asturian*
  - **Castilian/Spanish**
  - *Galician* ⑦
  - **Portuguese**
- Rhaeto-Romance
  - *Friulian* ⑫
  - *Ladin* ⑭
  - *Romansh* ⑬
- Romanian
  - *Arumanian*
  - **Romanian Moldovan**
- Sardinian
  - *Sardinian* ⑪

Finno-Ugric
- Ugric
  - **Hungarian**
- Sami
  - *Sami* ㉕
- Balto-Finnic
  - **Estonian**
  - **Finnish**
  - *Ingrian*
  - *Livonian*
  - *Võvo-Seto*
  - *Votic*

Turkic
- South
  - *Gagauz* ㉖

Basque
- *Basque* ㉔

Altaic

Basque

Uralic

23

Languages

The term "minority language" is often used in the sense of "regional language", a distinction between the two often being difficult to make. Indeed, the first term is often perceived in a derogatory manner and does not always match the reality of the situation. The second supposes that the language is regionalised and spoken in a defined region. Thus, the expression "less common language" is often substituted. The lesser-used languages are less practised than the other languages of the territory. In fact, Catalan is not a minority language in Catalonia since it is spoken by almost the entire population. Moreover, it is a language spoken by nearly ten million people. On the other hand, on a state scale this term can represent a definite reality. Certain regional languages can be equally spoken in two different states, like the Basque region which is recognised at different levels by both autonomous communities of the Euskadi and the Navarre but has no official status in Iparalde, i.e. the northern Basque region, which is part of the French state.

Equally, cross-border languages can be official in one state and considered a minority language in another. This is the case for German, Hungarian and Danish for example. German is the official language in Germany but it is in the minority in Belgium, Hungarian is the official language in Hungary but it is in the minority in Romania and Danish is for its part a minority in Germany.

Finally, the third case of minority languages in Europe concerns the languages that are not spoken in any particular region, such as Romani or Yiddish. They are dispersed or nomadic languages.

The list of regional languages is quite long. We estimate that 50 million citizens of the 450 million that make up the EU speak a lesser-used language. This table would not be complete if we did not consider the way a language is lived, often in a hostile, monolingual environment. Regional languages must often mix with other languages, which are official at state level. This creates a situation of bilingualism or diglossia.

Bilingualism has the tendency to favour one language in relation to another. Certain languages become the language of exterior communication, while others are used in more restricted circles, at home for example. This situation often contributes to the extinction of the spoken language in private. Thus, integral bilingualism is often difficult to impose, but vital for each language to live in equality. The only way to achieve this is to teach the languages spoken in the territory, the minority languages being preferred in the early years of learning (the solution of immersion teaching is advocated in these conditions). As a consequence, its spread in the media (television, radio, newspapers) and its use in social life (justice, administration) is essential. It involves an ambitious and voluntarist linguistic policy.

Regional languages

List of regional languages according to the European Bureau for Lesser-Used Languages

- *Aragonese* (Aragonés)
- *Armenian* (Hayerēn)
- *Aromanian* (Armâneti)
- *Asturian* (Asturianu)
- **Basque** (Euskera)
- **Breton** (Brezhoneg)
- **Catalan** (Català)
- **Cornish** (Kernewek)
- **Corsican** (Corsu)
- **Faroese** (Føroyskt)
- **Franco-Provençal** (Arpitan)
- **Friulian** (Furlan)
- **Frisian** (Frysk)
- **Galician** (Galego)
- **Irish** (Gaeilge)
- **Karaim** (Karaïm)
- **Ladin** (Ladin)
- *Limbourgian* (Limburgs)
- **Livonian** (Līvõ kēļ)
- *Low German* (Nedderdüütsch)
- *Luxembourgian* (Lëtzebuergesch)
- **Manx** (Manx)
- *Meänkieli* (Meänkieli)
- *Mirandese* (Mirandés)
- **Mocheno-Bernstoler**
- **Occitan** (Occitan)
- *Oïl Languages* (Oïl)
- **Pomak** (Помаци)
- **Romany** (Rromani ćhib)
- **Ruthenian** (Русинська / Rusyns'ka)
- **Sami** (Samegiella)
- **Sardinian** (Sardu)
- **Saterlandic** (Seeltersk)
- **Seto** (Seto)
- **Scots** (Scots)
- **Scottish Gaelic** (Gàidhlig)
- **Sorabian** (Serbsina)
- **Tatar** (Tatarlar / Татарлар)
- **Voro** (Võro)
- **Walloon** (Walon)
- **Welsh** (Cymraeg)
- **Yiddish** (שידיש / Yiddish)

Europe, minority, minimized or lesser-used languages.

Europe, minority, minimized or lesser-used languages

Barents Sea

ICELAND

Norwegian Sea

Faroian

Sami
Finnish

NORWAY
FINLAND
Finnish-
Karelian

SWEDEN
Swedish
Vepsian

Ingrian
Votic
Estonian
ESTONIA
RUSSIA

Scottish
Gaelic
Scots
Livonian
Russian

Irish
North Sea
DENMARK
LATVIA
Russian

IRELAND
Manx
Danish
LITHUANIA

UNITED KINGDOM
Frisian
Lithuanian
Polish
BELARUS

Welsh
Frisian
Kashubian

Cornish
Säterlandic
NETHERLANDS
Low Geman
Sorbian
POLAND
Ukrainian
Ukrainian

Atlantic
Ocean
Dutch
BELGIUM
GERMANY
Russian

Breton
Walloon
LUX.
Frankish
CZECH REP.
Ukrainian
UKRAINE

French
Alemannic
German
SLOVAKIA
Ruthenian
MOLDOVA

FRANCE
LIECHT.
AUSTRIA
Hungarian
Gagauz
Tatar

Galician
SWITZERLAND
Arpitan
Romansch Ladin
German
Slovene
Friulan
HUNGARY
ROMANIA

Asturo-
Leonean
Basque
Occitan
SLOVENIA
CROATIA
Romanian

Aragonese
BOSNIA-
HERZEGOVINA
Romanian
Serbian

PORTUGAL
ANDORRA
MONACO
SAN MARINO
Bosnian
Croatian
SERBIA

Castilian
SPAIN
Catalan
ITALY
MONTENEGRO
Albanian
BULGARIA
Black Sea

Corsican
Croatian
MACEDONIA
Bulgarian

Catalan
VATICAN
Franco-Provençal
Macedonian
Turkish

Sardinian
Albanian
ALBANIA
Arumanian
GREECE
TURKEY

Albanian
Greek
Greek

Mediterranean Sea

Albanian

0   500   1 000 km

MALTA

CYPRUS

Languages

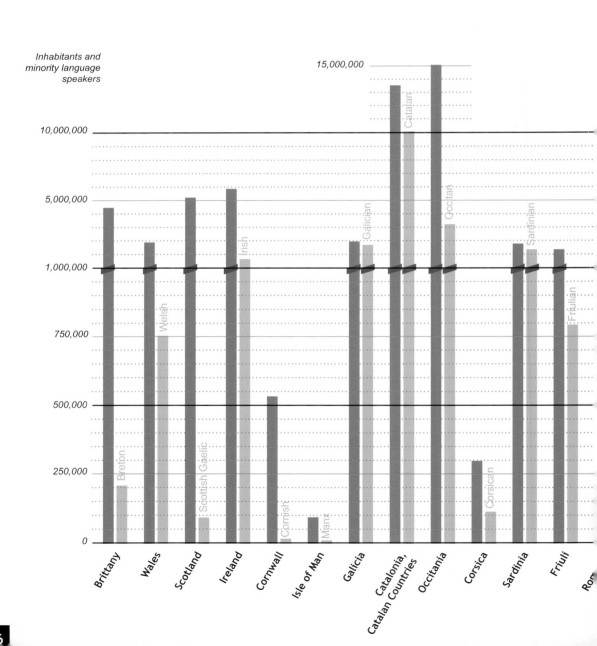

Inhabitants and minority language speakers

15,000,000

10,000,000

5,000,000

1,000,000

750,000

500,000

250,000

0

Brittany — Breton
Wales — Welsh
Scotland — Scottish Gaelic
Ireland — Irish
Cornwall — Cornish
Isle of Man — Manx
Galicia — Galician
Catalonia, Catalan Countries — Catalan
Occitania — Occitan
Corsica — Corsican
Sardinia — Sardinian
Friuli — Friulian
Ron

Population and number of native speakers of the languages of stateless nations. The order is that which is used in this work. This scale uses two levels from zero to a million and beyond a million. The situations of each stateless nation are totally different. Some have a number of speakers relatively equivalent to the total population. The Catalan region is an example. In a population of nearly 13 million, almost 10 million citizens speak Catalan. It is also the case of Galician in Galicia. However, this chart also shows the precarious situation of certain languages in the context of the total population. This is the case with Gaelic in Scotland, Kashubian in Kashubia and Breton in Brittany.

Total population

Number of native speakers
> *Assuming the highest**
> *Assuming the lowest*
*based on native speakers
"passive" users

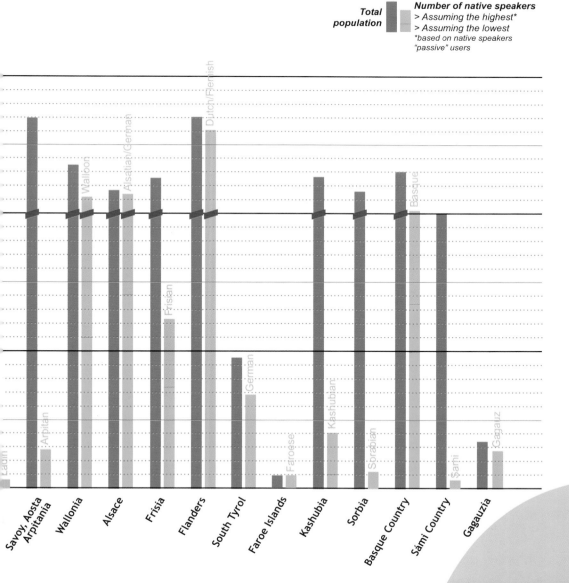

Flags

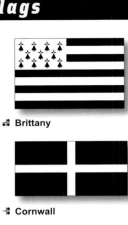
🍀 **Brittany**

🍀 **Wales**

🍀 **Scotland**

🍀 **Ireland**

🔩 **Cornwall**

🔩 **Isle of Man**

🍀 **Galicia**

🍀 **Catalan Countries**

🔩 **Occitania**

🍀 **Corsica**

🍀 **Sardinia**

🔩 **Friuli**

🔩 **Romansh**

🔩 **Ladins**

🔩 **Arpitania**

🔩 **Savoy**

🍀 **Aosta**

🔩 **Wallonia**

🔩 **Alsace**

🍀 **Flanders**

🔩 **Frisia**, Interfrisian flag

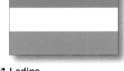
🍀 **Friesland**

🔩 **North Frisia**

🔩 **East Frisia**

Stateless nations have emblems, of which the flag is certainly the most characteristic. At all times the flags have been a means of identifying groups, communities, people or states. It is not about emblems frozen in history. Most often, there are recent emblems like the official state flag, such as those used by the Americans or the Germans, adopted during the Declaration of Independence in 1776 and the Revolutions of 1848 respectively. Others are older and their significance is sometimes discussed. They regularly draw on historical elements or characteristics of the communities they represent. The flags of stateless nations sometimes have an official status, but the majority of them are used only in a semi-official manner, even if they are almost universally accepted by the populations which they represent.

The flags are shown in the order of presentation of stateless nations in this work. A more detailed description of each stateless nation can be found on each page of this book.

 **South Tyrol**

 **Faroe Islands**

 **Kashubia**

 **Sorbia**

 **Basque Country**

 **Sámi Country**

 **Gagauzia**

Status

Official	● ❘ ●	Non-official
Institutional and/ or used by local institutions	● ❘ ● **Use**	Political and/or demonstrative

Supplementary flags used by the separatists,
differing from other versions in use (notably official)

Galicia

Catalan Countries

Flanders

Gagauzia

Political groups

The people are represented politically to defend their interests. Stateless nations are no exception to this rule. Thus, the political spectrum of minority peoples is as large as that of official states.

Indeed, whether in Brittany, Catalonia, Scotland or Friesland, state political parties must adapt to the local situation and often cooperate with regional, autonomist and also separatist parties.

Based on international texts, such as the "Declaration of the Granting of Independence to Colonial Countries and Peoples" (Resolution No. 1514), political parties demanding autonomy and independence have four main types of rights:

• the right to legally and officially practised languages and cultures that are theirs by teaching and dissemination,
• the right to control their economic and social development,
• the right to recognition as a people or nation
• the right to self-determination, for which the people are sovereign, and which is passed by referenda.

All tendencies are present in the political scene of stateless nations. They range from the most revolutionary on the far-right to the more sectarian on the extreme left, through progressive parties, claiming socialism or social democracy and on to conservative or liberal parties. This does not differ from the pattern found in the political arena of officially recognised states.

Claims about the right to self-determination differ greatly between people. All forms of claims regarding the desired status for the people that these parties wish to represent are found in this multitude of ideological behaviour. Federalists, regionalists, autonomists and separatists co-exist. The message conveyed by these political formations often corresponds strongly to the hopes of the population.

Thus, in Scotland, the Scottish National Party running the country wants a referendum on independence. In Euskadi, the Basque Nationalist Party and its former president want to do the same. Other parts of Europe have seen the emergence of coalitions between state and autonomist parties, such as Catalonia (in the sense of the Generality of Catalonia), where the Socialist Party (PSOE) cannot govern without the support of the Republican Left of Catalonia (ERC). This pattern also occurred in Galicia between 2005 and 2009 where the Galician Nationalist Bloc came to the rescue of the PSOE to prevent the ultra-conservative Popular Party from leading the country.

Moreover, national state parties are guilty of using election tricks to gain the votes of regionalists and autonomists. Thus, in the Brittany area the autonomists were associated with the socialists from 2004 to 2010. The fact is, as powerful as Scotland, Catalonia or the Basque Country are, the parties representing stateless nations have only varying electoral success. These successes are often difficult to achieve due to the media weight and financial resources of the major political organisations, an electorate loyal to the better-known parties and also electoral constituencies and means of voting favouring state parties, which don't always enable autonomist parties to present themselves in the best conditions.

In the European Parliament, most autonomist parties ally themselves with the progressive and moderate Social Democrat parties. They are gathered within the European Free Alliance (35 parties and 5 "observers"). This formation was combined with the Greens to form a political group with 55 elected from the 750 in the Assembly. This applies, for example, to those elected in the Scottish National Party (SNP), the Welsh Plaid Cymru, the Republican Left of Catalonia (ERC) or the Basque Eusko Alkartasuna (EA). Others, such as the Flemish separatists of the Nieuw-Vlaamse Alliantie (N-VA), moved from the conservative group Peoples Party and European Democrats to the Greens/EFA, the separatist Convergència i Democràtica Catalunya (CiU) and the Basque Nationalist Party (EAJ-PNV) are associated with the moderates' "Alliance of Liberals and Democrats of Europe".

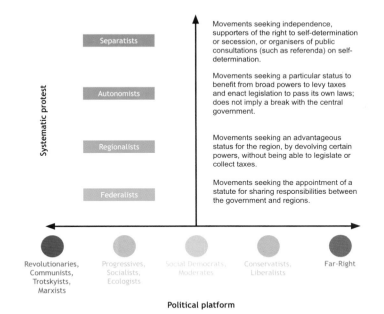

Separatists — Movements seeking independence, supporters of the right to self-determination or secession, or organisers of public consultations (such as referenda) on self-determination.

Autonomists — Movements seeking a particular status to benefit from broad powers to levy taxes and enact legislation to pass its own laws; does not imply a break with the central government.

Regionalists — Movements seeking an advantageous status for the region, by devolving certain powers, without being able to legislate or collect taxes.

Federalists — Movements seeking the appointment of a statute for sharing responsibilities between the government and regions.

Systematic protest (vertical axis)

Revolutionaries, Communists, Trotskyists, Marxists | Progressives, Socialists, Ecologists | Social Democrats, Moderates | Conservatists, Liberalists | Far-Right

Political platform

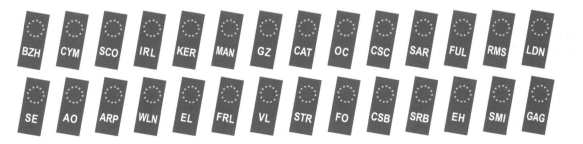

BZH CYM SCO IRL KER MAN GZ CAT OC CSC SAR FUL RMS LDN

SE AO ARP WLN EL FRL VL STR FO CSB SRB EH SMI GAG

The "Eurobands" that are found on the number plates for vehicles of all European countries (members of the European Union) have made an international code of one, two or three letters. European states now boast the most consistent ones: GB for Great Britain, D (Deutschland) for Germany, I for Italy. Stateless nations also have their distinctive codes. Many motorists have used them for many decades, at first on the international oval, and today on Eurobands. This is a sign of identification with a nation and is a contentious act.

In order: Brittany, Wales, Scotland, Ireland, Cornwall*, Isle of Man, Galicia, Catalonia, Occitania, Corsica, Sardinia, Friuli, Romansh*, Ladins*, Savoy, Aosta, Arpitan, Wallonia*, Alsace, Friesland, Flanders, South Tyrol, Faroe, Kashubia, Sorabia*, Basque Country, Sámi Country*, Gagauz* (*supposed).

Political groups

Exhaustive list of the political parties having elected representatives (on a regional or municipal level) or members of the European Free Alliance. Common names are listed in the table. The alternative denominations and the English translation are shown by a superscript number.

	Revolutionaries, Communists	Progressives, Socialists	Social Democrats	Conservatists, Liberalists	Far-right
Brittany		• Union démocratique bretonne (UDB) ■(EFA)[1]	• Parti breton ◆[2]		
Wales		• Forward Wales ■[3] • Wales Green Party ■[4]	• Plaid Cymru ■(EFA)[5]		
Scotland	• Scottish Socialist Party (SSP) [6] • Solidarity [7]	• Scottish Green Party ■[8]	• Scottish National Party (SNP) ◆(EFA)[9]		
Ireland		• Social Democratic and Labour Party (SDLP) ◆[10]	• Sinn Féin ◆[11]		
Cornwall			• Mebyon Kernow (EFA) ■[12]		
Isle of Man		• Mec Vannin ◆[13] • Manx Labour Party ■[14]		• Liberal Vannin Party (LVP) ■[15]	
Galicia	• Unión do Povo Galego [16] • Frente Popular Galega [17]	• Bloque Nacionalista Galego (ALE) ■[18]		• Terra Galega ■[19]	
Catalonia. Catalan Countries	• Esquerra Unida i Alternativa (EUiA) [20] • Candidatura d'Unitat Popular (CUP) [21]	• Esquerra Republicana de Catalunya (ERC) (EFA) ◆[22] • Iniciativa per Catalunya Verds (ICV) ■[23] • Bloc Nacionalista Valencià (BLOC) ■[24] • Partit Socialista de Mallorca (PSM) ■[25] • Unitat Catalana ■[26]	• Convergència Democràtica de Catalunya ■[27] • Unió Mallorquina ■[28]	• Unió Democràtica de Catalunya ■[29]	
Occitania		• Partit Occitan (PÒc) (EFA) ■[30]		• Partit de la Nacion Occitana (PNO) ■[31]	
Corsica		• I Verdi corsi ◆[32] • Corsica Libera ◆[33]	• U Partitu di a Nazione Corsa (EFA) ■[34] • A Chjama Naziunale ■[35]		
Sardinia		• Partito Sardo d'Azione (PSd'A) (EFA) ■[36]		• Partito del Popolo Sardo (PPS) ■[37] • Unione Democratica Sarda (UDS) ■[38]	

Friuli			• Movimento Friûl (MF) ▪39		
Ladins			• Moviment Politich Ladins ▪40		
Savoy / Aosta (Arpitania)		• Renouveau Valdôtain (RV) ▪(EFA-OBS) 41 • Vallée d'Aoste Vive ▪42 • Alé Vallée ▪43	• Mouvement Région Savoie (MRS) (EFA) ▪44 • Fédération Autonomiste (FA) ▪45 • Stella Alpina Valle d'Aosta ▪46 • Union Valdôtaine (UV) ▪47	• Ligue Savoisienne (EFA) ◆48 • Union Valdôtaine (UV) ▪49	
Alsace			• Unser Elsass (ex-UPA) (EFA) ▪50		• Alsace d'Abord ▪51
Faroe		• Tjóðveldi ◆52	• Miðflokkurin ▪53 • Sjálvstýrisflokkurin ▪54	• Fólkaflokkurin ▪55	
Frisia		• Fryske Nasjonale Partij (FNP) (EFA) ▪56	• Die Friesen (EFA-OBS) ◆57		
Flanders				• Nieuw-Vlaamse Alliantie (N-VA) (EFA) ◆58	• Vlaams Belang ◆59
South Tyrol		• Verdi-Grüne-Vërc ▪60		• Südtiroler Volkspartei (SVP) ▪61	• Union für Südtirol, (UfS) ▪62 • Die Freiheitlichen ▪63
Sorbia			• Serbska Ludowa Strona (SLS) ▪64		
Basque Country	• Aukera Guztiak 65 • Aralar 66 • Batzarre 67▪ Euskal Herrialdeetako Alderdi Komunista 68	• Eusko Alkartasuna (EA) (EFA) ◆69 • Abertzaleen Batasuna (AB) ▪70 • Eusko Abertzale Ekintza ◆71 • Ezker Batua-Berdeak ▪72	• Euzko Alderdi Jeltzalea (EAJ-PNV) ◆73		

1/ Unvaniezh Demokratel Breizh (Democratic Union of Brittany)
2/ Strollad Breizh (Breton Party)
3/ Cymru Ymlaen (Forward Wales)
4/ Plaid Werdd Cymru (Wales Green Party)
5/ The Party of Wales
6/ Pàrtaidh Uaine na h-Alba (Scottish Green Party)
7/ Solidarity
8/ Pàrtaidh Sòisealach na h-Alba (Scottish Socialist Party)
9/ Pàrtaidh Nàiseanta na h-Alba (Scottish National Party)
10/ Social Democratic and Labour Party
11/ "Ourselves"
12/ "Sons of Cornwall"
13/ "Sons of Man"
14/ Manx Labour Party
15/ Manx Liberal Party
16/ Union of Galician People
17/ Galician Popular Front
18/ Galician National Bloc
19/ Galician Ground
20/ Left Unitarian and Alternative Party
21/ Candidature of Popular Union
22/ Republican Left of Catalonia
23/ Catalan Green Initiative
24/ Valentian Nationalist Bloc
25/ Socialist Party of Majorca
26/ United Catalonia

27/ Democratic Convergence of Catalonia
28/ Majorcan Union
29/ Democratic Union of Catalonia
30/ Occitan Party
31/ Party of the Nation of Occitania
32/ The Green Corsicans
33/ Free Corsica
34/ Party of the Nation of Corsica
35/ National Call
36/ Sardinian Action Party
37/ Sardinian Peoples' Party
38/ Democratic Union of Sardinia
39/ Friulian Movement
40/ Political Movement of Ladinia
41/ Valdotain Renewa
42/ Lively Aosta Valley
43/ Go Valley
44/ Savoy Regional Movement
45/ Autonomist Federation
46/ Edelweiss Aosta Valley
47/ Valdotain Union
48/ Savoisian League
49/ Valdotain Union
50/ Our Alsace
51/ Alsace First
52/ Republican Party
53/ Centre Party

54/ Separatist Party
55/ Popular Party
56/ Frisian National Party
57/ The Frisians
58/ The Flemish New Alliance
59/ Flemish Interest
60/ The Greens
61/ The Popular Party of Southern Tyrol
62/ Southern Tyrol Union
63/ The Liberals
64/ Sorabian Popular Party
65/ All The Options
66/ Aralar
67/ Batzarre
68/ Basque Communist Party
69/ Basque Solidarity
70/ Union of Patriots
71/ National Basque Action
72/ United Left Greens
73/ Partido Nacionalista Vasco (Nationalist Basque Party)

No politcal party, regionalist, autonomist or separatist, identified for Romansh, Wallons, Sámi or Gagauz.

◆ **Separatist political parties**
▪ **Autonomist and regionalist political parties**
(EFA-OBS) **Political party members of the European Free Alliance or Observers**

Overview of stateless nations

There are thirty stateless nations in Europe. The people who comprise these often live in contrasting situations, which are not always comparable. However, an element is common to these people. It is the consciousness of belonging to a community. At various levels, they maintain the desire to preserve their identity and language. To promote and defend these desires, many have their own institutions. Scotland, sovereign until 1707, could regain its independence if its government is authorised to hold a referendum, which it desires. The Basque government is also poised to ask people's opinion on the issue. Other nations have a strong autonomy allowing them to legislate. For example, this is the case in Catalonia and Wales. Elsewhere the militant activism of the Bretons or Corsicans clashes with bigotry from a rigid state system. These are just a few examples of the situations presented in the following pages.

Stateless nations of Europe

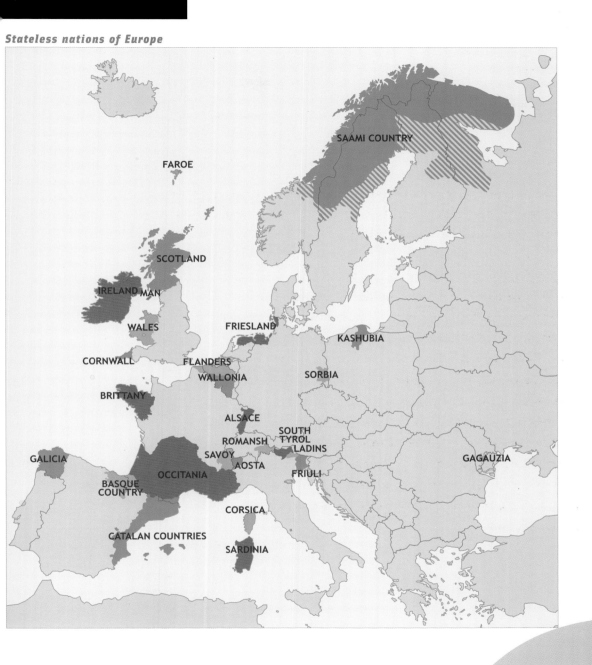

SAAMI COUNTRY

FAROE

SCOTLAND

IRELAND MAN

WALES

FRIESLAND

KASHUBIA

CORNWALL

FLANDERS

WALLONIA

SORBIA

BRITTANY

ALSACE

SOUTH
TYROL
LADINS

ROMANSH

GALICIA

SAVOY

AOSTA

GAGAUZIA

OCCITANIA

FRIULI

BASQUE
COUNTRY

CORSICA

CATALAN COUNTRIES

SARDINIA

Brittany, *cultural effervescence*

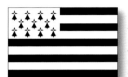

The Breton flag, *Gwenn ha du,* which literally means "white and black" was created by the autonomist architect Morvan Marchal in 1923. It incorporates the "mouchtetures d'hermine", the symbol of Breton sovereignty and the traditional colours since the 13th century. The number of bands symbolises the nine historic provinces that make up Brittany.

A peninsula at the tip of Europe, Brittany is bordered to the north by the English Channel and to the south by the Atlantic Ocean. It is one of six Celtic nations and is the only one to be found on mainland Europe. From the 4th century, the Britons began to settle on the island.

In the 9th century Brittany began to emancipate itself from its Carolingian neighbours. Nominoë, duke of Brittany and Erispoë, and his son, the king, expanded the territory and made it into the form it retains today. Torn between France and England, the Montfort dynasty (14th/15th centuries) managed to keep the country independent. It was then that Brittany saw its golden era, becoming an unchallenged maritime power. A kingdom then a duchy, Brittany was forced to unite with France by the union of its sovereignty in 1532. Having become a province, Brittany retains many privileges (specific legislation, tax collection).

During the French Revolution, it lost its rights and was reduced to 5 departments without identity. It wasn't until the 19th century that the Breton cultural movement began to fight for its culture, its language and for self-determination.

It is only in the 1970s that the teaching of Breton began, which had long been despised by the authorities. During this period, armed activism by the Front for the Liberation of Brittany intensified (1963). Having acquired few rights, the Bretons fight continuously for the reunification of arbitrarily divided territory and for the Breton and Gallo languages, which are in danger of extinction today. Without autonomous status, Brittany does not have the means to manage issues of concern, in regards to economic, cultural and linguistic diversity.

Timeline

4th–7th century • Bretons emigrate from the island of Brittany. They mingle with Celtic populations already present, while exercising political power.

9th century • Breton kingdoms unite under the authority of their sovereign, Nominoe.

14–15th century • War of succession sees the strengthening of the Monfort dynasty and the emancipation of Brittany.

1488 • The military defeats of the Duchy forces Brittany to join its neighbour, the kingdom of France.

15–17th century • The trade in cloth ushers in a Breton golden age.

1789 • Brittany loses all its rights under the Act of Union and begins a dark period, without a hold on its destiny. It no longer exists legally.

1941 • A "region" Brittany is created by the Vichy government led by Marshall Pétain, cutting off the Loire-Atlantique.

1970s • Emancipation thanks to the cultural movement. The Regional Council formally recognises Breton and Gallo as official languages of Brittany.

Identity card

Names: **Breizh[1], Bertaèyn[2], Bretagne[3]** (Brittany)
Population: **4,334,000 inhab.** note [1] *(2007)*
Area: **34,034 km²** note [1]
Languages: **Brezhoneg** [1] (Breton), **Galo** [2] (Gallo) *(without official status),* **Français[3]** (French) *(official)*
Number of native speakers: **206,000[1]** *(2007)*
State of guardianship: **France**
Official status: **Region without autonomous status in France**
Capitals: **Roazhon[1], Resnn[2], Rennes[3] / Naoned[1], Nauntt[2], Nantes[3]**
Historic religion: **Roman Catholic**
Flag: **Gwenn ha du[1]** (white and black)
Anthem: **Bro Gozh ma zadoù[1],** (Old Land of My Fathers)
Motto: **Potius mori quam foedari** *(in Latin),* **Kentoc'h mervel eget bezañ saotret[1],** (Death rather than staining)

Brief history

Like elsewhere in Europe, in the middle of the 19th century the Breton movement (*Emsav*) became aware of the cultural riches that exist in Brittany. Its leading figure is the Marquis T.-H. de la Villemarqué who collected folk songs, which he published under the name Barzaz Breizh. In the 1920s, an artistic movement was born, which included more than fifty artists in all fields (literature, music, visual arts, architecture). They were called *Seizh Breur* (Seven Brothers). Their goal was to combine tradition and modernity in art and give acclaim back to Brittany in a more militant way than their predecessors. By giving Bretons back a taste for their culture and languages, this movement has created a modern Breton, art-nouveau style, which can still be seen in contemporary design.

Brittany, the historic provinces

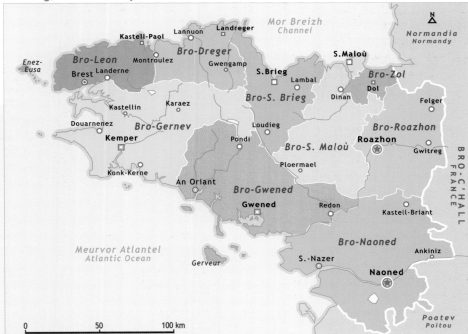

Brittany consists of nine historic provinces, original cultural entities maintaining a major cultural role known in Breton as *"bro"* (shown on map). Today, Brittany is made up of five departments, including the Loire-Atlantique, which was administratively separated under the collaborationist Pétain. Many islands surround it (Batz, Ouessant, Sein, Groix, Belle Isle, etc.). Normandy, Maine, Anjou and Poitou are found at its eastern border. The urban network comprises many cities, mainly located on the coast. To the east, Rennes, the administrative capital and Nantes, seat of the rulers, are the most emblematic and are considered the two historic capitals. To the west, Brest, a port city, has largely contributed to the reputation of Brittany as a great maritime nation. On account of its peripheral location at the edge of Europe, Brittany has suffered from a strong economic disadvantage, subsisting on agriculture and fishing. It began to develop upon the arrival of what is now called the "Breton model", based on the consensus of economists and politicians, particularly the CELIB during the 1960s.

Geography

Principal towns
(Breton / French)

An Oriant • *Lorient*
Brest • *Brest*
Gwened • *Vannes*
Kemper • *Quimper*
Montroulez • *Morlaix*
Naoned • *Nantes*
Roazhon • *Rennes*
Sant-Brieg • *Saint-Brieuc*
Sant-Maloù • *Saint-Malo*
Sant-Nazer • *Saint-Nazaire*

Régions
(Breton / French)

Bro Dreger • *Trégor*
Bro Gerne (Kerne) • *Cornouaille*
Bro Gwened • *Vannetais*
Bro Naoned • *Pays Nantais*
Bro Leon • *Léon*
Bro Roazhon • *Pays Rennais*
Bro Sant-Brieg • *Pays de Saint-Brieuc*
Bro Sant-Maloù • *Pays de Saint-Malo*
Bro Zol (Dol) • *Pays de Dol*

Geographical names

> "... 'drokfen ket evit teñzorioù, va bro, va yezh ha va frankiz."
> (Anjela Duval, Breton writer)
> "... I will not change for any treasure, my country, my language, my freedom."

Brittany, *cultural effervescence*

Brittany, the teaching of Breton

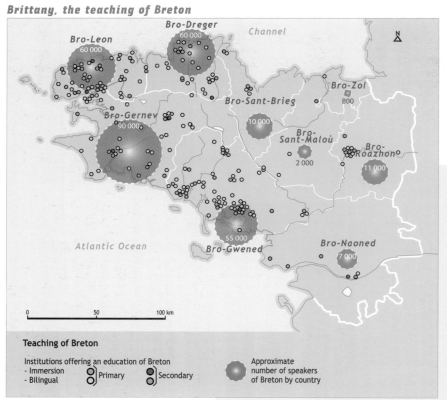

Teaching of Breton

Institutions offering an education of Breton
- Immersion
- Bilingual   Primary   Secondary

Approximate number of speakers of Breton by country

Brezhoneg / Galo

The Breton language is a Celtic language of the Brythonic branch. Spoken since the 5th century, the Breton language is still specific to Brittany. It is practised by more than 300,000 people, essentially to the west of Brittany. It is also spoken in the large towns to the east of Brittany (Rennes, Nantes). There are four variations, between which mutual understanding is mostly possible, though it is more difficult with the people of the Vannes area. Other variants are commonly called Cornish, Leonard and Trégorois. Breton does not benefit from official status, as France rejects any recognition of linguistic minorities. However, the situation is changing slowly. For its part, Brittany officially recognised Breton and Gallo (another language practised in the east of Brittany), but this recognition has only symbolic value. There are now over 16,500 students learning Breton (2002), which is low compared to the number of children enroled in schools. Breton, active in the field of information technology, remains fragile. Indeed, it is classified by UNESCO as an endangered language.

Languages

Anne of Brittany, last duchess of Brittany, statue in the castle of the duke of Brittany, in Nantes

The Breton administration has a Regional Council with no power to legislate. Despite the dynamic force of the Breton movement, it is mainly on cultural grounds that activists operate. However, Breton political parties always reinforce their positions. Indeed, the autonomist Breton Democratic Union has four regional advisers (between 2004 and 2009 the majority were Progressive Socialists / Greens). The Breton Party, in spite of its young age, has candidates in various elections and also has local officials. There are also some groups claiming federalism or anarchism. The extreme left is represented by a separatist party named the Breizhistance. The themes defended by the Breton parties are essentially the recognition of Breton people, the officialisation of the Breton language and the reunification of Breton territory into its historical configuration (the department of Loire-Atlantique is actually separated from the administrative region of Brittany despite polls indicating that 70% of the population desires reunification). In 2000, a CSA poll revealed that 23% of Bretons were strongly or somewhat in favour of independence.

The most representative autonomist or separatist Breton parties:
• **Unvaniezh demokratel Breizh** / Breton Democratic Union (UDB) *(Progressive Autonomist)*
• **Strollad Breizh** / Breton Party *(Separatist Social Democrat)*
• **Breizhistance /** Brittany Socialist Party *(Revolutionary Left)*

Politics now

39

Wales, *you said "Llanfairpwllgwyngyll..."*

According to the Romans, the red dragon, *Y Ddraig Goch*, was the war banner of the Breton people against the Anglo-Saxon invasions between the 5th and 6th centuries. Associated with the King Cadwaladr ap Cadwallon, the Welsh continued to use it over the centuries. In 1485, Henry Tudor used the red dragon on a green and white background. It officially became the flag of Wales in 1959.

Wales is a Celtic nation to the west of the British Isles. In spite of centuries of cultural oppression, a quarter of the population speaks Welsh, which today carries an official status. Political awakening is recent with the creation of a National Assembly in 1999.

The Welsh are Celts and are more precisely descended from Brythonic people. In the 5th and 6th century they were driven to the west of the British Isles by Anglo-Saxon invaders. It is because of the conflicts with their English neighbours that the different Brythonic kingdoms were united to form Wales.

In the 13th century, the attempted establishment of a sovereign state was thwarted by the assassination of the prince of Wales, Llywelyn ap Gruffydd, and by the conquest of the territory by Edward I of England in 1282. The revolts that followed were largely suppressed for more than a century, culminating in the liberation war of Owain Glyndŵr, 1400–04. In 1536, after a short period of independence, Wales was split by England and the language was outlawed.

In the 20th century the coalfield of the south of Wales became the most industrialised region of the world. It was in this same period that native speakers brought about a renaissance of Welsh nationalism. In 1925 the Nationalist Party of Wales appeared. The Cymdeithas yr Iaith Gymraeg (the Society of the Welsh Language) used civil disobedience in 1962 to obtain rights for the language. It was only in 1999 that the Welsh saw their efforts come to fruition with the creation of the Welsh Assembly, albeit with limited legislative powers. It did, however, allow them to make Welsh the official language of the country alongside English.

Timeline

940 • Welsh law codified by King Hywel Dda.

1282 • Assassination of Prince Llywelyn ap Gruffydd; English invasion.

1404 • After four years of war, Owain Glyndŵr establishes an independent Welsh parliament.

1536 • Annexing by the English under Henry VIII.

1847 • The government forbids the teaching of Welsh in schools. In 1870, the Welsh Not is established (punishment for children caught in the act of speaking Welsh).

1920s • Withdrawl of the Church of England and the creation of Urdd Gobaith Cymru; formation of the Welsh Nationalist Party (Plaid Cymru).

1960s • Start of the armed campaigns of MAC and the Free Wales Army; the Welsh Office is established; first Plaid Cymru Member of Parliament, 1966; first Welsh Language Act, 1967.

1997 • Majority vote for devolution; establishment of the National Assembly in 1998; first general election of Wales in 1999.

Identity card

Names: **Cymru[1], Wales[2]** (Wales)
Population: **3,004,000 inhab.** *(2004)*
Area: **20,760 km²**
Languages: **Cymraeg[1]** (Welsh), **English[2]** (English) *(official)*
Number of speakers: **750,000[1]** *(2010)*
State of guardianship: **United Kingdom**
Official status: **Principality of the United Kingdom with its own assembly**
Capital: **Caerdydd[1], Cardiff[2]** (Cardiff)
Historic religion: **Christian Methodist**
Flag: **Y Ddraig Goch[1]** (The Red Dragon)
Anthem: **Hen Wlad Fy Nhadau[1]** (Old Land of My Fathers)
Motto: **Cymru am Byth[1]** (Wales forever)

Brief history

In 1956, the Liverpool Corporation announced its intention to flood the valley of Tryweryn and the village of Capel Celyn, to provide water for Liverpool in England. Despite protests from the Tryweryn Defence Committee and Welsh deputies, British parliament endorsed this decision. The villagers were expelled from their houses and bodies were exhumed from the cemetery. In spite of the anecdotal character of this event, Tryweryn was a turning point in the modern history of Wales. A nation awoke. In 1963, the construction site in Tryweryn was shelled, marking the start of a long armed campaign. In 1965, the opening ceremony of the dam was invaded by thousands of protesters. It was in this era that the "society of the Welsh language" was created, launching 40 years of non-violent action. In 1996, Gwynfor Evans became the first MP of Plaid Cymru.

Wales, the traditional counties

Wales, the traditional counties

- N
- Caergybi
- Ynys Môn
- Bangor
- Caernarfon
- **Gwynedd**
- *Môr Iwerddon / Irish Sea*
- Bae Colwyn
- **Clwyd**
- Yr Wyddgrug
- Wrecsam
- Betws-y-Coed
- Llangollen
- Porthmadog
- Pwllheli
- Dolgellau
- Tywyn
- Y Trallwng
- Y Drenewydd
- *Bae Ceredigion / Cardigan Bay*
- Aberystwyth
- **Powys**
- Aberaeron
- Llandrindod
- Llanbedr Pont Steffan
- Llanfair ym Muallt
- Aberteifi
- **Dyfed**
- Llanymddyfri
- Aberhonddu
- Abergwaun
- *Môr Celtaidd / Celtic Sea*
- Tyddewi
- Caerfyrddin
- Hwlffordd
- Merthyr Tudful
- Glyn Ebwy
- Y Fenni
- Aberdaugleddau
- Penfro
- Llanelli
- Castell-Nedd
- Caerffili
- Pont-y-Pŵl
- Casnewydd
- Abertawe
- Aberafan
- Pen-y-bont ar Ogwr
- Porthcawl
- **Caerdydd**

- 1 - De Morgannwg
- 2 - Morgannwg Ganol
- 3 - Gorllewin Morgannwg
- 4 - Gwent

- *I W E R D D O N / IRELAND*
- *L L O E G R / ENGLAND*

0   50   100 km

Wales lies to the west of Great Britain. It shares its eastern border with England, while to the north, west and south, it is bordered by two seas – the Irish Sea and the Celtic Sea. The administrative history of Wales is complex. Historically, the country is made up of thirteen historical regions, which are called 'Siroedd' in Welsh. In 1972, a local government Act created eight regions based on this country, whose names are uniquely Welsh save for three of them which are bilingual names. In 1996, a reform took place to endow the new Welsh regions. Today, it is divided into nine counties, three towns and ten country divisions (the map represents the regions which were in force between 1974 and 1996) corresponding more to the historical reality. The biggest towns and the capital (Cardiff) are found in the south. Swansea and Newport, two ports famous for their role in the industrialisation of the country, have prospered thanks to the exploitation of iron ore.

Geography

Principal towns
(Welsh / English)

Abertawe • Swansea
Bae Colwyn • Colwyn Bay
Caerdydd • Cardiff
Caerfyrddin • Carmarthen
Caernarfon
Casnewydd • Newport
Penfro • Pembroke
Pont-y-Pŵl • Pontypool
Wrecsam • Wrexham
Yr Wyddgrug • Mold

Regions
(Welsh / English)

Clwyd
De Morgannwg • South Glamorgan
Dyfed
Gorllewin Morgannwg • West Glamorgan
Gwent
Gwynedd
Morgannwg Ganol • Mid Glamorgan
Powys

Geographical names

"Trwy ddulliau chwyldro yn unig y mae achub yr iaith Gymraeg."
(Saunders Lewis, Welsh writer)
"It is only by revolutionary methods that the Welsh language will be saved."

Wales, *you said "Llanfairpwllgwyngyll..."*

Cymraeg

Of the Celtic languages, Welsh is certainly the most practised language. Closely related to Cornish and Breton, it is part of the Brythonic languages. Many books, including grammar books and dictionaries were edited in the 17th and 18th centuries. It is at this time that the language was standardised. In 2001, there were just over 700,000 native speakers, corresponding to approximately 21% of the population. The north-west of Wales is traditionally an area where Welsh is more active. More than 50% of the population speaks Welsh in certain sectors such as Gwynedd. Thanks to devolution, Wales has a special policy which allows it to manage its own language policy. After the Government of Wales Act (1998), Welsh and English would be treated as equal. Thus, Welsh was strongly present in justice, public services, road signs, the media and all areas of public life. *Sianel Pedwar Cymru* (S4C), the Welsh television channel, broadcasts fully in Welsh. The BBC does the same in the field of radio. Although the UK has signed and ratified the European Charter for Regional and Minority Languages, its tradition of oppression of language minorities and the power of the English language, especially English immigrants, could jeopardise the future of the Welsh language.

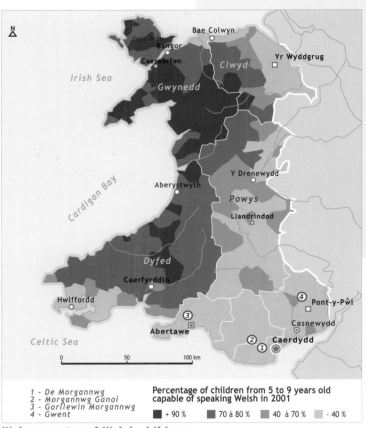

1 - De Morgannwg
2 - Morgannwg Ganol
3 - Gorllewin Morgannwg
4 - Gwent

Percentage of children from 5 to 9 years old capable of speaking Welsh in 2001

■ + 90 %　■ 70 à 80 %　■ 40 à 70 %　□ - 40 %

Wales, master of Welsh children

Memorial to the Welsh division of Mametz representing a red dragon, the emblem of Wales

Since 1999, some administrative powers were devolved to Wales, but they were limited and in contrast with Scotland, the Welsh Assembly had no lawmaking or tax collecting powers. In 1999, the new Labour Party obtained a running majority and in 2007 Plaid Cymru, the Welsh nationalist party, governed in a four-year coalition with Labour, but are now again in opposition. However, in a referendum held in 2011, the Welsh voted overwhelmingly for direct law-making powers for the National Assembly. The principal preoccupations of the Welsh remain the rights of workers, public services, the Welsh language, housing under pressure by what the Welsh term "English colonisation". The themes of decentralisation and the environment also trouble the Welsh political world. Recent opinion polls show that 32% of the Welsh are in favour of greater self-government. This is a relatively new development.

The most representative Welsh parties (some of which are localised elements of British parties):
• **Plaid Cymru** / Party of Wales *(Separatist progressive)*
• **Welsh New Labour** *(composed of British New Labour, progressive)*
• **Welsh Liberal Democrats** *(composed of British Liberal Democrat Party, pro-decentralisation)*
• **Welsh Conservatives** *(composed of British Conservative and Unionist Party, conservative, evolving on decentralisation issues)*

Politics now

Scotland, *eyeing independence*

The Cross of St Andrew has been the Scottish flag since the early 14th century. White on a blue background, it is commonly called 'The Saltire' after its heraldic name. The legend dates back to the 10th century, which would make it the oldest European flag still in use. It would appear in the sky on the eve of a victorious battle for King Angus against the Anglo-Saxons.

Scotland is a nation situated to the north of the British Isles. Largely autonomous today, a Scottish parliament elected by universal suffrage has managed affairs since 1999. Its separatist first minister wishes to organise a referendum on self-determination.

Scotland was initially populated by the Picts and the Scots, who were most likely Celts and from whom they take their name. Scotland did not have a strong Roman presence. The emperors Hadrian and Antonius built walls across the south of the country in defence of their empire, thus minimising Roman influence. In the 10th century, Domnall II (Donald II) became the first king of the Alban kingdom extending throughout the Gaelic and Scots territory. It was in the Middle Ages that the different kingdoms making up this region united to create Scotland, while also maintaining ties with neighbouring England. Over many centuries, there were successive wars between the two states. It was not until the 14th century that England recognised the independence of its neighbour, which by then had its own parliament. Even though Scotland lost its independence in 1707, polls regularly give the figure of 35% for Scots in favour of independence.

Today, a special feature of Scotland remains its use of the minority languages, Gaelic in the north-west and Scottish in the south-east. The Scottish nation cannot therefore be defined in linguistic terms. The Scottish independence movements, born in the 1920s (inspired at that time by their Irish neighbours Sinn Féin), are trying to regain their power by maintaining a unique culture made up of symbols known around the world.

Identity card

Names: **Alba**[1], **Scotland**[23] (Scotland)
Population: **5,094,800 inhab.** *(2005)*
Area: **78,772 km²**
Languages: **Gàidhlig**[1] (Scottish Gaelic), **Scots leid**[2] (Scots) *(official vote)*, **English**[3] (English) (official)
Number of native speakers: **58,400 to 92,400**[1] (2001),
1,500,000[2] (1996)
State of guardianship: **United Kingdom**
Official status: **Constitutive Nation of the United Kingdom with its own Parliament**
Capital: **Dùn Èideann**[1], **Edinburgh**[23]
Historic religion: **Anglican Christian and Presbyterian**
Flag: **Bratach-croise**[1], **Saltire**[23] / **Andrew's Cross**[3]
Anthem: **Flùir na h-Alba**[1], **Flouer o Scotland**[2], **Flower of Scotland**[3] *(other anthems are used)*
Motto: **Nemo me impune lacessit** *(Latin)*, **Cha togar m' fhearg gun dioladh**[1], **No one provokes me with impunity**[3]

Timeline

843 • Foundation (mythical) of the kingdom of Scotland by Cinéad mac Ailpin, king of the Picts and the Gaels.

1314 • Battle of Bannockburn (Allt a'Bhonaich), Scottish victory of Robert Bruce against the English, Scottish independence is preserved.

1603 • Union of the English and Scottish crowns. The king of Scotland James VI becomes James I of England.

1707 • Union of the English and Scottish parliaments, disappearance of the parliament in Edinburgh.

1746 • Battle of Cùil Lòdair (Culloden) which marks the end of Scottish-Gaelic and the clans of the Highlands.

1762 • Start of the Clearances, massive emigration of the Gaels of the Highlands under pressure by land owners who were looking to replace them with sheep, which were more profitable.

1999 • First session of the new Scottish parliament.

Brief history

Despite the English having had their eye on the coast of Scotland since the foundation of the kingdom in 843, we denote the wars of independence as being a series of conflicts at the end of the 13th and the beginning of the 14th century. The first war began with the invasion of Scotland by England in 1296 for dynastic reasons and ended with the Edinburgh-Northampton Treaty in 1328. The victories of William Wallace and Robert Bruce (at Bannockburn) date from this war. The second war of independence (1332–57), which commenced with a new English invasion, finally saw the Scottish troops venture into England. In both cases, Scotland's fate as an independent nation was strengthened. The Arbroath Declaration (signifying the attachment of Scotland to its independence) was signed by the Scottish nobles during the first war in 1320. It remains a reference today.

Scotland, the 10 traditional regions and the 2 islands

Scotland occupies the northern third of the island of Great Britain. Principally a mountainous area, the highest mountain of the island, Ben Nevis (Beinn Nibheis), in the Grampian Channel is found there, which stands at 1,344m. The country is made up of some 790 islands, of which only 10% are habitable, and 3,680 km of coastline. Among the larger islands are found Mull, Islay, Skye, Lewis, Juda to the west and the islands of Shetland and Orkney to the north. The country is traditionally divided into the Highlands and Lowlands and mountainous zones in the south (Southern Uplands). The maximal distance from north to south is 443 km and the maximal distance from east to west is 248 km, although few places are in fact more than 64 km from the sea. Since 1996, the country has been divided administratively into 32 councils (represented on the map), which can take an official name in Gaelic. The principal towns are (in order): Glasgow, Edinburgh, Aberdeen, Dundee, Inverness, Stirling.

Geography

Principal towns
(Scottish Gaelic / English / Scots*)
A' Bhruaich • *Fraserburgh / The Broch**
Cill Mheàrnaig • *East Kilbride*
Dùn Dèagh • *Dundee*
Dùn Èildeann • *Edinburgh / Embra**
(Édimbourg)
Dùn Phris • *Dumfries*
Glaschu • *Glasgow / Glesca**
Glean Rathais • *Glenrothes*
Grianaig • *Greenock*
Inbhir Àir • *Ayr*

Inbhir Nis • *Inverness*
Obar Dheathain • *Aberdeen / Aiberdeen**
Peairt • *Perth*
Sruighlea • *Stirling / Stirlin**

Regions (large groups)
(Scottish Gaelic / English / Scots*)
An t-Eilean Sgitheanach • *Island of Skye*
Arcaibh • *Orkney*
Gàidhealtachd • *Highlands*
Na h-Eileanan Siar • *Outer Hebrides*
Sealtainn • *Shetland*

Geographical names

> "Thig crioch air an t-saoghail, ach mairidh gaol 's ceol."
> (Scottish proverb)
> "Even after the end of the world, music and love will remain."

Scotland, *eyeing independence*

The kilt and the bagpipes, enduring symbols of Scotland

Languages

Gàidhlig / Scots

Scotland, like Brittany for example, is not bilingual but trilingual. Two languages are traditionally used besides English. One is the Gaelic language, Goidelic branch of Celtic and Scottish (also called Scots), a Germanic language similar to English. The best estimations show over 90,000 speakers of Gaelic, corresponding to only 2% of the total population. Mainly spoken in the Hebrides to the north-west of Scotland, Gaelic was made official in 2005, thanks to the re-establishment of the Scottish parliament following a referendum in 1999. Its status is equivalent to that of the Welsh. Scottish (or Scots) is spoken to a varying degree by more than a million Scots, who are often mistakenly thought to be speaking a tainted form of English. The Scottish have never had a great interest in Scots on account of their common origin with the English. Today, it is used in some schools to varying degrees. The situation could rapidly change with the current government, which is supportive of the language.

Scotland has been a part of the United Kingdom since 1707, the year in which the country lost its parliament (even though the crowns were united in 1603). It is a parliamentary monarchy, the head of state being Queen Elizabeth II. The Scottish parliament was restored in 1999 after a referendum in 1997. It is responsible for all internal affairs in Scotland, except for reserved domains (army, foreign affairs). Parliament also has limited powers in taxation, which were not used until 2008. In the 2011 General Election, the separatist Scottish National Party dramatically won an overall majority of seats in the Scottish Parliament. Its leader, first minister Alex Salmond, has pledged to hold a referendum on Scottish independence during his current term of office.

The most representative Scottish nationalist parties:
- **Scottish National Party** (SNP) *(Progressive separatist; in power since 2007)*
- **Scottish Socialist Party** (SSP) *(Separatist)*
- **Scottish Green Party** *(Separatist ecologist)*

The Cross of St Andrew, the Scottish flag

Ireland, *one objective: reunification*

The Irish flag is a vertical tricolour: three equal bands of green, white and orange. The green is the traditional colour of Ireland and represents the old Celtic and Anglo-Norman background of the population, the orange represents the more recent Protestant settlements, while the white symbolises the peace between the two communities. The principle of the flag dates from 1848, but was not recognised as the national flag until the Easter Rising in 1916.

Ireland is an island situated to the extreme north-west of Europe. It is the biggest of the six Celtic countries. The largest part of the island forms an independent republic, while the north-east remains under the control of the United Kingdom.

Ireland has been a Celtic country for a long time. The Gaels succeeded the megalithic civilisations who were closely related to those living in Brittany (the site of Newgrange was connected to that of Barnenez in Brittany). Never experiencing Roman colonisation, these Gaels were able to integrate different successive waves of Britons, Vikings, Anglo-Normans etc. who adopted the Gaelic language and Celtic civilisation. The English occupation, which started in the 12th century and peaked in the 18th, relegated the natives to second class citizens and favoured the plantation of British colonies, a policy exacerbated by the issue of religion. The Irish remained attached to Catholicism, while the new residents, who held political and economical power, were Protestants.

Paradoxically, the beginnings of the Irish political movement for the liberation of the island were the work of a Protestant lawyer, Wolfe Tone, who preconceived the union of Catholics and Protestants. These days, English is the dominant language on the island, but the Celtic culture remains a mainstay of the national conscience and is kept alive and regularly reinvented.

Today, the north is still governed by the United Kingdom. The conflict intensified from the 1960s onwards, the Irish Republican Army and the Unionist paramilitary groups largely defining this period. Nowadays, while a ceasefire is in effect, complete political resolution remains to be achieved.

Timeline

5th–6th century • Evangelization by St Patrick and vast cultural and religious development (Celtic Church).

1171 • Start of English domination which results in centuries of theft of land, "plantations" of Scottish and English Protestant colonies principally in the north-east, which sees Catholics relegated to second-class citizens.

1801 • Integration with the United Kingdom.

1846–1848 • "The Great Famine" results in misery, depopulation and mass migration.

1916–1922 • Uprising against British power.

1921 • Creation of a Free State.

1949 • Creation of the Republic of Ireland which covers 26 of the 32 counties of the island. Six counties of the north-east, dominated by the Unionists, remain an integrated part of the United Kingdom. Civil war between the provisional government opponents.

1998 • Agreement of peace on "Good Friday" which provides power sharing in Northern Ireland.

Identity card

Names: **Éire[1], Ireland[2]** (Ireland)
Population: **5,946,000 inhab.** note 2 (2006)
Area: **84,421 km² note 2**
Languages: **Gaeilge[1]** (Irish Gaelic), **English[2]** (official), **Scots[3]** (Scots) (without official status)
Number of native speakers: **540,000 to 1,800,000[1]**
States of guardianship: **Ireland, United Kingdom**
Official status: **Independent republic for 26 counties of 32; 6 counties of the north-east, under the name of Northern Ireland, form a province of the United Kingdom**
Capital: **Baile Átha Cliath[1], Dublin[2]** (Dublin)
Historic religion: **Roman Catholic**
Flag: **An Trídhathach[1], The Irish Tricolour[2]**
Anthem: **Amhrán na bhFiann[1], The Soldier's Song[2]**
Motto: **None**

Brief history

The rising against British power began in 1916 and the war of independence, which followed in 1921, led to a treaty partitioning the island of Ireland. Twenty-six of the 32 counties formed a "Free State" becoming a republic in 1949. Six of the nine counties of Ulster, dominated by the Unionists, remained loyal to London, these Unionists refused all sharing of power with the strong nationalist minority (43%), resulting in a movement for the equality of civil rights and a guerrilla war led by the Irish Republican Army (IRA). In 1998, negotiations lead to the "Good Friday" peace agreement. Sinn Féin became the principal nationalist party and the IRA eventually disarmed in 2005. The peace process now appears to be on track with the formation of a coalition government, in spite of the opposition of many Unionists.

Ireland, the 4 provinces and the 32 counties

An tAigéan Atlantach
Atlantic Ocean

Cúil Raithin
Leitir Ceanainn • Doire
Uladh
An Baile Meánach
Latharna
Dún na BnGall • An Ómaigh
Béal Feirste
Beannchar
Lios na gCearrbhach
Baile Nua na hArda
Port an Dúnáin
An Lorgain
Inis Ceithleann
An Caisleán Nua
Sligeach
Muineachán • Ard Mhacha
Rinn Mhic Ghiolla Rua
Béal an Átha
An Cabhán
Caisleán an Bharraigh
Dún Dealgan
Cathair na Mart
Connachta
Baile Átha Luain
Droichead Átha
An Muileann gCearr
Beal Átha na Sluaighe
Baile Átha Cliath
Gaillimh
Túlach Mhór
Cill Dara
An Nás
Biorra
Dún Laoghaire
Port Laoise
Laighean
An tAonach
Muir Éireann
Irish Sea
Dúrlas Éile
Luimneach
Cill Chainnigh
Inis Córthaidh
Caiseal
An Mhumhain
Cluain Meala
Loch Garman
Trá Lí
Port Láirge
Maigh Eala • Mainistir Fhear Maí
Dún Garbhán
Eochaill
Corcaigh
An Cóbh
Beanntraí
Cionn tSáile

0   50   100 km

Ireland is the third largest island in Europe. It lies to the north-west and enjoys a pronounced oceanic and temperate climate. A vast central bog land, dotted with numerous lakes and traversed by the Shannon, is surrounded by several hills and highlands (highest point: Carrauntoohill, 1,041 m). It is traditionally divided into four provinces (Munster, Connacht, Leinster and Ulster). Northern Ireland remains under British control. The economy of the island has for a long time depended on agriculture, with the north-east being the most industrialised. In the past, the country was an important ground for emigration. For a few decades and particularly since its entry into the European Union, this tendency has been reversed and the country became one of the wealthiest in the world before the global economic crisis struck (4th in the 2005 world rankings for PIB per capita at purchasing power), earning it the nickname "The Celtic Tiger".

Geography

Principal towns
(*Irish Gaelic / English*)
An Ómaigh • *Omagh*
Baile Átha Cliath • *Dublin*
Béal Feirste • *Belfast*
Beannchar • *Bangor*
Corcaigh • *Cork*
Doire • *Derry*
Dún Dealgan • *Dundalk*
Gaillimh • *Galway*
Loch Garman • *Wexford*

Luimneach • *Limerick*
Port Láirge • *Waterford*
Sligeach • *Sligo*

Regions
(*Irish Gaelic / English*)
An Mhumhain • *Munster*
Connachta • *Connacht*
Laighean • *Leinster*
Uladh • *Ulster*

Geographical names

Ireland, one objective: reunification

Gaeilge

Irish (or *Gaeilge*) is a Celtic language of the Goidelic group, like Scottish Gaelic. It is the first official language of the Republic of Ireland (since 1921) and became an official language of the European Union in 2007. Its usage has declined a great deal in its traditional strongholds in the west (*Gaeltachtaí*), but progressed in the towns, education and in the diverse aspects of modern life. Spoken by more than 1.2 million people, Irish is a daily language of 70,000 people. Thanks to efforts put in place by the Irish government and the Official Languages Act 2003, Irish and English have been placed on equal footing. For example, the television channel TG4 (formerly *Teilifís na Gaeilge*) broadcasts programmes in Irish. Despite these efforts, the Irish have a paradoxical attitude to their language and generally prefer to use English, the international language. Irish is thus in a critical situation.

Republican wall, Falls Road, Belfast, Northern Ireland

Celtic cross, Irish symbol

Politics now

The principal political problem remains the situation in Northern Ireland. Although the Republic of Ireland is run on a Western democratic model (even if it struggles to return the Irish language back to the place it deserves), the north is still only at the start of a process that could lead to a government representing all segments of the population. The rediscovery of the north by the south has encouraged a more positive and evolutionary solution to the problem, based on peace and social progress. This process began in 1995 through an agreement signed between Dublin and London on the management of affairs in the north and the Good Friday Agreement in 1998.

Representative Irish separatist parties:
• **Sinn Féin** *(Nationalist and Republican)*
• **Social Democratic and Labour Party** *(Moderate Nationalist)*

"Éire is ainm don Stát nó, sa Sacs-Bhéarla, Ireland."
(Article 1 of the Irish Constitution)
"The name of the State is Éire, or in the English language, Ireland."

Cornwall, a small-scale rebirth

The Cornish flag is made up of a white cross on a black background. Called "St Piran" or *Gwynn ha du* (white and black), by analogy with the Breton flag *Gwenn ha du*, it was originally the banner of St Piran, an Irish monk who visited Cornwall in the 6th century. Legend has it that he adopted these colours after seeing a tin plate decorated with a white cross on a black background.

Cornwall is one of the six Celtic nations and is the second-smallest Celtic language community after the Isle of Man. Its residents do not have the same recognition as the other people of the United Kingdom and they have yet to meet the challenge to resurrect their language.

For this reason, contrary to Wales and Scotland, they do not benefit from external recognition of their own identity. According to results published by the Morgan Stanley Institute in 2004, 44% of people questioned in Cornwall consider Cornwall to be English. The daily language is English, and Cornish rarely benefits from an equal status.

Considered a "dead" language, it has however become the daily language of more than a thousand people. This rebirth is an achievement that singles out this small population of Europe.

The name Cornwall comes from the Anglo-Saxon term *Cornu-Wealha*, literally signifying "Cornish-Welsh". The name *Kernow*, a Cornish term used to describe the Cornish people, is descended directly from the *Cornovii* people. Other sources say that Corineus, a Trojan warrior of the army of Brutus of Brittany, had left his name to the country.

For a long time, the exploitation of minerals and fishing has been two symbolic activities of Cornwall.

Today, as the Cornish language is protected by the government of the United Kingdom, the Cornish people continue to reclaim greater autonomy and demand to be considered as a nation of the kingdom. Controversy also surrounds the constitutional status of Cornwall: officially a "county", should it regain its status as Duchy, as considered by many Cornish people?

Identity card

Names: **Kernow[1], Cornwall[2]** (Cornwall)
Population: **526,300 inhab.** *(2006)*
Area: **3,563 km²**
Languages: **Kernewek[1]** (Cornish) *(without official status)*, **English[2]** (English) *(state official)*
Number of native speakers: **3,500[1]**
State of guardianship: **United Kingdom**
Official status: **County of the United Kingdom**
Capital: **Truru[1], Truro[2]** (Truro)
Historic religion: **Methodist Christian and Anglican**
Flag: **Gwynn ha du[1] / An Banner Sen Pyran[1]** (White and black / the banner of St Pyran)
Anthem: **Bro Goth Agan Tasow[1]** (Old Land of My Fathers)
Motto: **Onen hag oll[1]** (One and all)

Brief history

Violent rebellions were organised in Cornwall in 1497. As a result, these uprisings affected Cornish identity and language. They illustrate perfectly the difficult relations between the centre and the periphery. The popular uprising of 1497 saw the Cornish people protest against increased taxation, which had been introduced to finance the wars of Henry VII of England. This occurred despite the Cornish Stannary Parliament obtaining advantageous rights. Hoping to overthrow the king's power, Perkin Warbeck made a deal with the Cornish people in the same year, who had staged the uprising only three months earlier. Leading an army and promising to end exorbitant taxes if he took power, Warbeck obtained the support of the Cornish people. Defeated, he abandoned his army. Many Cornish people perished during this episode.

Cornwall, the ten traditional subdivisions

Geography

Cornwall is a very isolated area to the south-west of Great Britain. In fact, surrounded by the sea to the north, west and south, it finds itself cut off from the United Kingdom by the river Tamar. Thus, it forms a peninsula and is strongly exposed to the dominant winds of the Atlantic Ocean. The shoreline consists of cliffs dotted with sharm rias (or estuaries) and types of small fjords.

St Austell (S. Ostell) is the principal town with more than 30,000 inhabitants. The extraction of kaolin (clay) is one of the most important in Europe.

Geographical names

Principal towns
(Cornish / English)
Aberfal • *Falmouth*
Bosvenegh • *Bodmin Moor*
Pensans • *Penzance*
Rysrudh • *Redruth*
Sen Ostell • *St. Austell*
Truru • *Truro*
Ynysek Syllan • *Isles of Scilly*

Regions
(Cornish / English)
Karadon • *Caradon*
Keryer • *Kerrier*
Lysnowydh • *Lesnewith*
Pennwydh • *Penwith*
Pidar • *Pydar*
Powder • *Powder*
Strasnedh • *Stratton*
Tryger • *Trigg*

Language

Kernewek

The Cornish language is a language closely related to Breton and Welsh through its affiliation with Celtic languages of the Brythonic branch. Indeed, it is more removed than other Celtic languages of the Goidelic branch (Irish Gaelic and Scottish Gaelic and Manx). The Cornish people share around 80% of their vocabulary with Breton and 75% with Welsh. Until the end of the 18th century and probably the beginning of the 19th century, Cornish was a language of daily communication. Today, the number of native speakers is very small (a few thousand of neo-native speakers) but the language is in constant growth, and Cornish is again becoming the daily language of many speakers.

Politics now

Cornwall is considered as a ceremonial county of England by the British administration. According to the Constitution it is a royal Duchy of the United Kingdom. The political life of Cornwall is dominated by the Central Democrat Party (centre-left), which responds in various ways to questions of decentralisation, the Cornish language and the status of Cornwall. The lone autonomist party, the Mebyon Kernow, currently has a few representatives at most district councils and in certain municipalities.

Representative parties of Cornwall:
• **Mebyon Kernow** / Sons of Cornwall (MK) *(only political party of Cornwall, Social Democrat)*

"Me ne vidn cewsel Sawznek."
(Dolly Pentreath, last unilingual native speaker of Cornish)
"I do not want to speak English."

The Isle of Man, *the inter Celtic crossroads*

Dating from the 13th century, the Manx flag represents three legs in the form of a triskel on a red background. Its origin has been the subject of debate but the triskel often represents the three constitutive elements of life: air, water and fire. It could also represent the three personalities of the Celtic pantheon: Lugh, Daghda (Taran) and Ogme.

The Isle of Man is the smallest Celtic nation. Situated at equal distance between Scotland, Ireland, England and Wales, it has much autonomy but is not known as a sovereign state.

Dependent on the British crown, the Isle of Man is not part of the United Kingdom. Thus, even if the island is not independent and Queen Elizabeth II is the recognised sovereign there, it benefits de facto from a quasi-state status. Some abilities remain the prerogative of the United Kingdom, such as foreign affairs and defence. The parliament of the island is considered one of the oldest in the world and dates back to 979. It is known as the *Tinvaal* (Tynwald in English). It is made up of two rooms: the *Kiare as Feed* (Room of Keys), elected by direct suffrage, and the *Yn Choonseil Slattyssaghle*, legislative council, elected by indirect suffrage. Equally, it is one of the first European countries to have granted voting rights to women (1866).

Marked by Scandinavian influence, the Isle of Man nevertheless retains a strong Celtic culture. The last native speaker of Manx, Ned Maddrell, died in 1974. However, it is spoken as a second language by many thousands of Manx people. In spite of an important number of Britons installing a strong Anglicism, the Manx embarked on a campaign to reclaim their culture, notably music and dance, taught as extracurricular activities in schools.

As with the Faroe Islands, the Isle of Man benefits from a special regime which allows them to not be part of the European Union. The Manx pound is the money in circulation and the vigorous tax regime allows businesses to benefit from substantial advantages. Because of this it has become a true tax haven.

Timeline

500 BC • First Celts arrive on the island.

5th century • St Patrick, the Irish monk, brings Christianity to the Isle of Man.

9th–13th century • Scandinavian invasions and rule of the Norwegian kings, in particular Harald I, Magnus III and Håkon IV.

1275 • Battle of Ronaldsway; the Scottish drive away the Norwegian rulers.

1290 • England takes possession of the Isle of Man.

14th–18th century • The counts of Derby govern the island.

1866 • Creation of a local government. Beginning of Manx autonomy.

1960s • The Isle of Man becomes a tax haven in order to offset the economic crisis experienced by the island.

1974 • Death of Ned Maddrell, last native Manx speaker.

1990s • Opening of the first school in Manx.

Identity card

Names: **Ellan Vannin**[1], **Isle of Man**[2]
Population: **80,058 inhab.**
Area: **572 km²**
Languages: **Gaelg**[1] (Manx), **English**[2] (English) (official)
Number of speakers: **1,689** (2001)
State of guardianship: **United Kingdom**
Official status: **Dependency of the British crown**
Capital: **Doolish**[1], **Douglas**[2] (Douglas)
Historic religion: **Christian Anglican**
Flag: **Tree cassyn**[1] (The three legs)
Anthem: **Arrane Ashoonagh dy Vannin**[1] (O Land of My Birth)
Motto: **Quocunque Jeceris Stabit** (in Latin), **Aghterbee ceauee shiu eh, shassee eh**[1], (Whithersoever you throw it, it will stand)

Brief history

For a long time, the Scandinavians, most notably the Norwegians, reigned on the Isle of Man. In 1275, wishing to reinforce the authority of the Sudreyar, the island's royal family of Norwegian origin, the Manx opposed the Scottish army, who were attempting to take control. During the Battle of Ronaldsway, the two groups clashed. The Scots won, which led to the death of King Godfred Magnusson and the flight of his court to Norway. Due to this defeat, the Manx people were later integrated into the British crown. Relations between the two Celtic people, Manx and Scottish, remain marked by this event, even though today, inter-celtism enables partial reconciliation between the old enemies and the discovery of a common centre of interest for the rebirth and unity of Celtic culture in Europe.

The Isle of Man, the six administrative divisions "sheadings"

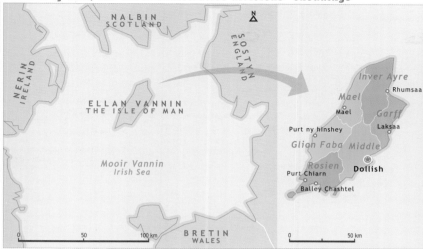

Geography

In the middle of the Irish Sea, the Isle of Man is made up of an island of more than 500 km² and three small islands (Caif, St Michael and St Patrick). Situated a little more than 50 km from Ireland, Scotland and England, it benefits from an oceanic climate which allows varied vegetation to be grown there: forests and pastures are interspersed. Its highest point, Sniall in Manx, Snaefell in English, reaches 621m. The island is divided into six sheadings, traditional administrative divisions: Glion Faba, Mael, Inver Ayre, Garff, Middle (the capital Douglas is found there) and Rosien.

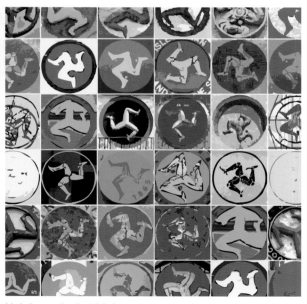

Variation on the the triskel

Principal towns
(Manx / English)
Dollish • *Douglas*
Garff • *Garff*
Glion Faba • *Glenfaba*
Inver Ayre • *Ayre*
Mael • *Michael*
Purt Chiarn • *Port Erin*
Purt ny h-Inshey • *Peel*
Rhumsaa • *Ramsey*
Rosien • *Rushen*

Regions
(Manx / English)
Garff • *Garff*
Glion Faba • *Glenfaba*
Inver Ayre • *Ayre*
Mael • *Michael*
Middle
Rosien • *Rushen*

Geographical names

"Gyn chengey, guy cheer."
(Universal proverb)
"Without language, no country."

Galicia, between Celtic and Iberian cultures

Dating from the 19th century, the Galician flag, a white background crossed by an oblique light blue band is inspired by the naval crest of the Corunna. Adopted by the Galician government in 1984, the official version bears the coat of arms, it is used only by the local authorities, while the version without arms is by the civilian population.

Galicia is an autonomous Spanish community defined as a "historic nation". It is situated at the north-western tip of the Iberian Peninsula.

Galicia distinguishes itself from Spain linguistically, historically and culturally. Its peripheral location has often spared it from significant assimilation. Galician, a Romance language, is related to Portuguese. The differences between the two languages are explained by a political context and different economies.

The oldest people known in Galicia are the *Oestrimnis* (people of the north-west), of which few archaelogical traces remain. In the 1st century BC,

the Celtic people arrived. Following that, under Roman rule, the territory took the name *Gallaecia*. The country was alternately ruled by the Suevi, the Visigoths and the Arabs. From 711, Gallicia embarked on alliances with neighbouring principalities began: Asturias, Léon and Castille. In this century the oppression of Galicia began, which the chronicles of time will eventually call "the taming and castration of the kingdom of Galicia".

Galician, a language of medieval lyricism, disappeared from all official documents. Over three difficult centuries, cultural and political movements struggled. During the 1st Spanish Republic, a project for the future of the Galician state was developed. Overwritten during the Franco dictatorship, the Galicians turned more and more towards separatist movements, which are struggling to catch up economically due to their peripheral location.

Although Galician is now used more and has the support of some media (newspapers, televisions), Castilian holds greater importance, endangering a fragile balance of languages.

Timeline

3rd century • The Roman emperor Diocletian creates the Province of Gallaecia.

411–585 • Kingdom of the Suevi of Galicia (period of prosperity).

559–570 • The Suevi king Theodemir divides the country into dioceses and provinces.

815–830 • Discovery of the tomb of St John the Apostle. Compostella becomes one of the biggest Christian centres for pilgrimage.

12th–13th century • Period of splendour for Galician literature.

1431 & 1467–69 • Anti-seigneurial revolts of the Irmandiñas (bourgeoisie, clergy and country people).

1622 • Re-establishment of Galician sovereignty following the 275 year supremacy of the Castilian town of Zamora.

19th century • The *Rexurdimento*, artistic and literary rebirth.

1980 • Approval by referendum on the status of the autonomy of Galicia, recognising Galician nationality.

Identity card

Names: **Galiza[1], Galicia[2]** (Galicia)
Population: **2,830,000 inhab.** [note 3] *(2007)*
Area: **33,277 km²** [note 3]
Languages: **Galego[1]** (Galician), **Castellano[2]** (Castilian) *(official)*
Number of native speakers: **2,400,000[1]** *(2005)*
State of guardianship: **Spain**
Official status: **Autonomous community**
Capital: **Santiago de Compostela[12]**
Historic religion: **Roman Catholics**
Flag: **Bandeira de Galiza[1]** (Flag of Galicia)
Anthem: **Os Pinos[1]** *(The Pines)*
Motto: **None**

Galicia has its own assembly with broad powers. The political life of Galicia has long been marked by Manuel Fraga Iribarne, head of Galicia from 1989 to 2005. A former minister under the Franco dictatorship and an ultra-conservative, he is one of the emblematic figures of the Popular Party, which is ultra-conservative. This paradoxical period is now over. Indeed, a coalition between the Socialist Party (PSOE) (32.5% of votes) and the Galician Bloc (19.6% of votes) has reversed the spiral of Galician conservatism. The Bloque Nacionalista Galego could now have a vice-president in the *Xunta de Galicia* (parliament).

The most representative Galician parties:
• **Bloque Nacionalista Galego** / Nationalist Bloc of Galicia (BNG) *(Progressive separatist)*
• **Terra Gallega** *(Separatist conservative)*
• **Nós-Unidade Popular** *(Separatist Marxist)*

Politics now

Galicia, the four provinces and Galician fringes

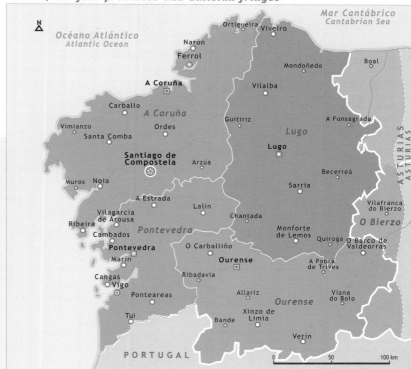

Galicia lies at the tip of the Iberian Peninsula. Surrounded by the Atlantic Ocean to the north and west, it borders the Asturias to the east and Portugal to the south, a country that it shares a common linguistic heritage with as well as privileged cultural relations. Divided into four provinces (shown on the map), the historic territory of Galicia extends east, officially into Asturias and Castile and León, where a part of the population still uses Galician. Made up of a number of villages, the population is spread over the territory. It is concentrated on the coast, in particular in the villages of La Corona and Vigo, the economic centres of the country. The better-known Santiago de Compostela, the cultural capital of Galicia, stretches far beyond the border of the country. The Pena Trevina reaches 2,124 m.

Geography

Principal towns
(Galician / Castilian)
Vigo • *Vigo*
A Coruña • *La Coruña*
Lugo • *Lugo*
Ourense • *Orense*
Santiago de Compostela • *Santiago de Compostela*
Pontevedra • *Pontevedra*

Ferrol • *Ferrol*

Regions
(Galician / Castilian)
A Coruña • *La Coruña*
Lugo • *Lugo*
Pontevedra • *Pontevedra*
Ourense • *Orense*

Geographical names

«Tivo Galiza reis antes que Castela leis.»
(Galician proverb)
"There were Galician kings before there were Castilian laws."

Catalan countries, *"We are a nation"*

The Catalan flag is the flag of the old kings of the crown of Aragon, which was also used by the Countess Ermessenda of Barcelona (around 1058). The number of red stripes varied until it was finally fixed at four. This royal directive gradually became the symbol most widely used by the Catalan people, identical to that of Aragon and Provence.

Catalonia, commonly called the Catalan countries, is a Romance nation stretching over 800 km. Lying at the extreme north-west of the Mediterranean Sea, it runs along the easternmost strip of the Iberian Peninsula, including the Balearic Islands. Apart from the principality of Andorra, the rest of the territory belongs to Spain and France.

The history of Catalonia is strongly related to Carolingian conquests (8th–9th centuries), which led to the formation of several counties, which then became a hereditary unit. Barcelona quickly became the cultural centre and its rulers were implicitly princes of Catalonia. After the union with Aragon (1137), the country stretched towards the south: Tortosa (1109), Lleida (1139), Mallorca (1229), Valencia (1232–44), Alicante (1296) and Minorca (1302). The Catalan crown was linked to the Habsburg dynasty, but after a period of splendour from the 14th and 15th centuries, trouble arose. After the War of Succession (1697–1715), northern Catalonia came under French rule (1659), which saw the loss of Aragon. From this period on, Spanish power would periodically deny Catalan identity.

It was not until the 19th century that the revival of nationalism was widely promoted by the industrial bourgeoisie, centred in Barcelona. Catalan politics was added to the literary rebirth, the highpoint of which was undoubtedly the experiences of the Association (1910–26) and the Generalitat of Catalonia (1931–39). In the 1960s a movement appeared in favour of uniting Catalan territories under the term "Catalan countries", inspiring the contemporary ideal of Catalan independence. In spite of these strong claims, the dominant trend has been a form of status quo limited to the defence of the strong regional claims supported by Catalonia's powerful political parties. This has not prevented 74% of Catalonians from voting yes in a referendum on the new status of autonomy in 2006.

Identity card

Names: **Països Catalans[1]** (Catalan Countries) **Catalunya[1], Cataluña[2]** (Catalonia)
Population: **13,712,983 inhab.** note 4 *(2006)*
Area: **70,520 km[2]** note 4
Languages: **Català[1]** (Catalan), **Castellano[2]** (Castilian), **Occitan[3]** (Occitan) *(official)*
Number of native speakers: **9,800,000[1]**
States of guardianship: **Spain, France, Italy**
Official status: **Independent state (Andorra), autonomous communities in Spain, department in France, a commune in Italy**
Capital: **Barcelona[12]** (Barcelone)
Historic religion: **Roman Catholic**
Flag: **La Senyera[1]** (The Signal)
Anthem: **Els Segadors[1]** (The Reapers)
Motto: **Som i serem[1]** (We are and we will be)

Brief history

The Catalonian *Renaixença* (renaissance) of the second half of the 19th century is considered a phenomenon halfway between the Provençal *Felibrige* (primarily a literary movement) and the Italian *Risorgimento* (clearly political). Thus, in spite of the efforts to normalise the Catalan language and culture, the general trend of Catalanism leans towards formation of a multinational Spanish state in a federal form. At the end of a period of decline (in the 18th century), called *Decadència*, this movement built on the recovery of Catalan as a language, not only by the promotion of diverse forms of art, theatre and literature, but also by reforming its orthography. The *Renaixença* stretched throughout the whole of the Catalan territory.

Catalan countries, territorial organisation

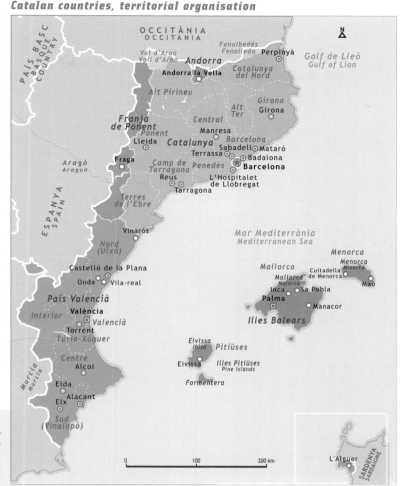

Covering an area of almost 70,000 km², the Catalan Country stretches for 800 km from north to south. Essentially a Mediterranean climate is found there, and there are high mountains like that of the great Cordilleras. To the north, the Pyrenees (Aneto, 3,404 m) dominate. This chain of mountains stretches more than 1,000 m to the south and along the Mediterranean. The Ebro constitutes the most important Catalan river. A great number of tributaries and smaller rivers form the drainage system of Catalonia. The urban mesh consists of large metropolises, whose two urban centres are Barcelona to the north and Valencia to the south. These two towns form larger groups, similar to metropolises, on account of their proximity to other cities. Alicante is the largest town in the south while in the north it is Perpignan. There are five major groups: Catalonia (which includes the former principality of Catalonia and northern Catalonia), the Franja de Ponent, the Valencian region, the Baleric Islands, Andorra and Alghero (Catalan town in Sardinia). The term *Països Catalans* (Catalan countries) describes this group. The map shows the territorial divisions into "vegueries" for the Generalitat of Catalonia (which are under development) and regions for the Valencian Community.

Geography

> "L'Esperit Català rebrota sempre i sobreviu els seus il·lusos enterradors."
> (Francesc Pujols, Catalan writer)
> "The Catalan spirit is reborn and survives its utopian oppressors."

Catalan countries, *"We are a nation"*

Català

Catalan is certainly the most spoken minority language in Europe. There are more native speakers of Catalan than there are native speakers of Danish, Slovenian or Estonian, which are national languages. Ten million people speak it. Thus, the term minority seems inappropriate in this case. Catalan is a Romance language closely related to Occitan, but has certain grammatical differences. It also shares common character traits with Ibero-Romance languages, like Castilian and Portuguese. The language is divided into two groups where intercomprehension is possible: western Catalan (following a regular line from north to south, from the Pyrenees to the Valencian region) and eastern Catalan (from the Roussillon to Tarragona and including the Balearic Islands and the town of Alghero in Sardinia). Although the knowledge of Catalan by newly arrived immigrants is important, its social use is decreasing in favour of the adoption of Castilian as an intercommunitary language, especially in the large agglomerations like Barcelona or Valencia. In the autonomous community of Catalonia, more than 5.7 million people speak it. A specific language of Catalonia, according to the Statute of Autonomy in 1979, Catalan is protected by a range of laws including the 2003 Linguistic Normalisation Law establishing Catalan in all acts of civil life, in addition to Castilian. It is this that has saved Catalan. Radio and television (TV3 and Canal 33) play their role as a vehicle for the language. In the Valencian community, thanks to the Statute of Autonomy of 1982, the authorities defend bilingualism even if in a more timid manner than in the Catalonian Generalitat: many Castilian speakers are hostile to the Catalan language. In northern Catalonia, the contempt of the French authorities regarding regional languages doesn't allow for much progress as in the south. Only a little more than 10,000 students learn it.

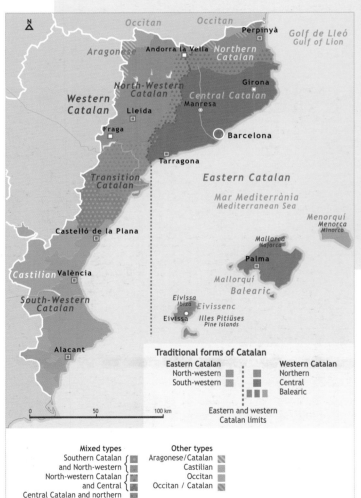

Catalan countries, the linguistic varieties

Traditional forms of Catalan

Eastern Catalan	Western Catalan
North-western	Northern
South-western	Central
	Balearic

Eastern and western Catalan limits

Mixed types
Southern Catalan and North-western
North-western Catalan and Central
Central Catalan and northern

Other types
Aragonese/Catalan
Castilian
Occitan
Occitan / Catalan

Due to the division of Catalonia between several administrative divisions, the political life is different from one region to the other. For example, Andorra is a sovereign state; the north has a general council without real powers. Despite the existence of statutes of autonomy in the principality of Catalonia, Valencia and the Balearic Islands, power is controlled by the Spanish government. According to polls, 20% of Catalonians would support independence (more than 35% in the Generalitat of Catalonia), but in these past years two battles have dominated the Catalan political scene. The Catalans have wished to be recognised as a "nation" like the Scottish, and they also fight for the Catalan language to be recognised at European level, a minority language more widely spoken than some official languages. In July 2010, after experiencing tensions with the central government regarding the Statute of Autonomy, 1.5 million Catalans protested in Barcelona to remind them that they had adopted autonomy four years earlier by referendum.

The most representative nationalist parties in Catalonia (complete list, see the table on pages 32–33)***:***
• **Convergència i Unió** / Convergeance and Union (CiU) *(Autonomist liberal and Social Democrat coalition)*
• **Esquerra Republicana de Catalunya** / Republican Left of Catalonia (ERC) *(Separatist progressive)*

Politics now

Catalan activists during demonstrations titled "We are a nation" which brought together tens of thousands of people in the streets of Barcelona

Occitania, a vast multifaceted area

The Occitan flag is made up of an Occitan cross (or Cross of Forcalquier, cross of the count of Toulouse), gold in colour on a red background. In the right-hand corner a seven-pointed star is often found in memory of the Occitan *Félibrige* literary movement.

Occupying a central space in Latin Europe, Occitania is a fully defined nation without official recognition, where a strong sense of southern identity persists despite the decline of the language.

Thirty-three French departments in eight administrative regions, Val d'Aran in the autonomous government of Catalonia and eleven Italian valleys, Occitania is a genuine central European area that occupies a third of the French state, from the Alps to the Pyrenees. For a long time, Occitania was a genuine bridge between the north and south of Europe. It was the cradle of the European Renaissance of the Middle Ages,

seeing the birth of the poetry of the Troubadours, who reinvented love and exported the Oc language throughout Europe. Nowadays, an Occitan-Catalan Euroregion has strong southern impulses in part of the territory, even if Provence prefers to look towards Piedmont and the Alps.

The term "Occitanian" has been used for a relatively short time (20th century) but its existence has been confirmed since 1290 to indicate ownership of the Oc language by the king of France. Today, the term "Occitan", is used by the majority of activists.

The language is one of the primary issues advocated by activists. Demonstrations in favour of this brought together 15,000 in Carcassonne in 2005 and more than 20,000 people in Béziers in 2007. Further regions developed political language projects in favour of the Occitan language (Midi-Pyrénées, Languedoc-Roussillon, Aquitaine, Rhône-Alpes but not in Provence, despite being the birthplace of the Occitanian linguistic and cultural renaissance in the 19th century). All regions combined, 80,000 students learn (or are aware of) Occitan today.

Timeline

123 BC • Conquest of the south of Gaul by the Romans

466 • The Visigoths, under the reign of their King Euric the Great (466–84) dominate their territory stretching to south-eastern Europe.

1209 • Pope Innocent III launches a crusade against the Albigensian heretics. In 1213, the Occitan defeat at the Battle of Muret is a symbol of the end of Occitan independence.

1790 • Abbé Grégoire launches his linguistic survey on "Patois". The Occitans are among the most numerous to respond.

1854 • Birth of the Maillane of Félibrige, a literary movement founded by Frédéric Mistral (Nobel Prize for Literature in 1904).

1907 • Revolt of the winegrowers in Languedoc. 70,000 people demonstrate in Montpellier in June, referring to the Crusade against the Albigensians.

2004 • 150 years of Félibrige. The Midi-Pyrénées and Languedoc-Roussillon create a Euroregion with the Catalan and Aragon regions.

Identity card

Names: **Occitània[1,5], Occitanie[2], Occitania[3,4]**
Population: **15,000,000 inhab.** note 5
Area: **190,000 km² note 5**
Languages: **Occitan[1]** (Occitan) *(without official status in France, status in Spain and Italy),* **Français[2]** (French), **Italiano[3]** (Italian), **Castellano[4]** (Castilian), **Català[5]** (Catalan) *(official)*
Numerb of native speakers: **500,000 to 3,000,000[1]**
States of guardianship: **France, Italy, Spain**
Official status: **Regions without autonomous status in France, Catalan country for the Val d'Aran, valleys of the Piedmont regions and Liguria for Italy**
Capital: **Tolosa[1]** (Toulouse), **Marseilha[1]** (Marseille)
Historic religion: **Roman Catholic**
Flag: **Crotz occitana[1]** (Occitan Cross)
Anthem: **Se canta[1]** (If it Sings), *other anthems are used*
Motto: **None**

Brief history

The crusade against the Albigians (1208–49) was the only crusade in European territory. It was decided upon by the Pope and the King of France to re-evangelise the county of Toulouse, which housed many Albigian "heretics", or Cathars (the name dates from the 19th century). It was primarily so that the King of France could annexe the southern territories. The inhabitants of Béziers were all massacred on 22 July 1290 and the atrocities would continue. The Occitano-Catalan troops (the count of Toulouse went to the king of Aragon-Catalonia) were defeated at Muret, in 1213, and Pierre II of Aragon was killed. The crusades led by Simon of Montfort increased their power in the region. A truce was imposed by the Pope in 1214, but Count Raymond VI raised an army in 1216 to regain Toulouse. Despite a series of victories, they were finally defeated and a peace treaty was signed in Paris in 1219. It signified the beginning of the annexing of the Occitan territories by France.

Occitania, the nine traditional regions

The geography of Occitan is complex: Occitan space stretches between two seas, the Mediterranean and the Atlantic Ocean, and on three mountainous massifs, the Alps, Massif Central (or Northern in Occitan manuals) and

the Pyrenees. Among the major rivers, there is the Garonne, the Rhône, the Loire, and the source of the Pô. Occitania is the largest stateless nation in Europe, with an area of 190,000 km² (which is the equivalent of about a third of the territory of France). Economically important plains are present around the Rhône and Garonne valleys. The terrain defines cultural and agricultural regions that are quite different, even if the mountains have never constituted the real language borders: the Val d'Aran is situated on the southern slopes of the Pyrenees, and Occitan is spoken as far as the plain of the Pô Valley in Italy.

Geography

Principal towns
(Occitan / French)
Ais • *Aix-en-Provence*
Albi • *Albi*
Arles • *Arles*
Avinhon • *Avignon*
Bordèu • *Bordeaux*
Clarmont d'Auvernha • *Clermont-Ferrand*
Carcassona • *Carcassonne*
Limòtges • *Limoges*
Marselha • *Marseille*
Montpelhièr • *Montpellier*
Niça • *Nice*
Nimes • *Nimes*
Rodès • *Rodez*
Tarbas • *Tarbes*
Tolon • *Toulon*
Tula • *Tulle*
Tolosa • *Toulouse*
Valença • *Valence*

Regions (large groups)
(Occitan / French)
Auvèrnha / Auvernhe • *Auvergne*
Daufinat • *Dauphiné*
Gasconha • *Gascogne*
Lemosin • *Limousin*
Lengadòc • *Languedoc*
Lengadòc Naut • *Haut Languedoc*
Niça • *Niçois*
Provença • *Provence*
Valadas • *Vallées occitanes*

Geographical names

"A perir tot entier, qué serviriá de náisser?"
(Victor Gélu, Occitan poet)
"To entirely perish, what would be the point of being born?"

Occitania, a vast multifaceted area

The Occitan language is now split between three European states where its politcal status varies considerably. In France, Occitania is divided between 33 departments and 7 regions. No particular status encompasses this area. The status of the Occitan region is that of the French regions: they have limited power, no special skills or political autonomy and cannot conduct cultural or linguistic policy that would violate the French constitution, which states that French is the only language of the Republic (although the legislation may soon change). In Italy, the Occitan minority has been recognised by law since 1999, and individual municipalities decide whether or not they belong to a minority. The 11 Occitan valleys of Italy are attached to the Piedmont and Liguria regions. In Spain, the Val d'Aran has been recognised by Catalonia since 1991 and has its own institutions (*Conselh Generau*). The Occitan Party is the most active of autonomist parties. It is present in a few municipalities and now has five representatives at regional level.

Occitan parties:
• **Partit Occitan** / Occitan Party (POC) *(Autonomist progressive)*
• **Partit de la Nacion Occitana** / Party of the Occitan Nation (PNO) *(Separatist)*
• **Anaram au Patac** *(Revolutionary)*

Occitania, composition of the territory

Occitan

Occitan is a Romance language belonging to the Gallo-Roman group, with French, Franco-Provençal and, of course, Catalan; a language with which certain Occitan dialects (Languedocian but also Provençal in particular) allow very good inter-comprehension. Born around the year 1,000, the language distinguishes itself from French by the more conservative traits: clearly, the Occitan language remained close to Latin and even closer to other Roman languages (Italian, Spanish, etc.). There are three variants, Gascon in the west, Languedocian-Provençal in the middle and south-east and Limousin-Auvergne-Upper-Provençal in the north. The number of native speakers is generally estimated as being between 500,000 and 7 million (taking into account the speakers knowing the language but not speaking it regularly), at the high end nearly 20% of the population (census data does not allow greater accuracy). It is spoken in the whole territory of Occitania, in the Val d'Aran in Catalonia and the valleys of the Piedmont Alps, where it has official status as a minority language. France refuses to give prominence to regional languages, where the Occitan language is now a concern for the future. Certainly the only encouraging fact is the 80,000 students who learn it or are starting to learn. However, its place in the media, on road signs and in administration is poor.

Activist poster for the Occitan language

Corsica, a turbulent story of a quest for freedom

The flag of Corsica is made up of the head of a Moor on a white background. When the Italian geographer Mainaldi Galerati mapped the land of Philip II, King of Spain, in the 16th century, this symbol was used for the first time and adopted by the Republic of Corsica in 1762. The white recalls the colour of the Virgin Mary, under the protection of independent Corsica, which was implemented in 1735. The current flag represents these two elements.

Rebel land, camped in the middle of the Mediterranean, Corsica, despite its small population, often makes its voice heard on the international scene. The national liberation movements are the legacy of Pasquale Paoli, one of the heroes of the Corsican nation.

The origin of the population of the island remains uncertain, however, the most convincing theory is probably the arrival of fishermen from what is now Tuscany. This first settlement on the island dates from 9000 BC. Throughout its history the Corsican people have forged a strong spirit. The will to live free and at peace is constant, but the scourge of the history of neighbouring powers has always managed to break the peace, for instance the period of independence in the 18th century when the Corsicans defeated the Genoese.

Nostalgic for the good times, the Corsican nationalist movement began in the 1960s as a regionalist movement and radicalised thereafter. The National Liberation Front of Corsica (FLNC) (1976) marks the division between the separatists and the autonomists.

These conflicts led to the creation of a special status for Corsica in 1991. The teaching of Corsican is now promoted, but the notion of "Corsican people", which would be indicated by this, was rejected by the French Constitutional Council, refusing to acknowledge that there may be other people on "her" territory.

Today, the political situation in Corsica is still tense. Thus, linguistic and separatist claims are still valid.

Timeline

1347 • Sambucucciu d'Alandu establishes the "Terra di u cumunu" whose main idea is equality and the distribution of wealth.

1553–64 • Sampieru Corsu tries to liberate Corsica from the Genoese.

1735 • Corsica is independent. Don Luiggi Giafferi and Ghjacintu Paoli are among the leaders of the nation.

1755 • Corsican constitution drafted by Pasquale Paoli.

1769 • Battle of Ponte Novu, French militarily takes over Corsica.

1943 • Corsica is freed from fascists, a year before France.

1970 • Revival, cultural and political renewal. Political renewal comes from the CRA brothers Simeoni.

1976 • Creation of the FLNC (National Liberation Front of Corsica).

Identity card

Names: **Corsica[1]**, **Corse[2]** (Corsica)
Population: **285,000 inhab.**
Area: **8,680 km²**
Languages: **Corsu[1]** (Corsican) *(without official status)*, **Français[2]** (French) *(official)*
Number of native speakers: **40,000 to 127,000[1]**
State of guardianship: **France**
Official status: **Local authority in France**
Capital: **Corti** (Corte)
Historic religion: **Roman Catholic**
Flag: **A Testa Mora / Bandera Corsa[1]** (The Head of the Moor / Flag of Corsica)
Anthem: **Diu vi salvi regina[1]** (God Bless the Queen)
Motto: **None**

Brief history

In 1755, Pasquale Paoli, one of the principal Corsican leaders against the power of Genoa, was proclaimed general of the nation. It was then that the first European democracy was born. The Corsican constitution made it a point of honour to be exemplary. It established the separation of powers and granted the right to vote to all citizens, including women. The government headquarters were in Corte, now considered the historical capital of Corsica. This period of independence was challenged by France, allied with the Republic of Genoa. A treaty was signed between the two states. The Corsicans, having been alerted to this, were definitively defeated by French troops in 1769, despite some previous victories.

Corsica's historical regions

[Map of Corsica showing historical regions]

U Mare Mediterràneu
Mediterranean Sea

Capi Corsu

Capi Corsu

Bastìa
San Fiurenzu
L'isula
Calvi · Balagna · Nebbiu
U Viscuvatu
Calvi · Bastìa
Calacuccia · Corti · Cervioni
Corti
Vicu · Aleria
Carghjese · Bucugnà
Aleria
Ghisunaccia
Aiacciu è
i trè valli
Aiacciu · Zicavu
Zonza
Rocca
Pruprià · Bunifaziu
Sartè · Purti Vechju

Bunifaziu

0   50 km

Geography

Corsica is a Mediterranean island stretching 183 km in length and 83.5 km wide. It is situated 340 km from Barcelona, 100 km from Nice, 55 km from Livorno and 8 km from Sardinia. Corsica has more than 1,000 km of coastline. It is a mountainous island, whose summit, the Monte Cintu, reaches 2,710 m. From these mountains flow the rivers that irrigate every valley, the two largest being u Golu (84 km long) and u Tavignanu (80 km long). The island has many lakes like u Ninu, u Melu and u Crenu. Coastal cities are among the most populated, Bastia and Calvi in the north, Ajaccio (Aiacciu) and Bonifaccio (Bunifaziu) in the south. Nestled in the heart of the mountains, Corte is the historic capital of Corsica. Corsican landscapes are very diverse and can go from snowy mountains to sandy beaches surrounded by clear sea in less than a two-hour drive. Corsica is traditionally made up of 'pieves', which are the parishes of origin. These are often grouped by historical regions, but may vary.

Principal towns
(Corsican / French)
Aiacciu • *Ajaccio*
Bastìa • *Bastia*
Bunifaziu • *Bonifaccio*
Calvi • *Calvi*
Corti • *Corte*
L'isula • *Île Rousse*
Purti Vechju • *Porto Vecchio*
San Fiurenzu • *Saint Florent*
Sartè • *Sartene*

Geographical names

Regions (Corsican / French)
Aiacciu è i trè valli • *Ajaccio et les trois vallées*
Aleria • *Aleria*
Balagna • *Balagne*
Bastìa • *Bastia*
Calvi • *Calvi*
Capi Corsu • *Cap Corse*
Corti • *Corte*
Nebbiu • *Nebbio*
Rocca Bunifaziu • *Rocca Bonifaccio*
Vicu • *Vico*

> "Quand'a cuscenza si discita nunda ùn pò l'assufucà."
> (Pasquale Paoli, Corsican politician)
> "When consciousness awakes, nothing can suppress it. It must be carried away."

Corsica, *a turbulent story of a quest for freedom*

Only the Corsican language
is left visible on these road signs

Corsu

The Corsican language is a Roman language of the Italo-Roman group. The diverse influences, Latin, Germanic, Arabic, Tuscan, have shaped a unique language, particular to the island of Corsica. The Corsican language is called "polynomic" because it contains specific features in areas of the island, which does not detract from its uniqueness. It was never official; even during independence, the language of the people was Corsican but the official language was Tuscan. More than 30,000 students learn Corsican which is very encouraging in regards to the total population of the island. It is estimated that 60% of the population speaks it. The law establishing the status of the territorial collectivity of Corsica (1991) endows the Corsican Assembly with broad powers including education. But these powers remain limited in view of French centralism. Even if Corsican is the first language of the country, it is now seriously threatened due to its vague status and its optional nature in education, not surviving through learning from an early age.

Today Corsica enjoys a special status granted after years
of struggle. Since 1982 the Corsican Assembly holds executive power and may propose legislation to the French government. In practice, no law or admendment has not been accepted. Tensions between central power and the Corsicans often make headlines. Since the failed 2003 referendum, there has been no dialogue between the nationalists and the French state. Despite calls for national political dialogue the situation seems to be at an impasse. The nationalist movement represents about 35% of voters in Corsica. Recently, the Corsican parties have been restructured. In the last elections (2010), the autonomists (FEMU in Corsica) and separatists (Free Corsica) represented 35.75% of the vote, or 25.89 % and 9.85 % respectively.

Principal Corsican parties:
• **Corsica Libera** / Free Corsica *(Separatist)*
• **Partitu di a Nazione Corsa** / Party of the Corsican Nation *(Autonomist)*
• **A Chjama Naziunale /** National Call *(Autonomist)*
• **A Manca Naziunale** / The National Left *(Autonomist)*
• **I Verdi Corsi** / The Corsican Greens *(Autonomist)*

Pasquale Paoli, hero of the Corsican nation, statue in Corte

Sardinia, "the first people" of the Mediterranean

The Sardinian flag, also called "Four Moors" appeared in the 14th century. It represented the kingdom of Sardinia in the Aragon crown. There exist different forms, heads looking right or left. The law of 15 April 1999 on the flag finally fixed the rules relating to its form.

Sardinia is the largest stateless nation within the Italian state. What may be regarded as 300 years of "cultural colonization" in Italy has had little effect on the characteristics of that country, where "Sardidadi", which can be translated as a sense of Sardinia, has not been shaken.

The Sardinians are often considered as one of the oldest indigenous people of Europe. Inhabiting this Mediterranean island for many centuries, they have been little influenced by Barbarian invasions or other people.

This relative isolation has made Sardinia a singular nation where linguistic and cultural traditions remain present. From the 11th to the 14th century, it was controlled by the Genoese, then the kingdom of Aragon (the town of Alghero, former capital, still speaks Catalan). Italian became the official language after Catalan in 1764.

It was not until the 19th century that Sardinian literature reached its peak, triggering an intense debate on language standardisation because of significant language differences. Sardinia has had autonomous status since 1948, which makes mention of linguistic rights, confirmed later by many texts. But in practice these have had little effect. Sardinian is considered a language in danger, despite the number of native speakers, since it is spoken in private and has little public visibility. The media use it but not much.

The autonomist movements have a long tradition in Sardinia. The autonomists of the Sardinian Action Party, founded in 1920, have always campaigned for the status of the Sardinian language, using sessions of the council (meeting) for this. Since then, other more radical parties have emerged. These are pro-independence parties with relative electoral success.

Timeline

17th century bc • The Nuragic civilisation commences, the Sardinians build more than 12,000 Megalithic towers.

227 bc • Sardinia becomes a Roman province.

1000 • Sardinia was ruled by kings and judges, Caralis, Arborea, Torres, Gallura. Period of independent splendour.

1409 • Sardinia belongs to the kingdom of Aragon until the Treaty of Utrecht is signed in 1713.

1720 • Philip V gives Sardinia to Austria, who then gives it to Victor Emmanuel II of Savoy.

1794–6 • Revolt against the king of Piedmont. The Piedmontese are driven out of Cagliari.

1948 • Implementation of the status of autonomous region.

1970–80 • Birth of movements for bilingualism and independence. The "Sardinian wind" begins to change attitudes.

Identity card

Names: **Sardigna (Sardinnya)[1], Sardenya[2], Sardigna[3]** (Sardinia)
Population: **1,662,758** (2007)
Area: **24,090 km²**
Languages: **Sardu[1]** (Sardinian), **Català[2]** (Catalan) (status of protection), **Italiano[3]** (Italian) (official)
Number of native speakers: **1,200,000[1]**
State of guardianship: **Italy**
Official status: **Autonomous region of Italy**
Capital: **Casteddu[1], Cagliari[3]** (Cagliari)
Historic religion: **Roman Catholic**
Flag: **Cuàturu Morus[1]** (Four Moors)
Anthem: **Su Patriotu Sardu a sos Feudatàrius** (The Sardinian Patriots tell feudalism)
Motto: **None**

Brief history

The destiny of Sardinia changed on 8 August 1720 when it surrendered to the Savoy family in Cagliari, who would later rule in Italy. Treated as a colony, Sardinia was familiar with revolts at the end of the 18th century. In 1793, the Sardinian parliament sent a delegation to Turin to ask for more power after defeating the French troops who had tried to invade the island. This promise, unfulfilled by Victor Emmanuel III, sparked revolts by the Piedmontese based in Cagliari, which were quashed swiftly.

Sardinia, four judicata and historic regions

Sardinia is the second largest Mediterranean island, 80% being made up of mountains and woods. The population is essentially concentrated in the region of Cagliari, the main town that is also the capital. Historically, it was made up of four autonomous regions, judiciaries, governed by the king elected by the Sardinian parliament. The judiciaries are divided into smaller regions, the *curadoria*. Since 2005, Sardinia has been divided into eight provinces (see following page), despite the commitment of the population to the many micro-regions that make up the country. Much of them are represented on the map. The Sardinian economy, based on tourism, profits from local knowledge, whether on wine or products derived from agriculture. The isolation of the island, while a benefit in preserving a heritage more than a thousand years old, can be a major handicap when travel or export is necessary. During the 1950s, the Italian state tried in vain to industrialise the region despite transport costs.

Principal towns
(Sardinian / Italian)
A Maddalena • *La Maddalena*
Altzachena • *Arzachena*
Aristànis • *Oristano*
Igrèsias • *Iglesias*
Biddexidru • *Villacidro*
Carbònia • *Carbonia*
Casteddu • *Cagliari*

Guspini • *Guspini*
Lanusè • *Lanusei*
Nùgoro • *Nuoro*
Othieri • *Ozieri*
Santu Antiogu • *Sant'Antioco*
Tàtari • *Sassari*
Tèmpiu • *Tempio*
Terranòa • *Oblia*

Historic regions
(Sardinian / Italian)
Gaddura • *Gallura*
Logudòro • *Logudoro*
Arborea • *Arborea*
(Arborée)
Casteddu • *Cagliari*
(Calaris)

Geographical names

> **"S'ira intendei pro s'indipendenzia chircada sempre..."**
> (Montanaru, Sardinian poet)
> *"I heard a pulse of anger for an independence always looked for..."*

Sardinia, "the first people" of the Mediterranean

The Sardinian political situation has changed greatly in recent years, since the region gained its autonomy. The separatist feeling is more and more prevalent among younger generations and it is now accepted that the Sardinians are a different "nation" in the Italian state. The current debate is about revising the special status of Sardinia, which dates back 60 years. It would give more power to the Sardinians. This project is supported by the Sardinian Council (legislative body).

The most representative Sardinian parties:
• **Indipendèntzia/Repùbrica de Sardigna** / Independence/Republic of Sardinia (IRS) *(Separatist)*
• **Sardigna Natzione Indipendentzia** / Sardinia Independentist Nation (SNI) *(Separatist)*
• **Partidu Sardu** / Sardinian Party (PsdAz) *(Autonomist)*
• **A Manca pro s'Indipendentzia** (aMp'I) *(Separatist)*

Politics now

Sardinia, linguistic varieties

Forms of Sardinian
- Sardo-Corsican { Sassarese / Gallurese
- Loguodorese { Loguodorese (Sardinian proper) / Central Loguodorese / Nuorese
- Campidanese { Campidanese

Other linguistic situations
- Catalan ■
- Ligurian ■

Language

Sardu
Sardinian is a Roman language of the family of Indo-European languages. It is not however like the other languages of the group, such as Italian, French or Catalan, and differs so much so that it is often linguistically isolated. Two variations dominate: Campidanese (and its own dialects) and Loguodorese (variation spoken in the north) (Gallurese is very close to Corsican). Inter-comprehension between the variations of the language is relatively easy. The first documents published in Sardu date from the 11th century. It is estimated that of the 1.6 million Sardinians, 1.3 million know the language, which is exceptional for a minority language. Despite the autonomous status agreed in 1948, protection of the Sardinian language is low. However, regional law on the promotion and enhancement of culture and the Sardinian language (1997) provides broad protection in theory but in practice, whether judicial, administrative or media, Sardu is virtually absent from all areas of public life. Worse still, its teaching is almost non-existent, the ubiquity of Italian endangering the language. Despite the large number of speakers, the future of Sardu is more worrying due more to the rural character of society than to widespread awareness. The voluntary sector is working on its promotion following the example of Wales or Catalonia.

The head of a Moor represents Sardinia, similar to Corsica

Friuli, *border of empires*

The Friulian flag depicts a yellow eagle on a blue background. It incorporates the emblem of the patriarch of Aquileia, the origin of this name being eagle (Latin *Aquila*).

Friuli is numerically the most important Rhaeto-Romance nation. In fact, Friulians, along with the Romansh and Ladins, make up three historic nations of Romance culture in central Europe.

Like a large number of minority peoples, the Friulians are distinguished by their language. It is also due to their rich history that Friulians are eligible for special status in an Italy anxious to develop regional autonomy.

Initially populated by the Celts and the Carni, Friuli was colonised by the Romans before becoming a buffer zone between the Barbarians and the Roman Empire. It is during the Middle Ages, in the 8th century, that Friuli acquired legal status for the first time. It was a duchy during the reign of King Alboin of Lombardy. From the 12th century, and for six further centuries, Friuli had a parliament representing the municipalities, the nobility and the clergy. From the 11th to the 14th century, under the administration of the diocese of Aquileia, Friuli saw a period of exceptional democratisation, particularly with the creation of the parliament. During the rule of Lombardy and that of the Franks, the Friulians experienced a difficult period when they were governed by the Venetians, who depleted their lands. They lost their institutions under the oppression of Napoleon Bonaparte, who put an end to the legislative privileges of the duchy in 1805. From the congress of Vienna in 1815 and during the First World War, Friuli was shared between Austria and Italy.

From 1918, demands for autonomy became more pressing, but Italian fascism did not allow any progress. After the Second World War, through the efforts of the Autonomist Association of Friuli, a region called Friuli-Venetia-Giulia was created, however, this did not meet the hopes of the autonomists. Populated by 90% of Friulians, different languages are spoken there, mainly Friulian, but also Ladin, German and Slovenian.

Timeline

2nd century BC • Settling of the Romans followed by the Celts.

31–14 BC • Apogee of Aquileia, second capital of the Roman Empire and Friuli.

7th century AD • The Lombards create the duchy of Friuli.

1077–1420 • The bishop of Aquileia controls Friuli and creates a parliament.

1420 • Annexing of Friuli by the Republic of Venice.

1516 • The Austrians take control of east Friuli.

1805 • Napoleon Bonaparte sells the whole of Friuli to the Austrians and puts an end to the duchy.

1815–66 • Friuli is part of the kingdom of Lombardy-Venetia.

1922–45 • Under the fascist Italian regime, the Friulians are victims of a campaign of forced assimilation.

1960 • First pro-autonomist movement.

1963 • Creation of the autonomous region of Friuli-Venetia-Giulia.

Identity card

Names: **Friûl[1], Friuli[2], Friaul[3], Furlanija[4]** (Friuli)
Population: **1,308,766 inhab.** note 6 *(2007)*
Area: **8,538 km² note 6**
Languages: **Furlan[1]** (Friulian), **Italiano** (Italian) *(official)*, **Deutsch[3]** (German), **Slovenščina[4]** (Slovenian), **Ladin[5]** (Ladin) *(without official status)*
Number of native speakers: **794,000[1]**
State of guardianship: **Italy**
Official status: **Autonomous region in Italy**
Capital: **Udin[1], Udine[2]** (Udine)
Historic religion: **Roman Catholic**
Flag: **Bandiere dal Friûl[1]** *(Flag of Friuli)*
Anthem: **None**
Motto: **None**

Brief history

'*Joibe grasse*' (Fat Thursday) of 1511, is the name of a popular revolt started in Udine by the citizens dying of hunger, helped by farmers throughout Friuli. These insurgencies, violently repressed by the Venetian authorities forever marked the history of Friuli and its relations with its dominant Venetian neighbour. Between 1550 and 1600 the population of Friuli decreased from 200,000 to less than 100,000 inhabitants. This is one of the events marking the long drawn-out history between neighbours eager for power but not inclined to share wealth.

Friuli, the five provinces and the spoken languages

Friuli is often confused with the Friuli-Venetia-Giulia region. Historically Friuli belongs more or less to the Italian region separated by its mid-point, namely Mandamento di Portogruaro (or Mandament di Puart in Friulian) and the community of Sappada, now incorporated into Venetia. Friuli is a buffer region, i.e. it links different states – Italy to the east, Austria to the north (Carinthian Alps) and Slovenia to the east (Giulian Alps). To the south, the Adriatic Sea provides access to the Mediterranean. Udin (in Friulian) (Udine in Italian) is the capital. It is situated in the middle of the country, consisting of plains and hills to the centre and south and massive alpine mountains to the north of which Monte Coglians (2,780 m)

is the highest. Friuli traditionally has five provinces: Udin, Pordenon, Gurize, Triest and Mandament di Puart (shown on the map). The most spoken minority language is Friulian, although German is spoken in the north, Slovenian to the east and Venetian to the south-east.

Geography

Principal towns
(Friulian / Italian)
Cividât • Cividale del Friuli
Cjaurlis • Caorle
Glemone • Gemona del Friuli
Gurize • Gorizia
Muja • Muggia
Monfalcon • Monfalcone

Pordenon • Pordenone
Puart • Portogruaro
Sacîl • Sacile
San Vît dal Timent • San Vito al Tagliamento
Spilimberc • Spilimbergo
Tisane • Latisana
Triest • Trieste
Tumieç • Tolmezzo

Udin • Udine

Regions
(Friulian / Italian)
Gurize • Gorizia
Pordenon • Pordenone
Mandament di Puart • Mandamento di Portogruaro
Udin • Udine

Geographical names

"Se ducj nus bandonin, nus judarin bessôi."
(Luigi Faidutti, Friulian parliamentarian of the 16th century)
"If we are abandoned by all, we will help ourselves."

Romansh, *the poor Swiss relative*

The Grison flag does not explicitly represent the Romansh people. It is a flag made up of coats of arms of "three leagues" that are tied to the 15th century and form the canton of the Grisons. The Romansh identify with this flag.

Although the term stateless nation is questionable in the case of the Romansh, these Rhaeto-Romance people in the Alpine region are distinguished by their language. They are related to the Ladins and the Friulians. Since the end of the Roman Empire they have been part of the canton of Grisons. However, their territory has been greatly eroded.

Thus, the Romansh do not claim their own territory, but populate many valleys of the canton of Grisons. They are scattered into five regions. The remainder of the population speaks German or Italian. The Romansh have only recently obtained the use of their own language.

Descendants of Latin populations, the Romansh were able to preserve their culture because of their location in the heart of the Alps. Under the pressure of Walser populations, originally German speakers of Vallais, their territory has been largely eroded, leaving the place to a multi-cultural community.

Since 1938, Romansh has had the status of a national language in Switzerland, without the benefit of an official status. It took the efforts of many associations in 1996 to get it. Thus, surprisingly, without claiming any territory, the Romansh can teach their language by immersion in all primary schools, with German being gradually introduced.

Unfortunately, the small Romansh community faces the exodus of its citizens: 40% of the Romansh population live outside the traditional territory. Maintaining the language is difficult in these conditions. Romansh consciousness is beginning to emerge in recent years, however, especially through relations with their Rhaeto-Romance neighbours.

Timeline

15 BC • The Romans conquer the Rhaetic territory. Appearance of the Rhaeto-Romance language and culture, strongly influenced by Latin.

1464 • After the Great Fire of Chur, the capital of the Canton of Grisons, the town is completely Germanised.

16th–17th century • The Reformation stimulates the use of a written Romansh language.

19th century • Increased awareness of the value of the Romansh culture.

1938 • Romansh becomes the national language.

1996 • Romansh becomes an official language in Switzerland.

1997 • Ratification of the European Charter for Regional and Minority Languages, allowing an increased presence of Romansh in public life.

2007 • The Canton of Grisons engages in the development of a real language policy in favour of the Romansh language.

Identity card

Names: **Rumantschs dal Grischun[1], Romantschen in Graubünden[2], Romanci dei Grigioni[3]** (Romansh of Grisons)
Population: **187,920 inhab.** [note 7] (2006)
Area: **7,105 km²** [note 7]
Languages: **Rumantsch[1]** (Romansh), **Deutsch[2]** (German), **Italiano[3]** (Italian) *(official)*
Number of native speakers: **35,095[1]** (2000)
State of guardianship: **Switzerland**
Official status: **Canton**
Capital: **Cuira[1], Chur[2], Coira[3]** (Coire)
Historic religion: **Roman Catholic and Protestant**
Flag: **Bandiera dal Grischun** (Flag of the Grisons)
Anthem: **None**
Motto: **None**

Brief history

Romansh (*Rumantsch grischun*), is recognised as one of the four Swiss languages (with some exceptions) since the official vote of 1996. The *Lia Rumantscha* largely participated in this dynamic. A body established in 1919, it aims to disseminate the Romansh language throughout public life. It is particularly through the efforts of language standardisation (i.e. finding a common base for different varieties in the area) that the preservation of the Romansh language is now possible. Since 2003, the Cantonal parliament of Grisons has established Romansh as a written language in all schools, which has allowed the publication of a number of handbooks. This rebirth is due to a voluntary policy by the authorities of the Canton of Grisons and the fact that the language has been made official. Multilingual Switzerland proves that its model of preserving a minority language is effective.

Grisons, the 11 districts and Romansh settlements

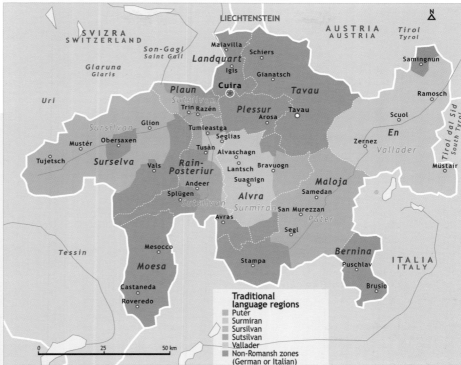

Map labels:
LIECHTENSTEIN
SVIZRA / SWITZERLAND
AUSTRIA / AUSTRIA
Tirol / Tyrol
Son-Gagl / Saint Gall
Glaruna / Glaris
Uri
Maiavilla
Schiers
Landquart
Igis
Gianatsch
Samingnun
Plaun
Cuira
Tavau
Ramosch
Sutsilvan
Trin · Razén
Plessur
Tavau
Sursilvan
Glion
Arosa
Scuol
Sursilvan
Tumleastga
En
Tirol dal Sid / South Tyrol
Mustér
Obersaxen
Seglias
Zernez
Vallader
Tujetsch
Tusàn
Alvaschagn
Müstair
Surselva
Vals
Lantsch
Bravuogn
Rain-Posteriur
Andeer
Suagnign
Maloja
Splügen
Samedan
Sutsilvan
Alvra
San Murezzan
Puter
Avras
Surmiran
Tessin
Mesocco
Segl
Bernina
Moesa
Stampa
Puschlav
ITALIA / ITALY
Castaneda
Brusio
Roveredo

Traditional language regions
- Puter
- Surmiran
- Sursilvan
- Sutsilvan
- Vallader
- Non-Romansh zones (German or Italian)

Scale: 0 — 25 — 50 km

Surrounded by Austria, Liechtenstein, Italy and the cantons of Uri, St Gall and Glaris, the canton of Grisons was initially populated by Celts. This particular area of south east Switzerland lies entirely in the Alps, St Moritz and Davos being two of the most well-known ski resorts in the world. This Alpine landscape also explains the low population density, which is 26 inhabitants per km². Largely populated by German speakers in the north and Italian speakers in the south, only the central part extending from the borders of Uri to those of the Tyrol speak Romansh, the native Rhaeto-Roman language. Widely dispersed and living in Alpine valleys, the Romansh are still seeing their territory shrink. For example, Chur, the Canton capital, is now largely populated by German speakers. Five linguistic regions make up the Romansh territory: from west to east – Surselvan, Sutsilvan, Surmiran, Puter and Vallader. Only rarely would Romansh speakers identify themselves with their territory, often preferring to see it as a linguistic community inside the canton of Grisons.

Geography

Geographical names

Principal towns (Romansh / German)
Alvaschagn • *Alvaschein*
Cuira • *Chur*
Gianatsch • *Jenaz*
Mesocco • *Mesocco*
Müstair • *Münster*
Mustér • *Disentis*
Puschlav • *Poschiavo*
Razén • *Rhäzüns*
San Murezzan • *St. Moritz*
Scuol • *Schuls*
Seglias • *Sils im Domleschg*
Tavau • *Davos*
Tujetsch • *Disentis*
Tusàn • *Thusis*

Regions (Romansh / German)
Alvra • *Albula*
Bernina • *Bernina*
Plaun • *Imboden*
Plessur • *Plessur*
En • *Inn*
Landquart • *Landquart*
Malögia • *Maloja*
Moësa • *Moesa*
Rain-Posteriur • *Hinterrhein*
Surselva • *Surselva*
Tavau • *Prättigau-Davos*

"Stai si defenda!"
(Romansh proverb)
"Stand up and fight for your rights!"

Romansh, *the poor Swiss relative* / Ladins, *minorities within a minor*

Grisons, linguistic practices

za da tschanter per iffaunts,
itzplatz, danke schön!
grazie!
ercie beaucou
thanks!

Multilingual road sign. Romansh is first

Languages
Romansh
German
Italian

Romansh
majority
Near German
Near Italian

Other situations
Bilingual Romansh / German
monolingual German
on former territories
Bilingual Romansh / German
Bilingual Italian / German

0   25   50 km

Romansch

In the canton of the Grisons German predominates and is spoken by nearly 70% of the population, followed by Romansh (15%) and Italian (10%) as well as other languages. Thus, the predominant situation of German puts the Romansh language in peril. Romansh is a Rhaeto-Romance language, descended directly from Latin. In fact, many dialects are practised (Puter, Surmiran, Sutsilvan, Vallader). A national language according to the Swiss constitution of 2000, Romansh now benefits from a more comfortable status, the language policy being managed directly by municipalities. *Rumantsch Grischun*, a variety taught in school, is now taught in 102 of the 208 municipalities in the canton.

Language

Zoom

Created in 1920, the Ladin flag was used for the first time to protest against the Treaty of Versailles, which did not recognise Ladin specificity. It represents the Ladin environment (the prairies, the forests, the snow and the sky).

The Ladins, like the Romansh people and the Friulians, are Rhaeto-Romans. Divided between three provinces under Italian administration (South Tyrol, Trentino and Belluno in Venetia), they populate the Dolomite valleys. The term Ladin is derived from the word "Latin", the Ladin language being considered a resurgence of Vulgar Latin spoken in the Alps. Recognised as a minority language, Ladin should enjoy special protection, particularly for its use in education, administration and dissemination in the media and justice. Unfortunately, this is wishful thinking, with Italy only partially applying the provisions it pledged to take. Threatened for centuries by the influx of Germanic people, Ladins survived because their relative isolation enabled them, among others, to resist the fascist regime of Mussolini, who considered the Ladins as speakers of an Italian dialect. The Ladin domain was, in fact, transferred to Italy after the Treaty of Versailles, having been attached to Austria. Only since 1988 have the Ladins been using a unified language and a standardised orthography. Traditionally, five valleys are considered as Ladin. They are the Val Badia, Gherdäina, Fascia, Fodom and Anpezo. The territory of Cadore adds to that although nowadays it has very few Ladins. The Ladins call their territory *Ladino*, a term that is not ordinarily translated in English.

Ladins, the 5 valleys and the Ladin speakers territory of Cadore

Identity card

Names: **Ladinia[1][3], Ladinen[2]** (Ladinia)
Population: **35,711 inhab.** [note 8] *(2006)*
Area: **1,140 km²** [note 8]
Languages: **Ladin[1]** (Ladin), **Deutsch[2]** (German), **Italiano[3]** (Italian) *(official)*
Number of native speakers: **30,000**
State of guardianship: **Italy**
Official status: **No status**
Capital: **Urtijëi** (Ortisei, principal town)
Historic religion: **Roman Catholic**
Flag: **Bandira di Ladins[1]** (Flag of the Ladins)
Anthem: **None**
Motto: **None**

Principal towns
(Ladin / Italian)
Auronzo di Cadore • *Auronzo di Cadore*
Cianacei • *Canazei*
Cortina de Anpezo • *Cortina d'Ampezzo*
La Plié •
Lorenzago di Cadore • *Lorenzago di Cadore*
Mareo • *Marebbe*
Moena • *Moena*
Pieve di Cadore •
Rocca Pietore • *Rocca Pietore*
San Martin de Tor • *San Martino in Badia*

San Vido • *San Vito di Cadore*
Sëlva • *Selva di Val Gardena*
Urtijëi • *Ortisei*

Regions
(Ladin / Italian)
Anpezo • *Ampezzo*
Cadore • *Cadore*
Fascia • *Fassa*
Fodom • *Livinallongo*
Gherdëina • *Gardena*
Gran Ega • *Val Badia*

Geographical names

Savoy and Aosta, *heart of the Arpitan people*

The flag created by the Arpitan Cultural Alliance uses the Burgund colours, the twelve stars symbolising the European dimension of the linguistic region, decorated in the traditional *rozon*. Another flag dating from the 1970s exists that is essentially used by the Apritain Movement of the Aostal Valley. It uses the Valdotain colours, Valais and Savoy – red, black and white – and three stars that represent them.

Arpitania designates the area where Arpitan is the traditional minority language. Inhabited since the Paleolithic era, the country lies on the borders of three European states – France, Italy and Switzerland.

Various Celtic tribes settled on Arpitan land, the most famous being the Allobroges. They found themselves rapidly integrated into the kingdom of Burgundy, comprising Burgundy and Sapaudie (Savoy). It is at the heart of the kingdom

that the Arpitan language developed from Latin.

The concept of Arpitania dates from the 1970s. A Valdotain party, the Arpitan Movement uses the old term "Arpitan", formed from the root of the pre Indo-European "alp", in its modern variant dialect "arp", which referred to the mountain pastures. The confusion generated by the term "Franco-Provençal" invented in 1873 was then cleared up and it defined the language according to its phonetic characteristics.

The term "Arpitan" therefore specifies the language according to the social characteristics of the people who speak it: it is the language of the Arpians, the shepherds. Arpitan consciousness developed in the 20th century, when groups of speakers of the vernacular language took the initiative to organise international meetings on a regular basis in one or the other regions of Arpitania. Although aware of speaking the same language, though rich in local characteristics, residents continue to claim to represent their historic region, Savoy and the Aosta Valley being the two most symbolic regions of this vast territory.

Identity card

Names: **Arpitania[1][3], Arpitanie[2], Arpitanien[4]** (Arpitania)
Population: **7,000,000 inhab.** note 9
Area: **60,000 km²** note 9
Languages: **Arpitan[1]** (Franco-Provençal), **Français[2]** (French), **Italiano[3]** (Italian), **Deutsch[4]** (German, Walser German)
Number of native speakers: **140,000[1]** *(1998)*
States of guardianship: **France, Italy, Switzerland**
Official status: **No particular status (departments in France, cantons in Switzerland, autonomous region in the Aosta Valley in Italy**
Capital: **Chamèri[1]** (Chambéry), **Aosta[1]** (Aosta)
Historic religion: **Roman Catholic and Protestant**
Flag: **Lo rozon[1]** (The rosette)
Anthem: **Les Allobroges[2]** *(Savoy)*, **aMontagnes valdôtaines[2]** *(Aosta)*
Motto: **Fier et a l'abada tanqu'a la fin[1]** (proud and free until death)

Timeline

443 • Foundation of the kingdom of the Burgunds in Sapaudia.

888 • Second Kingdom of Burgogne: cradle of the Arpitan language, stretching around the area of Lyon-Geneva.

1860 • Savoy is annexed by France after a Napoleonian "plebiscity" (99.8%)

1943–5 • The Aosta Valley is liberated by the armed struggle of the fascist yoke.

1948 • The Aosta Valley becomes an autonomous region.

1973 • Birth of Arpitan conscience: a Valdotain movement proposes a new spelling for the language and demands the union and the freedom of Arpitainia.

2000 • After the breakthrough of the 1998 elections where there was a leaning towards independence, a CSA poll reported that 23% of the inhabitants of Savoy would support independence.

1998–2003 • The linguist Dominique Stich provides a standard orthography to Arpitan, the ORB, providing a tool for mutual comprehension in writing between the many variants.

Brief history

One of the highlights of the history of Arpitania remains the annexation of Savoy by France. This term is preferred to that of "incorporation" used in school textbooks. Despite the long or short periods of occupation, Savoy was often independent or at the forefront of bigger territories. It was not until 1860 that Savoy became French after the Treaty of Turin and a referendum now considered flawed (99.76% of the 130,839 voters voted for incorporation). The Treaty of Turin was in fact a deal between France and the kingdom of Piedmont-Sardinia, who wished to unify Italy to retain the favour of their French neighbours. The most ironic thing being that this kingdom was ruled by the house of Savoy. This treaty is considered to be null and void by many Savoyards as its demands were not adhered to.

Arpitan, the subdivisions (Savoy, Aosta, Romandy and Rhôdany)

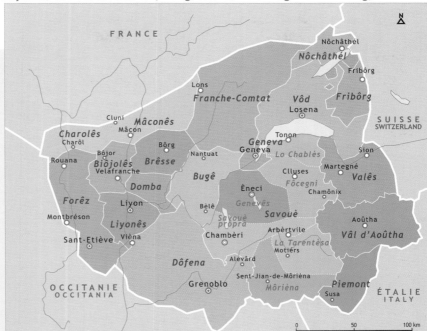

Arpitania is the territory of people of the Franco-Provençal language, also called Arpitan. In the west are the mountains and plains of Forez, the Pilat, the mountains of Vivrais, Beaujolais and Lyonnais. In the middle, the territory is crossed from north to south by the Rhône Valley, which marks the historic border between France and Savoy. From both sides, there are large areas in low relief (Bresse, Dauphiné, Dombes) and hilly areas (Bugey). The region is mountainous in the east also (Jura and the Alps). Further east still, in the Aosta Valley and in Valais we find Mont Blanc – bordering Savoy – Mont Rosa, the Matterhorn, Gran Paradiso and Rutor

Head. All of Arpitania is distinguished by the presence of Arpitan. Lyon is the principal city of this vast Alpine and pre-Alpine space. Other cities like Grenoble, Geneva, Lausanne or Saint Étienne mark the territory made up of many countries (18 shown on the map above) and divided between three states (France, Switzerland and Italy).

Geography

Principal towns
(Arpitan / French)
Aoûtha • *Aoste (Aosta)*
Arbèrtvile • *Albertville*
Bôrg • *Bourg-en-Bresse*
Chambèri • *Chambéry*
Chamônix • *Chamonix*
Èneci • *Annecy*
Fribôrg • *Fribourg*
Geneva • *Genève*
Grenoblo • *Grenoble*
Liyon • *Lyon*
Lons • *Lons-le-Saunier*
Losena • *Lausanne*

Mâcon • *Mâcon*
Nôchâthél • *Neuchâtel*
Pontarliér • *Pontarlier*
Sant-Etièvе • *Saint-Étienne*
Sion • *Sion*
Velafranche • *Villefranche*

Regions
(Arpitan / French)
Brêsse • *Bresse*
Bugê • *Bugey*
Dôfenâ • *Dauphiné*
Forêz • *Forez*
Franche-Comtât • *Franche-Comté*

Fribôrg • *Fribourg*
Geneva • *Genève*
Liyonês • *Lyonnais*
Nôchâthél • *Neuchâtel*
Mâconês • *Maconnais*
Piemont • *Piémont*
Poulye • *Pouilles*
Savouè • *Savoie (Savoy)*
Vâl d'Aoûtha • *Val d'Aoste*
Valês • *Vallais*
Vôd • *Vaud*

Geographical names

"Je ne sé pè ün usé de cage."
(Arpitan proverb)
"I am not a bird who lives in a cage."

Savoy and Aosta, heart of the Arpitan people

The flag of Savoy shows the coat of arms of the house of Savoy. There is the cross of St John, white on a red background, which is one of the oldest known flags.

Belatedly incorporated into France by the Treaty of Turin in 1860, Savoy has maintained and still actively maintains a strong attachment to its former glories. The dynasties of Savoyard sovereigns date from the 11th century. Dukes since the 15th century, they extended their lands to Sicily and Sardinia in 1720 to create the states of Savoy, a power recognised at European level. Its original name in Latin, *Sapaudia,* which means 'fir tree' in French, makes reference to the many conifers inhabiting the slopes of high mountains. A real buffer territory between the Frank, Italic and Germanic worlds, Savoy made up part of Lorraine before becoming a sovereign state in the 16th century. In 1919, the French state put an end to the neutrality of Savoy, contrary to the terms of the Treaty of Turin. It was condemned by the international tribunal in 1932 without having any real effect. This turbulent history explains the success of the Savoisian separatist and regional movements (terms they prefer to Savoyard, which is pejorative). The Savoy Region Movement founded in 1971 has been campaigning since then for more autonomy. Since the start of the 1990s, competing political parties (including the now famous Savoy League) have had many electoral successes. In fact, in a recent poll, 23% of Savoyards were in favour of independence. Made up of six provinces (Ducal Savoy, Chablais, Faucigny, Tarentaise, Maurienne, Genevois), Savoy is part of the whole of Arpitana. The native speakers of Arpitan and Franco-Provençal are numerous.

Savoy, the six traditional provinces

Lo Chablès • *Chablais*
Fôcegni • *Faucigny*
Genevês • *Genevois*
Môrièna • *Maurienne*
Savouè propra • *Ducal Savoy*
La Tarentèsa • *Tarentaise*

The flag of the Aosta Valley is a bi-colour of black and red. It was used for the first time in 1940 but officially adopted in 2006.

Aoste

Part of the whole of Arpitania as well as Savoy, the Aosta Valley is a specific area because of several unique features. First, it is included in the Italian state, where it has had special autonomous status since 1948. Arpitan (Franco-Provençal) is practised by a large part of the population. With an area of 3,263 km², the Aosta Valley borders the canton of Valais to the north, Savoy to the west, separated by Mont Blanc and Piedmont to the south and the east. A region of mountains, the Aosta Valley is named after Augusta Praetoria, the capital having been created in honour of Augusta. The Burgundians reigned for over five centuries from the 5th century, followed by the Lombards and the Franks. Incorporated into Savoy from the 11th century, the Aosta Valley has always retained a large degree of autonomy as a duchy, even after it became part of Italy in 1861. Under the fascist yoke, a policy of assimilation had grave consequences on linguistic practice: French was no longer taught from 1925 and place names were replaced with Italian names in 1939. After the end of the war, Federico Chabod, the Valdotain president, obtained a special status for the Aosta Valley. Populated by little more than 120,000 people, the Aosta Valley, whose official languages are Italian and French, is nowadays a prosperous region maintaining greater ties with its Arpitan neighbours.

Regional issues

Arpitan

Arpitan (also called Franco-Provençal, not to be confused with Provençal) is spoken in the pre-Alps and in Savoy, to the south of Romandy and in the Aosta Valley. It is one of the principal Gallo-Romance languages. Discovered only in the 19th century, there has been no consensus on its particularities and borders. Its rich literature started from the end of the 13th century and has continued without interruption up to the 21st century. The Valley of Lys, between Aosta and Piedmont, is populated with descendants of a German-speaking population – the Walser. It does not benefit from widespread promotion, unlike other minority languages. Unfortunately its future seems very uncertain.

Language

Wallonia, the survival of an Oïl people

The Walloon flag is "a bold red rooster on gold". It was designed by Paulus in 1913. The colours are those of the principality of Liège, which was an independent state from the 10th to the end of the 18th century and whose eponymous diocese coincided with the linguistic area of Wallonia.

Wallonia is situated on the margins of the Roman and Germanic worlds. Linguistically, the Walloons, as well as the Picards and the Normans, make up part of the Oïl people. Politically, however, they are marked by a history of conflicts between micro-territories and unions in larger groups.

Populated initially by the Celtic tribe of the *Belgii*, Wallonia was conquered by Caesar and was strongly Romanised. After the collapse of the Roman Empire, Wallonia saw the emergence of the kingdom of the Franks, as well as the Carolingian dynasty, of Liégeoise origin, mixing its history with that of northern France. Following the Treaty of

Verdun, it returned to Lorraine and then integrated into the Germanic Holy Roman Empire. After a feudal period dividing it into independent micro-territories that were regularly in conflict, vast counties and duchies were created (Namur, Brabant, Luxembourg, Hainaut), controlled by the Burgundian power, Spain, and then Austria.

The principality of Liège became involved in the French Revolution and France profited from annexing the region and dividing it into departments, based on provinces. Integrated with the Netherlands in 1815, Wallonia rebelled in 1830, leading to the creation of Belgium, born of an arranged marriage requiring the co-existence of two very different people: the Walloons and the Flemish.

The Industrial Revolution made Wallonia rich in natural resources, until its decline in the 1960s. Belgium turned towards federalism. The Walloons wanted economic autonomy so that they would no longer depend on the Flemish majority. The movement accelerated until the abolition of federalism in the 1990s.

Timeline

AD 57 • The Romans invade Belgian Gaul.

5th century • The Franks settle in the country that will become the centre of their future kingdom.

843 • Treaty of Verdun, Wallonia is incorporated into Lorraine.

15th century • Burgundian rule over the country except for the principality of Liège. Spanish then Austrian annexation.

1795 • Following the French Revolution, Wallonia is annexed to the Republic (creation of the departments of Jemappes, the Dyle, Sambre-et-Meuse, Forêts and Ourthe).

1815 • Defeat at Waterloo, the Walloons are fighting with the Napoleonic troops. Wallonia is annexed to the kingdom of the Netherlands.

1830 • Formation of Belgium, made up of Wallonia and Flanders.

End of the 20th century • Wallonia becomes a region in the framework of Belgian federalism. It has widespread autonomy and possesses a parliament and government.

Identity card

Names: **Waloneye[1], Wallonie[2], Wallonien[3], Wallonië[4]** (Wallonia)
Population: **3,413,000 inhab.**
Area: **16,845 km²**
Languages: **Walon[1]** (Walloon) *(recognised)*, **Français[2]** (French), **Deutsch[3]** (German) *(official)*, **Vlaams/Nederlands[4]** (Flemish/Dutch)
Number of native speakers: **600,000 to 1,120,000[1]** *(1998)*
States of guardianship: **Belgium, France**
Official status: **Federal region in Belgium, No status in France**
Capital: **Nameûr[1]** (Namur) [note 20]
Historic religion: **Roman Catholic**
Flag: **Li cok walon[1]** (The Walloon Rooster)
Anthem: **Li tchant des Walons[1]** (The Song of the Walloons)
Motto: **Walon todi[1]** (Always Walloon)

Brief history

If the Walloons have been a people for a long time, it was not until 1950 that this cultural notion took its own political dimension. In that year, the "royal question" divided Belgium. In a referendum, the Belgians were asked if they wanted the return of King Leopold III, whose behaviour during the war had been questioned. The Walloons voted "No" while the Flemish voted "Yes". Because of their demographic weight the latter allowed the king to return. This return was accompanied by serious riots in Wallonia, which resulted in three deaths at Grâce-Berleur when the police fired at the crowd. A "Walloon government" assembled in Liège and wished to declare independence. Léopold III eventually abdicated but the tensions between the Walloons and the Flemish were never resolved. Following that, tensions increased and provisionally led to federalism.

Wallonia, the five provinces, the German-speaking community and Brussels

Situation linguistique
(original languages)
- Walloon / Picard / French
- German
- Walloon / German
- Walloon municipalities for the Dutch
- Walloon municipalities for the French

Without access to the sea, Wallonia is enclosed between Flanders and the Netherlands to the north, Germany and Luxembourg to the east and France to the south and west. It is made up of two large geographical areas separated by the Sambre-et-Meuse furrow, the two main rivers of the region: to the north-west the plateaus of Hainaut, Brabant and Hesbaye, to the south-east the high plateaus of Condroz, the Famenne, the Ardenne

and Gaume. An economically developed region with an indigenous population, the "Walloon ridge" crosses the country of Tournais, through Mons, Charlerois, Namur, Huy, Liège as far as Verviers. To the east of Wallonia, we find the High Fens, populated by German speakers.

Geography

Principal towns
(Walloon / French)
- Brussele • *Bruxelles*
- Lîdje • *Liège*
- Mont • *Mons*
- Nameûr • *Namur*
- Tchårlerwè • *Charleroi*
- Tournè • *Tournai*
- Vervî • *Verviers*
- Wareme • *Waremme*
- Wåve • *Wavre*

Regions
(Walloon / French)
- Hinnot • *Hainaut*
- Lîdje • *Liège*
- Lussimbork • *Luxembourg*
- Nameûr • *Namur*
- Roman Payis • *Brabant wallon*

Geographical names

"C'est todi les ptits k'ont spotche."
(Walloon proverb)
"It's always the small things that one crushes."

Alsace, land of the Alamanni

The Alsatian flag carries the name of *Rot un Wiss* (red and white). These colours are present in the coat of arms of cities and Alsatian families. The *Rot un Wiss* appeared towards 1872, to affirm the Alsatian identity, with regards to the German authorities and then the French. It was made official by the Alsace-Lorraine parliament in 1912.

Alsace is a former geographical reality, but its political unity is relatively recent. Since the 19th century, Alsace has been trying to assert its identity between two great powers – France and Germany – who covet the territory for its wealth.

The Alsace people arose slowly during the Middle Ages. In this century, Alsace was primarily a geographical and cultural reality and non-political because its territory was divided up into fiefs under the authority of the Holy Roman Empire. The Franco-Germanic Wars (1870–1, 1914–18 and 1939–45) placed Alsace between the two great powers. Alsace became a political reality after its annexation to the German Empire in 1871 and in 1911 it acquired autonomous status. After 1918, Alsace led a staunch fight against the central French state to maintain its characteristics. In this century, two-thirds of the Alsace deputies were autonomist. Unfortunately, after the Second World War, in cultivating the amalgam "Alsace = Nazi", the French state accelerated its policy of assimilation.

The Alsatian people are a Germanic people, who could be considered southern Germans.

Today, Alsace is once more a rich region, benefitting from locally specific law and a German dialect that still persists. However, these elements are threatened by the Jacobean character of the French state, which isolates it from the Rhine area. The Alsatian people work hard to make their demands heard even if German is taught nowadays in the schools. Moderate separatist movements have begun to emerge, raising awareness of the specificity of Alsatian culture and promoting interest in preserving it.

Timeline

378 • The Alamans and the Franks drive out the Romans. Alsace is at the centre of Alamannia.

9th–10th century • Treaty of Verdun and the Treaty of Mersen: Alsace is successively incorporated into Lorraine and then the Germanic Holy Roman Empire.

1648 • Annexation of Alsace to France. Alsace has to leave the Holy Roman Empire.

1871 • Franco-Prussian War: Alsace and Moselle are incorporated into the German Empire.

31 May 1911 • Alsace-Lorraine obtains politically autonomous status.

1914–18 • The Alsatians fight in the German army. French victory in 1918. Expulsion of Alsatians under ethnic criteria.

24 May 1926 • Creation of the Home Federation, structure of political coordination for obtaining autonomous status.

1939–45 • Deportation of part of the population of Gascogne. Annexation of Alsace by the Third Reich. Liberation in 1944–5.

Identity card

Names: **Elsass**[1][2], **Alsace**[3] (Alsace)
Population: **1,829,000 inhab.**
Area: **8,280 km²**
Languages: **Elsässisch**[1][2] (Alsatian, Germanic and Franconian variant of German, used as a written standard[2]) *(without official status)*, **Français**[3] (French) *(official)*
Number of native speakers: **700,000 to 1,100,000**[1]
State of guardianship: **France**
Official status: **Region in France**
Capital: **Strossburi**[1], **Straßburg**[2] (Strasbourg)
Historic religion: **Roman Catholic and Protestant, Jewish**
Flag: **Rot un Wiss**[1], **Rot und Weiß**[2] (Red and White)
Anthem: **Elsässisches Fahnenlied**[2] (Song of the Alsatian Flag)
Motto: **None**

Brief history

On 8 May 1926, the manifesto of the Home Federation appeared in the Alsatian newspaper *Die Zukunft*. Published by representatives of moderate and autonomist parties, it called for autonomous status for Alsace. In response, Paris launched an unprecedented wave of repression: banning newspapers, laying-off staff and making arrests. On 22 August 1926 in Colmar, an autonomist parade fell into a trap prepared by police and royalists: separatist protesters were violently attacked and arrested (Bloody Sunday). On Christmas night 1927, the main autonomists responsible were arrested and incarcerated for "conspiracy against state security". Convicted without evidence in Colmar, they were then released by the Assize Court of Besançon.

Alsace, the two regions and Frankish Moselle

Geography

Alsace is a region stretching from the north to the south along the Rhine valley. It is defined to the east by the Rhine (Baden), to the west by the crest of Vosges (France), to the north by the river Lauter (Palatinate) and to the south by the Jura mountains (Switzerland). It consists of many different areas: the plain of Alsace, drained by the river Ille, the marshy area of Ried, which lies between the Rhine and the Ille marking the former floodplain of the Rhine, the Vosges mountains (highest point: Grosser Belchen/Grand Ballon 1, 424 m). Two metropolises, Strasbourg and Mulhouse, shine on the two historic regions of Low and Upper Alsace. Comprising a network of average-sized towns (Guebwiller, Colmar, Sélestat, Saverne), the Vosges are home to vineyard, of worldwide repute.

Principal towns
(German / French)
Hagenau • *Haguenau*
Kolmar/Colmar • *Colmar*
Mülhausen • *Mulhouse*
Saarburg • *Sarrebourg*
Schlettstadt • *Sélestat*
Strassburg • *Strasbourg*
Zabern • *Saverne*

Regions
(German / French)
Oberelsass • *Haute-Alsace*
Unterelsass • *Basse-Alsace*
Hardt • *Hardt*

Hanauer Land • *Pays de Hanau*
Ried • *Ried*
Kochersberg • *Kochersberg*
S'Krumme Elsass • *L'Alsace Bossue*
Sundgau • *Sundgau*
Weissenburg • *Outre-Forêt*
Vogesen • *Vosges*

Geographical names

"Das Elsass ist wie ein Klo, immer besetzt!"
(Tomi Ungerer, Alsatian painter)
"Alsace is like the toilets, always occupied!"

Alsace, land of the Alamanni

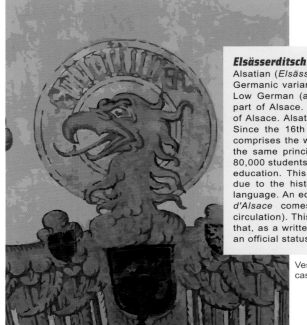

Language

Elsässerditsch

Alsatian (*Elsässerditsch*) is a collection of Germanic variants. The most important of these dialects is Low German (also spoken in Baden), used in the largest part of Alsace. High German is used equally in the south of Alsace. Alsatian has been spoken since the 6th century. Since the 16th century, standard German (High German) comprises the written expression of Alsatians, according to the same principle in Switzerland for example. More than 80,000 students learn it including 50,000 in primary bilingual education. This enthusiasm for German is understandable due to the historical ties the Alsatians maintain with this language. An edition of the newspaper *Dernières Nouvelles d'Alsace* comes out each day in this language (10% circulation). This favourable situation shouldn't hide the fact that, as a written standard, Alsatian German does not have an official status in France.

Vestige of the link of Alsace with Germany, here in the castle of Haut-Königsburg.

Today, Alsace is considered a French region. In this context, certain areas have a specific law, a unique situation for a metropolitan region, except for the case of the Territorial Collectivity of Corsica. Moreover, to national law is added a local law which specifically concerns greater municipal autonomy, a right to work and a more advantageous social system (social security) as well as a specific system for religious worship, hunting, justice etc. Despite this interesting heritage, the autonomist parties (of those the former People's Union of Alsace) poll modestly, often becoming the opposition of the far-right (Alsace First; ADA), who coat themselves in a regionalist sheen. The formation of a new political force in 2009, uniting the UPA and the dynamic association "Fer's Elsass", could give new impetus to Alsatian autonomism.

Principal Alsatian parties:
- **Unser Land** (Our Country) *(Autonomist, Social Democrat)*
- **Parti Fédéraliste d'Alsace** / Federalist Party of Alsace *(Federalist)*
- **Nationalforum Elsaß-Lothringen** / National Forum of Alsace-Lorraine *(Separatist)*

Politics now

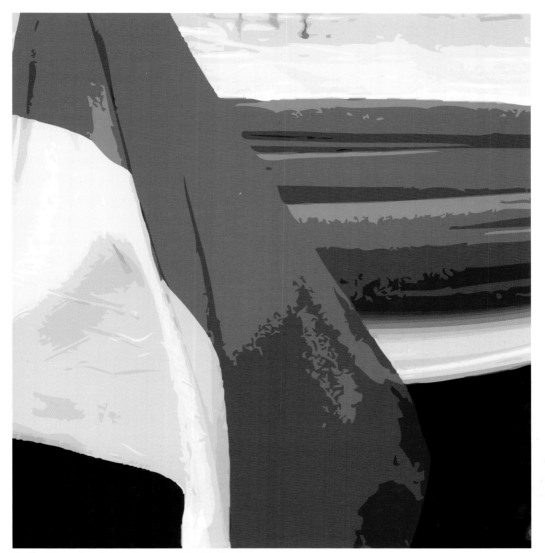

Rot un Wiss, red and white, the name of the Alsatian flag

Frisia, nostalgic people of the North Sea

Since the 11th century, the lily has represented Frisia. At the end of the 18th century the Frisians created the flag of lilies, adopted officially by the province of Fryslân in 1958. In 2007, the *Groep fan Auwerk* proposed a flag to the Inter-Frisian Council that represents the whole of the Frisian regions: the lily for the west and different colours for the east and north. As this flag has not been officially adopted, a contest is currently being launched to provide the Frisians with a unified flag.

Part of Germany and the Netherlands, the Frisians are rich in their differences. Three regions are distinguished: the west, the east and the north. They speak three different languages with a common root: the Anglo-Frisian group.

Frisia is situated in an area that stretches from the River Ijssel to the German-Danish border. Between these two points, the Frisians inhabit a 60 km strip bordering the coast. Frisia is mentioned in Roman times by the historian Tacite, under the name of *Frisii*. In the 6th and 7th centuries, the Frankish chronicles also mention the kingdom of the Frisions. King Aldegisi was the first acknowledged king. His successor, Redbad, a pagan king, defeated Charles Martel at the Battle of Cologne. Around the year 700, the Frisian territory stretched from Bruges (Belgium) to the Weser in Germany. After 1500, Frisia, conquered by other states, was divided up and though the language disappeared from these regions, the feeling of belonging to Frisia remained strong there.

Today, Ljouwert with its 95,000 inhabitants is the biggest city in Friesland. In Friesland (Fryslân), there are 350,000 natives of Frisian, in east Frisia, there are 2,000 people who speak the language in Saterland (east Frisian) and in north Frisia (Nordfriisklön), 10,000 speakers. The Frisian vocabulary permeated by Low German is spoken there. In the province of Groningen, the language used is very close to western Friesland. But the feeling of being Frisian is not very strong among the people of Groningen.

Identity card

Names: **Fryslân[1], Fraschlönj[2], Friislon[2], Friisklun[2], Fräislound[3], Freesland[4], Friesland[5 6], Frisland[7]** (Frisia / Friesland)
Population: **2,300,000 inhab.** [note 10]
Area: **14,000 km² [note 10]**
Languages: **Frysk[1]** (western Frisian), **Frasch[2]** (northern Frisian, Mooringer Frasch written standard[2]), **Seeltersk/Fräisk[3]** (Saterlandic/Eastern Frisian), **Nedersaksisch/Plaatdüütsch[4]** (Low Saxon/Low German), **Deutsch[5]** (German), **Nederlands[6]** (Dutch), **Dansk[7]** (Danish)
Number of native speakers: **360,000 to 700,000[1]** *(2004),* **10,000 to 15,000[2]** *(1999),* **2,250[3]** *(1998)*
States of guardianship: **Germany, Netherlands**
Official status: **Province in the Netherlands, Kreise in Germany**
Capitals: **Ljouwert[1], Leeuwarden[6] / Hüsem[2], Husum[5] / Grunnen[4], Groningen[6] / Auerk[3], Aurich[5]**
Historic religion: **Protestant**
Flag: **Ynterfryske Flagge[1]** (Interfrisian flag)
Anthem: **De âlde Friezen[1]** (The Old Frisians)
Motto: **None**

Brief history

In 1345, William IV of Holland and John, duke of Beaumont, attempted to conquer Frisia by crossing the Zuiderzee with a large naval fleet. Helped by Dutch, French and Flemish knights, they docked on the Frisian shore (Starum, Laaksum) and planned to use the St Odulphus monastery as an assembly point. Having no horses, preferring to carry building materials, the knights ransacked the abandoned villages. The troops of William IV were routed by the Frisian peasants who had been driven into impassable swamps. It is there that William IV lost his life. When John of Beaumont, ally of the Dutch, learned the news, he ordered the retreat. This date marks the resolution of the small people of Frisia against their "great neighbours". More than an act of war, it was an act of bravery to control their destiny.

Frisia, historical territories

Formation of Friesland
Areas of Frisian language
Historic Frisian domain
Frisian area claimed
Extension of the Frisian domain
Historic in Holland

Frisia is found on the banks of the North Sea. Officially divided between two states (the Netherlands and Germany), its historic territory is vast. Today, three reclaimed spaces are once again Frisian: Province of Friesland, East Frisia / Saterland and North Frisia. To these are added the territories of Frisian culture, such as the province of Groningen, the hinterland of Wilhelmshaven and the historical regions of Wuster and Rüstringen near Bremerhaven. Partially formed over the course of the last two glacial periods, this is an area of polders (areas reclaimed by the sea). Upon arrival, the first people created small hills where they lived (w(i) erden). They built ditches to protect themselves from the sea, thus modelling a particular landscape, flat with numerous pastures. The Wadden Sea stretches the length of Frisia from the west towards the north, approximately 500 km. The Frisian Islands form an archipelago which stretches over the entire coast. There are four towns with more than 50,000 inhabitants: Ljouwert: 91,000, Groningen: 180,000, Emden: 51,000 and Wilhelmshaven: 86,000. The majority of Frisians live in the smaller towns or in the countryside.

Geography

91

Frisia, nostalgic people of the North Sea

The Frisian flag was officially adopted by the province of Fryslân in 1957. Comprising four oblique bands on a white background, the red waterlilies, often confused with hearts, have been used since the 11th century. The flag in this version has been used by the Frisian movements since the 19th century.

Regional issues

In 1997, the province of Friesland changed its name and officially became Fryslân, a Frisian name that replaced the Dutch name used until this date (Friesland). *Fryslân* is the Frisian region with the most local native speakers of Frisian. Few differences exist between the dialects of this region. Thus in 1879, the first Frisian orthography was adopted. In 2007, 94% of Frisians declared an understanding of their language and 74% were able to speak it, 75% could read it and 25% could write it. Thus, to be a polyglot is normal for the Frisians. Local life is punctuated by the language, which is broadcast on radio and television. Ice-based sports are one of the distinctive elements of the western Frisians, especially ice skating and *fierljeppen* (*Pultstockspringen* in German), which consists of jumps, helped by poles, above the river. The harsh winters permit the use of frozen canals as large ice rinks. This is what the Frisians call *Alvestêdetocht* (English: Eleven Cities Tour), i.e. a 200 km stretch of ice connecting 11 towns. Finally, the famous Frisian cows or the equally well-known Frisian horses enhance the reputation of the region.

Variants of Frisian
- Aasters
- Hylpersk
- Klaaifrysk
- Noardhoeksk
- Skiermûntseagersk
- Skylgersk
- Súdwesthoeksk
- Wâldfrysk

Other languages
- Stellingwerfsk (Low German)
- Biltsk, Amelansk, Midslânsk, Flylânsk (Dutch)

Friesland, the 31 communities and spoken languages

Principal towns
(Frisian / Dutch)
Frjentsjer • *Franeker*
Harns • *Harlingen*
It Bilt • *Het Bildt*

It Hearrenfean - *Heerenveen*
Ljouwert • *Leeuwarden*
Smellingerlân • *Smallingerland*
Snits • *Sneek*

Geographical names

North Frisia was the first region of Friesland to have its own political party. The Union of Electors of South Schleswig was founded in 1948. There is a political representation for the Danish and Frisian minority in the German province of Schleswig-Holstein. In the Dutch province of Friesland, the Frision Nationalist Party was founded in 1962. Polling at 10% in provincial elections, it has five seats and governs a left coalition. A second political party of western Friesland is being created. It is called De Friezen.

- **Fryske Nasjional Partij** / Frisian Nationalist Party (FNP)
- **De Friezen - Die Friesen** / The Frisians
- **Partij voor het Noorden** / Party of the Nordics
- **Südschleswigsche Wählerverband** / Union of the Schleswig of the South

Frysk, Frasch, Fraïsk...

There is not just one language, but many languages that are spoken in Frisia. Frisian in different forms is spoken throughout the whole of the domain of Frisia. It is a Germanic language, long-time cousin of English, of which written traces have been found in runes dating from the 5th century. Low German or Low Saxon is also spoken. With regards to Frisian, there are three pockets. One to the west of the province of Fryslân, the other to the centre in Saterland and the last to the north of northern Frisia. To the west, in the province of Fryslân, it is spoken by 400,000 of the 600,000 inhabitants. Today the language is protected (Convention on the Frisian Language and Culture 2001) but its advancement still requires the effort of written practice, which is obligatory in primary education. At the centre of this area, it is spoken by a few thousand people in the four Saterlandic communes. In North Frisia, the number of native speakers is around 10,000, but the different language variants (seven) render it difficult for teaching. Its protection in this region could involve the use of a standard, which today tends to be the variety of the Mooring region. Thus the three varieties of the Frisian language will certainly have a very different future. The future of western Frisian is now assured if the efforts and enthusiasm of the population is confirmed. In contrast, the weak protection from which the two varieties on German soil benefit risks the disappearance of this treasure forever.

The sea of Watten, the first plan of the Frisian flag

"Bûter, brea en griene tsiis, wa' t dat net sizze kin is gjin oprjocht Fries."
(Frisian proverb)
"Butter, bread and green cheese, if you are not able to say that, you are not a true Frisian."

Frisia, nostalgic people of the North Sea

The northern Frisian flag is called the 'yellow-red-blue'. Inspired by the coat of arms of North Frisia, this vertical triband symbolises the sleeping sun on the Watten Sea.

North Frisia (or 'Nordfriesland' in German) is now integrated into the region of Schleswig-Holstein. As its name indicates it is at the most northern part of Frisia. North Frisia is traditionally made up of two distinct territories: a continental part and many islands and peninsulas, the main ones being Söl, Feer, Öömrang and Noordströön. Until 1864, North Frisia made up part of Denmark. After being conquered by Germany, three districts were created: Südtondern, Husum and Eiderstedt. In 1970, the three districts were grouped into one, giving a historic coherence to North Frisia. The Frisian language is spoken in this region by 10,000 native speakers. There are many variants that can be classed into two large groups: continental and insular. They correspond to several phases of settlement in this region, which began in the year 700. The *"Mooringer Frasch"*, i.e. "the Mooring Frisian" plays the role of lingua franca, even if different variants are taught in school.

Regional issues

North Frisia, linguistic variants

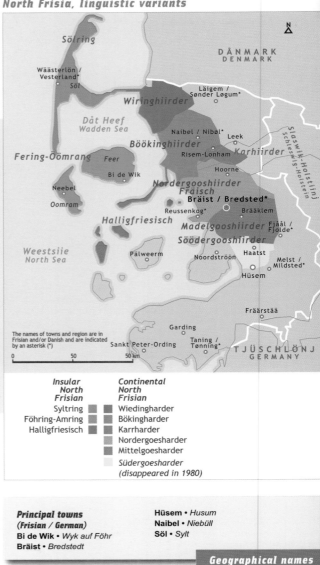

The names of towns and region are in Frisian and/or Danish and are indicated by an asterisk (*)

Insular North Frisian	Continental North Frisian
Syltring	Wiedingharder
Föhring-Amring	Bökingharder
Halligfriesisch	Karrharder
	Nordergoesharder
	Mittelgoesharder
	Südergoesharder (disappeared in 1980)

"Rüm hart, klaar kiming."
(Frisian proverb)
"Wide heart, clear horizon."

Principal towns
(Frisian / German)
Bi de Wik • *Wyk auf Föhr*
Bräist • *Bredstedt*

Hüsem • *Husum*
Naibel • *Niebüll*
Söl • *Sylt*

Geographical names

94

According to Eastern Frisians, they use a vertical riband of black-red-blue. They are the colours of the ruling families of Frisia that are found on their coat of arms.

East Frisia remained an autonomous principality until 1744. It is made up of four districts: Auerk, Emden, Lierre and Wittmund. A little more to the east lie the districts of Freesland, Wilhelmshaven and Ammerland. These are historically connected to East Frisia and, from an inter-Frisian perspective, have an important role to play. 700,000 people live in East Frisia. The major towns are Auerk, Emden, Lierre and Wilhelmshaven. The lone region of Saterland (*Seelterlound* in Frisian) practises the Frisian language called Saterlandic. The other native language spoken nowadays is Low German, of which the Frisian variant is distinctive. Even if the Frisian sentiment is strong in this region, it was only in the 1990s that a real movement began to emerge. In 2007, a political party called "*Die Friesen*" was set up in order to support Frisian ideas. Apart from specific landscapes and styles, East Frisia is distinguished in cultural terms by the practice of an atypical sport: Boßeln, where the players have to throw a ball over a distance of 10 km. The player who makes the fewest throws wins. Frisia is also known for its tea culture, like the English. This activity gives Frisia its cultural vibrancy and the Frisian friendliness is renowned. All visitors are welcomed to tea, morning, noon and night.

East Frisia, the eight territorial subdivisions

Noordsee / North Sea
Oostfreeschen Inseln / Eastern Frisian Islands
Waangeroog
Spiekeroog
Langoog
Baltrum
Nördernee
Waddehsee / Wadden Sea
Juist
Borkum
Nörden
Dorm
Esens
Freesland
Wittmund
Jever
Willemshaven
Willemshaven
Mainhaaf
Auerk
Auerk
Wittmund
Jadebusen
Wiesmoor
Zetel
Grootfehn
Oostfreesland / Oostfraislaand*
Emden
Emden
Hesel
Dollert
Jemgum
Leer
Leer
Leer
Weener
Seelterlound*
NEDDERLANNEN / ETHERLANDS
Strukelje*
Roomelse*
Schäddel*
Seedelsbierich*
DÜÜTSCHLAND / GERMANY

Principal towns
(Low German / German)
Ammerland • *Ammerland*
Auerk • *Aurich*
Emden • *Emden*
Leer • *Leer*
Nörden • *Norden*
Twüschenahn • *Bad Zwischenahn*
Willemshaven • *Wilhelmshaven*
Weener • *Weener*
Westerstäe • *Westerstede*

Wittmund • *Wittmund*

Principal towns
(Saterlandic / German)
Roomelse • *Ramsloh*
Schäddel • *Scharrel*
Seedelsbierich • *Sedelsberg*
Strukelje • *Strücklingen*

Geographical names

"Eala Frya Fresena."
(Frisian motto)
"Stand up, free Frisians."

Flanders, *the long march towards emancipation*

The *Vlaamse Leeuw*, the Flemish Lion, with black claws and tongue, represents Flanders. This symbol was used in the Middle Ages by the counts of Flanders. It is endorsed by the separatists and autonomists. The official flag of the province of Flanders has a black lion with red claws and tongue. This last version was officially adopted in 1990.

Populated by more than 7 million inhabitants including Brussels, Flanders can be considered as the Netherlands of the south. This is the gateway to the Germanic world on the North Sea. Since the beginning of the 14th century, the Flemish have protected their identity in the face of attempts at forced linguistic assimilation.

That which we now call Flanders has never been united in a single state. In the Middle Ages, the territory was divided between many feudal states, the most important being the county of Flanders, the duchy of Brabant and the county of Loon. The county of Flanders belonged to the French crown, while other territories were part of the Germanic Holy Roman Empire, except for the county of Loon, which was part of the principality-bishopric of Liège. Later, the county of Flanders and the duchy of Brabant made up part of the twenty-six provinces, roughly corresponding to the current Bénélux. The latter were dependent on Charles V. In 1581, after the Reformation, the twenty-six provinces declared their independence, except for the southern Netherlands (Belgium) which remained under Spanish and Catholic rule. Between the 16th and 18th centuries, conflicts between the French, the Austrians and the Spanish in Flanders led to the creation of a new kingdom, through the congress of Vienna, uniting both the Netherlands and present-day Belgium. But during the Belgian revolution, Belgium broke away and French became the only official language, forcing the Flemish to resist.

Despite significant advances after the Second World War, the Flemish remained weak. Only in 1971, with the creation of the Council of the Dutch Cultural Community was some autonomy granted, re-enforced by the creation of a parliament in 1980. Today, following the political crisis in Belgium, the question of Flemish independence arises again.

Timeline

58–51 BC • Julius Caesar conquers Gaul and lays the foundations of the Roman-Germanic language.

1302 • Battle of the Golden Spurs. An army of Flemish citizens defeats the army of the king of France, Philip IV (the Fair).

1568–1648 • Revolt of the seventeen provinces of the Netherlands against the Spanish kingdom.

1815 • Congress of Vienna. Creation of the United Kingdom of the Netherlands.

1830 • Belgian revolution, separation of Belgium from the northern part of the Netherlands.

1914–18 • Flemish movement for peace following the atrocities of the war.

1971 • Creation of the Council of the Dutch Cultural Community in Belgium. In 1980, the council is transformed into a Flemish parliament.

2007 • Political crisis in Belgium. The Flemish wish for more autonomy. The Walloons wish for a status quo.

2010 • Historic victory for Flemish separatists. The New Flemish Alliance wins 29% of votes in Flanders.

Identity card

Names: **Vlaanderen**[1], **Flandre**[2] (Flanders)
Population: **7,000,000 inhab.** [note 11]
Area: **16,000 km²** [note 11]
Languages: **Vlaams/Nederlands**[1] (Flemish/Dutch) *(official)*, **Français**[2] (French)
Number of native speakers: **6,000,000**[1]
States of guardianship: **Belgium, France**
Official status: **Region and community in Belgium**
Capital: **Brussel**[1] (Brussels) [note 20]
Historic religion: **Roman Catholic**
Flag: **De Vlaamse Leeuw**[1] (The Flemish Lion)
Anthem: **De Vlaamse Leeuw**[1] (The Flemish Lion)
Motto: **None**

Brief history

On 11 July 1302, the Battle of the Golden Spurs took place in Groeninge near Kortrijk. The urban population army ("communiers") summarily defeat the French. After the battle, the golden spurs of the French knights were collected and hung in the tower of the Church of Our Lady in Kortrijk, hence its name. The exact reason for this conflict was the imprisonment of Count Guy I of Flanders by the king of France, Philip IV the Fair, on accusations of treason. The king seized the county and appointed French officials to Bruges to lead the new conflicts. The king then formed an army of knights that was defeated. In the 19th century, Hendrik Consience wrote the "Lion of Flanders", based on this battle, thus developing a strong sense of identity. Today, 11 July is the day of national celebration in Flanders.

Flanders, the five provinces, Lille Flanders, Westhoek and Brussels

Flanders is situated in the centre of Europe, on the edge of the North Sea. It is a crossroads between France to the west, Wallonia to the south, the Netherlands to the north and Germany to the east (a few kilometres from a narrow strip belonging to the Netherlands). It is called the "flat country", despite a few hills that are found in the south. Along with the Netherlands and Bangladesh, Flanders is one of the most densely populated areas in the world. The economic centre of Flanders was located to the west, especially in Bruges and Ghent, which were the equal of Paris or London. Later, when their power diminished, the centre of gravity moved towards the east, in particular to Antwerp and Brussels. Antwerp was developed thanks to the Industrial Revolution, which also saw the construction of the first railway between Brussels and Mechelen. At the end of the 20th century, Flanders successfully launched into new technologies and services, ensuring its economic prosperity today.

Geography

Geographical names

Principal towns
(Dutch / French)
Aalst • *Alost*
Antwerpen • *Anvers*
Brugge • *Bruges*
Brussel • *Bruxelles*
Dowaai • *Douai*
Duinkerke • *Dunkerque*

Gent • *Gand*
Hasselt • *Hasselt*
Kortrijk • *Courtrai*
Mechelen • *Malines*
Oostende • *Ostende*
Rijsel • *Lille*
Robaais • *Roubaix*
Toerkonje • *Tourcoing*

Regions
(Dutch / French)
Antwerpen • *Anvers*
Limburg • *Limbourg*
Oost-Vlaanderen • *Flandre orientale*
Rijsels-Vlaanderen • *Flandre lilloise*
Vlaams-Brabant • *Brabant flamand*
West-Vlaanderen • *Flandre occidentale*
Westhoek • *Westhoek*

Today, the Flemish government has the ability to manage culture, education, the environment, agriculture, communication and, for a large part, health and the economy. In other domains, such as defence or justice, there is little or no power and it has to cooperate with the Belgian federal government. A large number of parties exist Flanders. Since the legislative elections of 2010, the parliament is dominated by moderate separatists of the N-VA. The latter wish that the bulk of the powers be entrusted to the regions, a preliminary step towards independence. The detestable party of the far-right Vlaams Belang (English: Flemish Interest) necessitate other parties to form unnatural but necessary coalitions, bringing conservatives and progressives together, to prevent the spread of Vlaams Belang ideologies.

Principal separatist Flemish parties:
• **Nieuw-Vlaamse alliantie** / New Flemish Alliance (N-VA) *(Separatist conservative)*
• **Vlaams Belang** / Flemish Interest (VB) *(Far-right separatist)*

Politics now

> "Schild en vriend."
> "Shield and friend."
> (This expression, difficult for a French speaker to pronounce, was used in 1302 to distinguish the Flemish soldiers from the French soldiers)

97

South Tyrol, *Austrians at heart*

Officially adopted in 1983, the flag of South Tyrol uses some details similar to the flag of the Austrian Tyrol. The red eagle is simplified and found in a white shield. The white and red colours are the colours of the Tyrol.

South Tyrol or Südtirol is a German-speaking territory in the north of Italy, to which it is reluctantly linked historically. Austrians at heart, the South Tyroleans today benefit from a strong autonomy, permitting them to live their lives free from interference.

Inhabited since the Mesolithic era, there exist traces of human presence on South Tyrolean land. Part of the Roman Empire from 59 AD onwards, the Germanic people succeeded them, in particular Bavarians and Lombards of the 6th–9th centuries. From the 10th century, South Tyrol became a stronghold, a base of the Germanic Roman Empire in the Alps.

Ruled by the Habsburgs in the 14th century, it wasn't annexed to Italy until 1918, after the Treaty of Saint-Germain. The fascist regime led to a strong repression of Tyroleans from 1922. Hitler and Mussolini agreed and "offered" two options to the Tyroleans. Stay and be Italianised or head towards Germany and be stateless.

After the Second World War, an automonous status for South Tyrol was negotiated in Paris (Gruber-De Gasperi Agreement). It did not come into effect immediately. In parallel, Italy organised the arrival of many migrants from southern Italy. This situation of quasi-colonisation frustrated the local populations. From 1957, the Committee for the Liberation of South Tyrol (BAS) organised armed struggles initially directed against public buildings. Thanks to the intervention of Austria before the UN Security Council the question of South Tyrol was finally discussed impartially and conciliation was facilitated. Autonomy is now effective. The Tyrolean political parties dominate the political scene allowing it to benefit from an advantageous status and from co-officially speaking the German language.

Identity card

Names: **Südtirol**[1], **Alto-Adige (Sudtirolo)**[2] (South Tyrol)
Population: **487,673 inhab.** *(2006)*
Area: **7,400 km²**
Languages: **Deutsch**[1] (German), **Italiano**[2] (Italian) *(official)*
Number of native speakers: **345,000** *(2001)*
State of guardianship: **Italy**
Official status: **Autonomous province in Italy**
Capital: **Bozen**[1], **Bolzano**[2] (Bozen/Bolzano)
Historic religion: **Roman Catholic**
Flag: **Südtiroler Fahne**[1] (Flag of South Tyrol)
Anthem: **Andreas-Hoferlied**[1] / **Südtirollied**[1] (Song of Andreas-Hofer / Song of South Tyrol)
Motto: **None**

Brief history

During the Napoleonic wars, Tyrol was annexed by Bavaria, then allied with France. Andreas Hofer spearheaded a resistance movement to liberate the country. Supported a number of years later by Emperor Franz II of Austria (1809), the Tyrolean rebellion was put into full effect. Defying the Bavarians in Sterzing, Hofer became a charismatic figure of Tyrolean patriotism. There were successive victories and defeats. Napolean crushed the Austrians who took back the advantage. In a few months, Hofer succeeded in defeating the invaders. A price was put on his head. Captured, he was executed in Mantua in February 1810. Having become a martyr in Austria, his remains were transferred to Innsbrück in 1823. The Tyrolean anthem now bears his name in the Austrian Tyrol and unofficially in South Tyrol.

South Tyrol, the eight Ladin districts and territories

South Tyrol is found perched in the Alps. Bordered to the north and east by Austria, a country with which it has strong links, its neighbours are Switzerland to the west and Italy (Lombardy, Trentin and Venice) to the south. The boundary between Austrian Tyrol and South Tyrol, imposed after the First World War was designed on the main peaks of the Alps. The Brenner Tunnel (2,020 m) allows contact between the two parts of historic Tyrol. South Tyrol is divided into eight districts (Bezirksgemeinschaft): Bozen, Burggrafenamt, Eisacktal, Puster, Salten-Schlern, Überetsch-Unterland, Vinschgau, Wipptal. Its capital Bozen is found in the centre of the country. The largest part of the population is found between an altitude of 300 and 1,200 m. The vast Alpine pastures and the high pastures enhance the reputation of this region of Europe.

Geography

Principal towns
(German / Italian)
Bozen • *Bolzano*
Leifers • *Laives*
Meran • *Merano*
Brixen • *Bressanone*
Brunek • *Brunico*
Glurns • *Glorenza*
Neumarkt • *Egna*
Sterzing • *Vipiteno*

Regions (German / Italian)
Pustertal • *Val Pusteria*
Wipptal • *Alta Valle Isarco*
Burggrafenamt • *Burgraviato*
Vinschgau • *Val Venosta*
Salten-Schlern • *Salto-Sciliar*
Überetsch-Südtiroler Unterland • *Oltradige-Bassa Atesina*
Eisacktal • *Valle Isarco*

Geographical names

"Wer rastet, der rostet."
(Tyrolean proverb)
"He who sits, rusts."

The Faroe Islands, *insurmountable archipelago of the Atlantic*

The Faroese flag is a Scandinavian cross, symbolising the Christian heritage of the island. The colours are close to those of Norway and Iceland, to which they are culturally related. The white background symbolises the snow-white foam of the sea and the waterfalls, the red cross the blood of people, and the blue symbolises the expanse of the sky on the endless sea.

Subjected to the harsh climate of the North Atlantic, the Faroe Islands appear as a small dot on the map between Scotland, Norway and Iceland. Despite their size, the Faroe Islands are organised into a quasi-state and have their own institutions. The Faroese people work hard to control their destiny by developing a strong sense of belonging and a language spoken by the entire population of the island.

The Faroese people, distant descendants of the Vikings, have always defended their culture and their independence while struggling for survival on inhospitable land originally populated by sea birds and sheep.

The Faroe Islands are self-governed according to the old Scandinavian practices of electing a representative assembly. The Norwegian king was initially recognised as sovereign and by an accident in history the Faroese are today under the control of the Danish monarchy, which leaves them to govern themselves.

Conflicts linked to fishing have long monopolised the attention of the Faroese who enjoy a rich fishing source. Relations with their neighbours today, however, are more or less peaceful.

Because their geographical distance places them far away from the central power and a sense of consensus, the Faroe Islands have developed great legal expertise. Elected by the people since 1948, parliament (Løgting) is officially recognised as a legislative authority. For example, the Faroe Islands are not part of the European Union and may in some respects conduct their own foreign policy in some areas. The question of independence arises now in a more meaningful manner and could make its reappearance in debates in the coming years.

Timeline

9th century • Introduction of Scandinavian people and those from the British Isles.

11th century • Recognition of Christianity by the Løgting Assembly.

1270 (circa) • Treaty with the king of Norway recognising his supremacy on the island while retaining the right to self-government.

1380 • Union of Norway and Denmark, little by little the administrative capital becomes Copenhagen.

1814 • Danish rule. The Løgting is not convened for 50 years.

1856 • The Løgting meets and is able to take legislative action.

1948 • After the de facto independence during the war and a referendum in favour of seccession, the Faroe Islands retains extensive autonomy.

2004 • All the political parties agree to a constitutional process to reduce the influence of Danish power.

Identity card

Names: **Føroyar[1], Færøerne[2]** (The Faroe Islands)
Population: **48,378 inhab.** *(2007)*
Area: **1,399 km²**
Languages: **Føroysk[1]** (Faroese), **Dansk[2]** (Danish) *(official)*
Number of native speakers: **48,378[1]**
State of guardianship: **Denmark**
Official status: **Autonomous island belonging to Demark**
Capital: **Tórshavn**
Historic religion: **Lutheran and Calvinist**
Flag: **Merkið[1]** (The Emblem)
Anthem: **Tú alfagra land mítt[1]** (You, my magnificent country)
Motto: **None**

Brief history

After the Second World War, the Faroe were recognised quickly for their efforts during this difficult period. Indeed, the allies settled there so as to prevent the Germans setting up a base. In 1948, the Faroese organised a referendum for independence. The people opted for this solution but, following parliamentary elections, the choice of a trade solution with Denmark was finally chosen in order to achieve a gradual independence. Since this period, the Faroe islands have remained divided between loyalty to the fact that Denmark provides large subsidies and a desire for instant secession. This ambivalence was observed in the drafting of the new constitution in 2004, where Danish subsidies were renounced while gradually the promised independence was reached, whilst also respecting the shared feelings of the public on this issue.

Geography

The Faroe Islands are made up of 18 volcanic islands between the Shetland Islands (Scotland), Iceland and Norway. The population is located on the six biggest islands. Their privileged position in the North Atlantic offers them unrivalled fishing resources. The seabed contains many minerals and possibly oil. The Faroe Islands benefit from a temperate climate thanks to the warm currents of the Atlantic. Thus the vegetation is essentially made up of grass herbs. The thermal contrasts due to low pressure create a pleasant ambience, inspiring artists of all genres. The housing consists of little coloured houses located on the coast and notably in Tórshavn (the capital) which takes its name from the ancient god of thunder "Thor", and the word "havn", harbour.

Faroe, the six regions

Geographical names

Principal towns
(Faroese / Danish)
Fuglafjørður • *Fuglefjord*
Hvalba • *Hvalbø*
Klaksvík • *Klaksvig*
Leirvík • *Lervig*
Miðvágur • *Midvåg*
Sandur • *Sand*
Sørvágur • *Sørvåg*
Tórshavn • *Thorshavn*
Tvøroyri • *Tværå*

Vágur • *Våg*
Vestmannav • *Vestmannahavn*

Regions
*(Faroese / Danish) *English*
Eysturoy • *Østerø (Island of the East*)*
Norðoyar • *Norderøerne (Island of the North*)*
Sandoy • *Sandø (Island of Sand*)*
Streymoy • *Strømø (Island of Running*)*
Suðuroy • *Suderø (Island of the South*)*
Vágar • *Vågø (Island of the Bay*)*

Politics now

The Løgting, parliament of the Faroe Islands, has a very strong autonomy, to which all political parties are committed. Depending on the political circumstances, they often advocate cutting all links with Denmark. Economic and social politics equally divide the parties, creating a very diverse political landscape, even if non-adherance to the European Union remains unanimous. The system of "Scandinavian" social protection is also one of the big cohesive factors for the Faroe Islands. These numerous lines of parliamentary political fracture often create unpredictable coalitions, without real party logic.

Principal Faroese parties:
- **Tjóðveldi** / Republican Party *(Socialist separatist)*
- **Sambandsflokkurin** / Unionist Party *(Federal liberal)*
- **Fólkaflokkurin** / Popular Party *(Conservative separatist)*
- **Javnaðarflokkurin** / Social Democratic Party *(Progressive federalist)*
- **Miðflokkurin** / Central Party *(Separatist)*
- **Sjálvstýrisflokkutin** / Separatist Party *(Liberal separatist)*

"So leika bátar sum skip."
(Faroese proverb)
"The yachts sail better than large boats."

Kashubia, the Slavs of the Baltics

The Kashubian flag represents the colours of their coat of arms which features a black griffin on a yellow background. These two colours are found on the official coats of arms of most towns and suburbs in Kashubia. Today this flag is used by Kashubian regionalists.

Direct descendants of Slavic tribes of Pomerania (meaning countries along the sea, in this case the Baltic), the Kashubians are able to reiterate their identity in a more open Poland. Often assimilated into the Poles, they are distinguished by their language. *Kaszub* **is the name of the coat, which they traditionally wore.**

Living between different states, sometimes German, sometimes Polish, the Kashubians survived under the Communist regime that tried to assimilate them. The Kashubian families had to speak their language in secret but managed to preserve it and pass it on. For a long time Gdańsk, the main city of Kashubia, was better known under the German name Dantzig.

Today, the Kashubians aspire above all to safeguard their language, but movements for the creation of a Kashubian region are emerging, even if Kashubia has never been a sovereign state. Despite a low number of native speakers, the majority of the population consider themselves Kashubian. Permission to use the language in conjunction with Polish since 2005 has reinforced this sentiment.

Nowadays taught to 6,000 students, Kashubian is an optional subject for the school-leaving exam since this date.

Many associations for the promotion of Kashubian culture have been formed over the past few years. The principal organisation is the Kashubian-Pomeranian Association. *Odroda*, another association, fights for the rebirth of Kashubian culture.

Timeline

13th century • First mention of the Kashubians on the seal of Barnim.

13th century • The duke of Pomerania is named the duke of Kashubia.

1648 • The kings of Sweden are "dukes of Kashubia".

1843 • The Prussians take control of Kashubia. The Kashubians emigrate en masse to North America.

1919 • Preferring to be Polish rather than German, the Kashubian activist Antonie Abraham declares "There is no Kashubia without Poland and no Poland without Kashubia."

1939–1945 • Summary executions of Kashubians by the Nazis.

1945 • The Kashubian, germanised by force between the 14th and 19th centuries, are expelled from Poland during liberation.

1990 • Movements in favour of the Kashubian language are reborn after the fall of the Communist regime in Poland.

Identity card

Names: **Kaszëbë**[1], **Kaszuby**[2] (Kashubia) note 19
Population: **2,515,000 inhab.** note 13 *(2006)*
Area: **6,870 km²** note 13
Languages: **Kaszëbsczi**[1] (Kashubian) *(without official status)*, **Polski**[2] (Polish) *(official)*
Number of native speakers: **50,000 to 300,000**[1]
State of guardianship: **Poland**
Official status: **None**
Capital: **Kartuzë**[1], **Kartuzy**[2] (Kartuzy)
Historic religion: **Roman Catholic**
Flag: **Fana Kaszëbsczi**[1] (Kashubian Flag)
Anthem: **None**
Motto: **None**

Brief history

The Kashubian movement is basically structured with regards to the language. The first activist in favour of the language, Ceynowa Florian, worked largely on linguistic standardisation, notably on orthography and grammar. This work dates from 1879. Initiating literary journals, e.g. Zrzësz Kaszëbskô, these activists facilitated a distribution of the language up to the present day. Thus today, teaching has been able to expand and the number of students totals 6,000, which is unfortunately very few in relation to the total number of scholars. The Polish authorities, reluctant to install an official bilingualism, have nonetheless ratified the European Charter for Regional or Minority Languages. Bilingual signs were installed in the 2000s, but the latter were quickly damaged by people opposed to all forms of multiculturalism in Poland.

Kashubia, the nine powiats

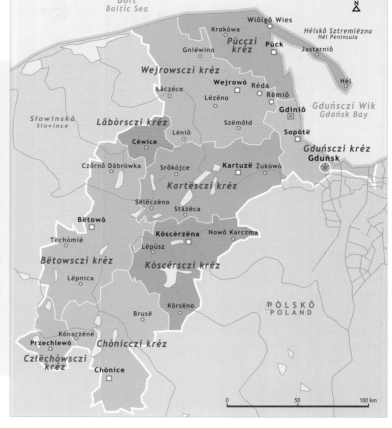

Kashubia has never had a defined status. It is a Pomeranian territory, literally "along the sea". Pomerania and Kashubia have always been divided up among many regions or states (Poland, Denmark, Saxony, Brandenburg, Prussia, Sweden and Germany). Gdansk is certainly the most emblematic city. Traditionally, Kashubian society revolved around fishing and agriculture, explained by its position near the Baltic Sea. The city of Gdansk was rapidly turned over to industrial activities. The principal Kashubian cities are Gdansk, Wejrowo, Karuze (considered the de facto capital), Betowo, Koscerzena and Chonice. Kashubia represents almost the whole of the new voivoide (administrative division) of Pomerania. It brings together 9 of 15 districts (powiat) in this region, sometimes only partially.

Principal towns (Kashubian / Polish / German)

Bëtowò • *Bytów, Bütow*
Chònice • *Chojnice, Konitz*
Gdiniô • *Gdynia, Gdingen*
Gduńsk • *Gdańsk, Danzig*
Kartuzë • *Kartuzy, Karthaus*
Kòscérzëna • *Kościerzyna, Berent*
Pùck • *Puck, Putzig*
Sopòtë • *Sopot, Zoppot*
Wejrowò • *Wejherowo, Neustadt in Westpreußen*
Wiôlgô Wies • *Władysławowo, Großendorf*

Geographical names

"Je ju wiôldżi czas, cobë niżóden Kaszëba sã nie wstidzёł pò kaszëbskù gôdac."
(Florian Cenôwa, Kashubian writer)
"It is high time for the Kashubians to not be ashamed to speak Kashubian."

Sorbia, *rebirth after oppression*

The flag of the Sorbs, representing the pan-Slavic colours, is made up of three horizontal bands of blue, red and white. It was used for the first time in 1948. Today, it appears as the flag of the Sorbian community in the laws relating to their protection in Brandeburg and in Saxony.

The Sorbs, who call themselves Wends, are the last survivors of the Slavs of the east German territory. They occupy a large part of that which is eastern Germany today and western Poland.

The Sorbs live in Lusatia, straddling two German states (Brandenburg and Saxony where they are recognised as a minority), near the Czech and Polish borders. Using two distinct language variants, Low Sorbian in Lower Lusatia and High Sorbian in Upper Lusatia, the Sorbians have suffered throughout their history because of Germanic domination, until they received some recognition after the Second World War. Estimated at more than 300,000 people today, only a fraction of the population are registered as being Sorb according to language. Sorbian is spoken by 30,000 people mainly in Upper Lusatia.

Apart from the Nazi regime, it was under the yoke of the DDR that the Sorbs have suffered most. While appearing to be protected, the Sorbs actually lost more than 40% of their territory, which was given over to lignite mines and power plants.

After the collapse of the Communist bloc, the Sorbs became aware of the richness of their identity, and enjoyed expressing their culture, notably thanks to the "*Domowina*" association, forbidden under the Nazi regime. Since 1998, certain nursery schools teach Sorbian by "immersion". Unfortunately, bilingual teaching is not widespread, which is a risk for the survival of the language.

Since 2003, a political party has formed to defend Sorbian interests. This is the "Serbska Ludowa Strona – Wendische Volkspartei", polling modestly.

Timeline

400–600 BC • First Wende population and creation of "rondins" (a particular form of housing).

950–13 BC • Start of Christianisation and the Germanisation of Wende tribes.

14th–18th centuries • Progressive assimilation of Sorbian territories.

1700 • First Bible edited in Low Sorbian.

18th–19th centuries • Boom of literature and the associative sector.

1900 • First bans on the use of the language in Lower Lusatia.

1933–45 • Under the Nazi regime, deportation of Sorbian activists to Siberia.

1948 • First "Sorbian law", protecting de facto the Sorbian minority while destroying the territory.

1998 • After the fall of the Berlin Wall, massive efforts to spread and conserve the Sorbian culture and language.

Identity card

Names: **Serbja**[1'], **Serby**[1'], **Sorben / Wenden**[2] (Sorbia) note 19
Population: **1,400,000 inhab.** note 14
Area: **10,800 km²** note 14
Languages: **Serbšćina/Serbska**[1] (Sorbian) (Hornjoserbsce[1'], High Sorbian / **Dolnoserbski**[1'], Low Sorbian) *(without official status)*, **Deutsch**[2] (German) *(official)*
Number of native speakers: **60,000**[1]
State of guardianship: **Germany**
Official status: **None**
Capitals: **Chóśebuz**[1'], **Choćebuz**[1'], **Cottbus**[2] *(Lower Lusatia)* / **Budyšin**[1'], **Budyšyn**[1'], **Bautzen**[2] *(Upper Lusatia)*
Historic religion: **Protestant and Roman Catholic**
Flag: **Chorhoj Serbow**[1'] (Sorbian Flag)
Anthem: **Rjana Łužica**[1'] **/ Rědna Łužyca**[1'] (Magnificent Lusatia)
Motto: **None**

Brief history

Sorbian history is one of subjection. In 938, the Margrave of Merseburg invited the chiefs of the Wende tribes, ancestors of the Sorbians, to peace negotiations. However, this invitation turned into a massacre and the Wende princes were decapitated, beginning a forced Germanisation. The height of the Sorbian persecution was reached during the Nazi regime, with Sorbian patriots being exiled by force. It was only in 1945 that the East German dictatorship actually promoted Sorbian culture, not without the condition of adhering to the regime. These good times were not without their consequence for the Sorbian culture and language. After the fall of the wall, some hastily made the link between Communist dictatorship and the protection of the Sorbian minority. Today the situation is improving but remains critical. Obligatory teaching could perhaps save the language.

Lusatia, historic territory and Sorbian people

Regions
(Low Sorbian / Upper Sorbian / German)
- Górna Łużyca/Hornja Łužica = Upper Lusatia
- Dolna Łużyca/Delnja Lužica = Lower Lusatia
- Lusatia (off field Sorbia)
- Historic Lusatia

Geography

The Sorbs are found in Lusatia, a region straddling Germany, Poland and the Czech Republic. Two towns separate this small territory: Bautzen in the south, the capital of Upper Lusatia and Cottbus in the north, and the capital of Lower Lusatia. The Sorbian language is very present in the south. Strongly marked by the coal industry, Lusatia embarked on converting fallow land to create recreational areas. Artificial lakes have been recently created. In addition to these two territories, Saxony and Brandeburg are recognised as bilingual (the two German states in which Sorbs are located), Lusatia is historically more extensive. It spills over into Poland to the east and the Czech Republic to the south. The Sorbian populations do not live there anymore.

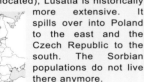

Principal towns (Sorbian / German)
Baršć • *Forst*
Běla Wóda • *Weißwasser*
Biskopicy • *Bischofswerda*
Budyšin • *Bautzen*
Chósebuz • *Cottbus*
Gródk • *Spremberg*
Kameńc • *Kamenz*
Kalawa • *Calau*
Łukow • *Luckau*
Lubin • *Lübben*
Lubńow • *Lübbenau*
Niska • *Niesky*

Wětošow • *Vetschau*
Wójerecy • *Hoyerswerda*
Zły Komorow • *Senftenberg*

Regions (Sorbian / German)
Błota • *Spreewald*
Dolna Łužyca • *Niederlausitz*
Slepjański stron • *Schleifer Region*
Łužyska Góla / Hola • *Lausitzer Heide*
Hornja Łužica • *Oberlausitz*
Hornja Łužiske Hory • *Oberlausitzer Bergland*

Geographical names

"Ja Serski som, a Serski budu, a Serski pśeceń wóstańom."
(Sorbian song)
"I am Sorbian, I will be Sorbian and I will always remain Sorbian."

Sorbia, *rebirth after oppression*

Bucolic landscape of Lusatia

Serbska

Sorbian is divided into two varieties – Low Sorbian and High Sorbian. It is a western Slavic language, related to Polish and Czech. Sorbian is spoken by almost 30,000 to 60,000 registered people in a region made up of 490,000 people. It enjoys a relatively small status, granted by the two German states of Brandenburg and Saxony. However, these states display a voluntary policy, in particular where it concerns the promotion of the language. Primary education does not enable its circulation, which is often carried out by the family. Nevertheless, a daily newspaper *Domowina* has created a real link between native speakers of this Slavic language.

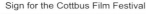

Sign for the Cottbus Film Festival

Sorbs are recognised as a minority in Germany although this recognition is tentative. A sort of status quo exists, which is for the Sorbs not to engage in the political arena, as if that were taboo. This attitude of mistrust with regards to the public is possibly due to the turbulent history of the region. The fact is that representatives of major cultural associations in the region had voted, until recently, against the creation of a specific party. In 2005, the Popular Party of Sorbia (Serbska Ludowa Strona (SLS) Wendische Volkspartei) appeared on the political scene. It is considered a part of the Sorbian minority in Lusatia, claiming a true linguistic independence and a re-enforcement of German federalism. Fearing greater assimilation through the merging of Berlin and Brandeburg, the SLS rejects this option.

Politics now

The Basque Country, *always fighting for their rights*

The Basques used the term *Ikurriña* to name their flag. It was created in 1896 by Sabino Arana Gori, considered the founder of modern Basque nationalism. It represented Biscay and was adopted in 1936 as the flag of the Euskadi government before being adopted by the whole of Basque. The white cross of St Andrew is positioned on a green cross representing the oak of Guernica and a red background representing the Basque people.

Euskal Herria is the term that describes the whole of the Basque Country. It is a cultural region to the west of the Pyrénées, torn between Spain and France. Seven provinces make up this nation's historic Bay of Biscay.

The Basques are considered descendants of the Paleolithic people of Western Europe, which makes them one of the oldest people on the continent. During Roman occupation, the Basque tribes were already present.

There is no doubt that Basque was already spoken at the start of the Middle Ages between Ebra and Garonne in the region called Biscay. After the Muslim invasions and the Frankish expansion, the territory was broken up. The Basque Country known under the name of Navarre was partially annexed by the kingdom of Castille in 1512–21. However, the Basque provinces benefited from relative autonomy until the French Revolution in the north and the Carlist Wars in the south.

Despite a statute of autonomy being acquired in 1936, the civil war put an end to the first democratic advances. Guernica, the former Basque capital was bombarded by the Germans allied to the Spanish nationalists. Despite a different approach by Basque movements to achieve independence, desired by the former nationalist government, the Basque parties continued to gain the votes of their compatriots, in a context of enthusiasm for the Basque language, which is popular with them.

Timeline

198 AD • The Basque Country is occupied by the Romans.

602 • First appearance of the name of "Vasconia".

824 • Foundation of the kingdom of Navarre.

1200 & 1379 • Álava, Guipúzcoa and Biscay are occupied by Castilla.

1449 & 1451 • Soule and Labourd are conquered by France.

1545 • First Basque book.

1789 • The French Revolution suppresses the freedom of the provinces (Iparralde).

1833–74 • Carlist Wars.

1841 • Paccionda Law: end of the kingdom of Navarre.

1936–9 • Spanish Civil War. Acts of violence against the Basques.

1978 • Statute of Autonomy of the Southern Basque Country (Statute of Guernica).

1982 • Statute of Autonomy of Navarre (Ley de Amejoramiento del Fuero), revised in 2001.

Identity card

Names: Euskal Herria[1], País Vasco[2], Pays basque[3] (Basque Country)
Population: **3,007,661 inhab.** note 17 (2006)
Area: **20,947 km²** note 17
Languages: **Euskara[1]** (Basque), **Castellano[2]** (Castilian), **Français[3]** (French) *(official)*
Number of native speakers: **665,800 to 1,234,000[1]**
States of guardianship: **Spain, France**
Official status: **Autonomous regions in Spain, no status in France**
Capital: **Iruñea[1], Pamplona[2]** (Pamplona)
Historic religion: **Roman Cathoilic**
Flag: **Ikurrina[1], Ikurriña[2]** (Symbol)
Anthem: **Eusko Gudaria[1]** (The Basque Fighter)
Motto: **Zazpiak bat[1]** (Seven makes one)

Brief history

The Basque sense of identity has its source in the 9th century and is based on the *Fueros* charter giving people specific freedoms. Constantly torn between several states, the Basque Country maintained its liberties until the French Revolution, which abolished them in the north. In 1876, the Spanish royal power abolished them completely in the south. The Basque Nationalist Party (PNB) was born during this period. The Spanish Civil War, which started in 1936, brought Franco to power (1939). Opposed to all ideas of autonomy, his regime claimed many civilian casualties. The Basque autonomous government was exiled to Bayonne and the resistance was established. It is at this time that ETA (Euskadi ta Askatasuna) was created. In 1979, after the death of Franco, the Basque Country acquired autonomous status. However, the situation remained tense, particularly in regards to the subject of self-determination, which creates debate in Basque society.

Basque Country: the seven historical provinces

The geography of the Basque Country is complex. The country is made up of seven historic provinces: Araba, Biscay (Bizkaia), Guipúzcoa (Gipuzkoa), making up part of the autonomous Basque community of Euskadi, Navarre, the only constituent that is an autonomous community and the three northern provinces (Labourd, Basse-Navarre and Soule). Pamplona is considered the historic capital of the Basque Country, while other towns, such as

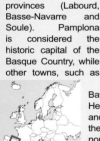

Bayonne, Bilbao, Gasteiz-Vitoria or Saint-Sebastian extend throughout the whole territory. Iparralde and Hegoalde are two names, which characterise the division of the Basque Country between two states, Spain and France. The first linked to the northern Basque Country and the second to the south. The geography of the Basque Country is also characterised by a strong toponymy marked by mountainous landscapes in the north, bordering the Atlantic Ocean and the flatter, arid landscapes of the south, particularly the nature parks and the semi-deserts of the Bardenas Reales.

Geography

Principal towns (Basque / Castilian or French*)

Angelu • *Anglet**
Baiona • *Bayonne**
Barakaldo • *Baracaldo*
Bilbo • *Bilbao*
Donibane Garazi • *Saint-Jean-de-Pied de-Port**
Donostia • *San Sebastián*
Eibar • *Éibar*
Gasteiz • *Vitoria*
Getxo • *Guecho*
Irun • *Irún*
Iruñea • *Pamplona*
Leioa • *Lejona*

Maule-Lextarre • *Mauléon-Licharre**
Miarritze • *Biarritz**
Tolosa • *Tolosa*
Zarautz • *Zaraut*

Regions (Basque / Castilian or French*)

Hegoalde (Southern Basque Country / Spain)
Araba • *Alava*
Nafarroa • *Navarre*
Gipuzkoa • *Guipuzcoa*
Bizkaia • *Vizcaya*
Iparralde (Northern Basque Country / France)
Lapurdi • *Labourd**
Nafarroa Beherea • *Basse Navarre**
Zuberoa • *Soule**

Geographical names

«Hizkuntza dela-eta, ez da inor gutzietsiko.»
(Article 6 of the Statute of Autonomy of Euskadi)
"No person shall be discriminated against because of language."

The Basque Country, *always fighting for their rights*

Language

Euskara

The Basque language (Euskara) is an isolated case in Europe. It belongs to neither the most common Indo-European family nor the less widespread families, which are the Finno-Ugric or Turkic-Altaic languages. There are traditionally seven variants and many sub-variants. However, intercomprehension is largely possible, especially since the writing system is unified. More than 33% of Basques speak their language, which is traditionally spoken more in the north. Nowadays, in the autonomous regions (i.e. the Euskadi regions), Basque is taught as a first language in schools. Indeed, the statute of autonomy of 1979 places Basque and Castilian on equal footing and the Basques are very attached to this right. The fundamental law on the use of Euskara reinforces their rights in the field of administration, justice and public services. ETB (*Euskal Telebista*), a television channel created in 1984, broadcasts in Basque. In Navarre, where 10% of Basques speak their language, the government has traditionally opposed the growth of Basque, not being restricted to follow the measures which their statute of autonomy affords them, i.e. the recognition of Basque as a second language. In the north, under the French administration, the situation is more tense, with the French monolingual system of teaching leaves little room for the Basque language. The future of the Basque language will probably depend on the results of a referendum expected in the next few years in Euskadi, but only for one part of the territory.

Basque Country, linguistic varieties

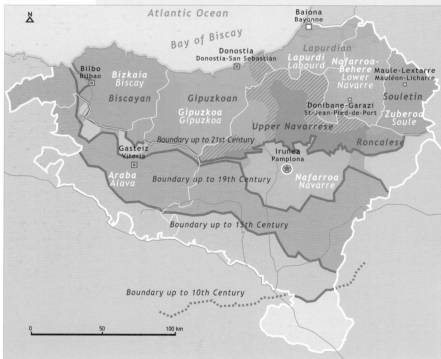

Basque nationalism in its modern form has existed since the 19th century. It is based on the right of the Basque people to self-determination and to their independence. The Parliament of the three autonomous provinces of Euskadi – Araba, Bizkaia and Gipuzkoa – has twice decided in favour of self-determination, in 2002 and 2006. As this right is not guaranteed in the Spanish Constitution of 1978, the issue continues to be keenly debated in the country. Many remain loyal to the Madrid government, but a majority favour more autonomy or secession and 59% of Basques are in favour of holding a referendum on the subject.

Principal Basque parties:
• **Eusko Alderdi Jeltzalea - Partido Nacionalista Vasco** / Nationalist Basque Party (EAJ/PNV) *(Separatist Social Democrat)*
• **Eusko Alkartasuna (EA)** / Basque Solidarity *(Progressive separatist)*
• **Aralar**,split from Batasuna *(Revolutionary separatist)*

Giant demonstration in the Basque Country

Sápmi, shepherds of the Boreal Lands

The Sámi flag is red, blue, green and yellow. It builds on the drum of the shaman and the poem "Paiven parneh" (Son of Sun, surname that the writer Anders Fjellner (1795–1876) gives to the Sámi). The circle represents the sun (red) and the moon (blue).

The Sámi have one of the most extensive territories in Europe. This land, called "Sápmi", stretches from the north of Sweden, Norway, Finland and on the Kola peninsula in Russia. Their language, Sami, is spoken in many groups.

For thousands of years, the Sámi lived on hunting and fishing to the north of the European continent. It wasn't until around the year 900 AD that they began to herd tamed reindeer, henceforth considered their traditional way of life. They maintain a special relationship with nature, living in harmony with it. Thus, the Sámi community was traditionally based on the *siida*, i.e. the units and collectivities of common law (not necessarily familial), which use their own council and administration, allocating hunting grounds and fishing.

The colonisation of Sápmi (Lapland) and the exploitation of resources were considerably increased over the course of the 13th and 14th centuries, causing many states to claim their sovereignty over this region. The first stage of this division split the territory the length of the mountain ridges from the region of Jämtland to Finnmark The border between Sweden and Finland was established in 1809 and that between Norway and Russia in 1826.

Over the course of the past two centuries, the Sámi have been the victims of repression and negligence of the people who ruled them, who considered them to be inferior. For example, the well-known term "Lapon" is used in a derogatory manner by the population ("lapp" being an old Scandinavian term used to describe a worn piece of clothing or "lape" in vernacular Finnish). The banning of cultural expression and the speaking of the Sami language intensified in the 19th century. It is only since the 1980s that the Sámi have made a remarkable return to the public scene, allowing them to develop their autonomy peacefully and to enforce their identity.

Identity card

Names: **Sápmi/Sámeednam[1], Sameland/ Lappland[2 3], Lappi[4], Лапландия/Laplandiya[5]** (Sápmi / "Laponia") [note 19]
Population: **2,979,938 (of which 100,000 Sámis)** [note 18]
Area: **669,646 km²** [note 18]
Languages: **Sámegielat[1]** (Sami/Lapon), **Svenska[2]** (Swedish), **Norsk[3]** (Norwegian), **Suomi[4]** (Finnish), **Русский/Russkiy[5]** (Russian) (official)
Number of native speakers: **25,000[1]**
States of guardianship: **Sweden, Norway, Finland, Russia**
Official status: **Represented by a parliament in Sweden, Norway and Finland, no particular status in Russia**
Capital: **Giron[1], Kiruna[2]** *(Sweden)* **/ Kárášjohka[1], Karasjok[3]** *(Norway)* **/ Áanaar[1], Inari[4]** *(Finland)*
Historic religion: **Christian and Animist**
Flag: **Sámi leavga[1]** (Sámi Flag)
Anthem: **Sámi soga lávlla[1]** (Song of the Sámi People)
Motto: **Sámieatnan sámiide[1]** (A Sámi Land for the Sámi People)

Brief history

The first joint conference of the Sámi parliamentaries took place in Jåhkåmåhkke on 24 February 2005. The representatives of the Sámi parliaments in Norway, Sweden, Finland and Russia participated. It was during this historic event that they assert that the Sámi are a united people, whose unity cannot be challenged by state borders. The declaration states, among other things, the right to self-determination by the Sámi people and the fact that important work is to be carried out to complete the "Nordic Sámi contract". Since this date, the Sámi parliaments have met every three years.

Timeline

1600 • Denmark, Sweden and Russia establish tax in the north of the Sámi territory.

1751 • Despite the establishment of a border between Norway and Sweden-Finland, rights are granted to the Sámi to live and move freely.

1852 • The town of Guovdageaidnu experiences one of the rare Sámi rebellions against the Norwegian oppressor.

1963 • The Sami language is newly authorised in Norwegian schools.

1979 • Controversy around a hydroelectric project in Norway, which enables the Sámi to have new rights. Creation of the first Sámi sport federation.

1986 • The Sámi conference decrees that Sápmi is Sámi territory and should be treated with respect and care. Creation of the national anthem and the flag.

1989–96 • First Sámi parliaments in Norway, Sweden and Finland, with limited powers.

2005 • Law on the Finnmark, granting extensive rights to Sámis in the northernmost part of Norway.

Sápmi, historic regions and territories under Sami administration

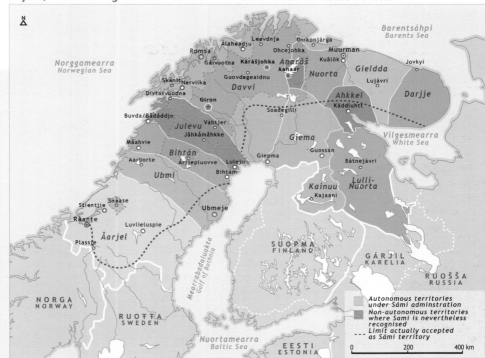

The territory of the Sámi is called Sápmi. It corresponds to the north of Scandinavia, Finland and the Kola Peninsula in Russia. Essentially made up of arctic landscapes, the boreal forests (taiga) and the arid plains (tundra) follow one another. The forests of taiga are principally made up of conifers, dominated by larch, spruce, fir and pine. The tundra is a landscape of lichens and

cropped vegetation, a source of food for the reindeer. The coast, where the big towns are located, benefits from a more temperate climate. To the north, the coast is not covered with ice-sheets because of the effect of the warm current of the Gulf Stream from the south of the Atlantic. Islands and fjords dominate the coastal landscape. The Gulf of Bothnia is covered with ice all winter. A long chain of mountains follows the coast from north to south and separates the areas, which were previously used by nomads to herd reindeer.

Geography

Principal towns (Sami / Norwegian[1], Swedish[2], Finnish[3] or Russian[4])

Aanaar • Inari[3], Enare[2]
Bådåddjo • Bodø[1]
Giron • Kiruna[1,2], Kiiruna[3]
Guovdageaidnu • Kautokeino[1,2], Koutokeino[3]
Jåhkåmåhkke • Jokkmokk[1,2], Jokimukka[3]
Kárášjohka • Karasjok[1,2], Kaarasjoki[3]
Leavdnja • Lakselv[1]
Lujávri • Ловозеро[4] (Lovozero), Luujärvi[3]
Luvlieluspie • Östersund[2]
Muurman • Мурманск[4] (Mourmansk)
Ohcejohka • Utsjoki[1]
Råante • Trondheim[1]
Romsa • Tromsø[1]
Snåase • Snåsa[1]
Váhtjer • Gällivare[1], Jällivaara[3]

Regions (Sami / English)
Åarjel • South
Ahkkel • Akkala
Anarâš • Enare
Bihtán • Pite
Darjje • Ter
Davvi • North
Gieldda • Kildin
Giema • Kemi
Julevu • Lule
Kainuu • Kainuu
Nuorta • Skolt
Ubmi • Umi

Geographical names

"Sabmá suolggai Sámieanan. Duottar leabbá duoddar duohkin, jávri seabbá jávrri lahka."
(Isak Saba, Sámi poet)
"Sápmi stretches gently. Mountain after mountain, lake after lake."

Sápmi, *shepherds of the Boreal Lands*

The reindeer, a symbol of the traditional lifestyle of the Sámi

Sámegiella

The Sami language is a group of 12 Finno-Ugric linguistic variants, belonging to Finnish (six are still active, three are in serious danger of extinction and three are extinct). Three groups are dominant (to the south, Ume and southern Sami; Pite, Lule and Sami to the north; to the east, Enare, Skolt, Akkala, Kildin, Ter, Kemi and Kainuu). Significant differences exist between these three linguistic groups. Inter-comprehension is difficult, if not sometimes impossible. The variants of Akkala, Kemi et Kainuu are extinct and those of Ume, Pite and Ter are in serious danger of extinction. Northern Sami is the most common variety and is often used for radio programmes as well as in numerous publications. It is becoming the language of communication of the Sámi people.

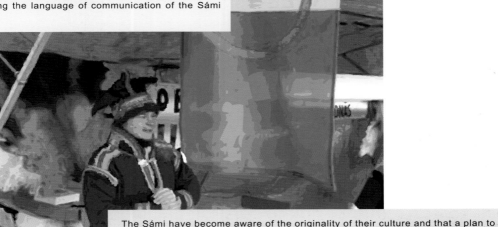

Sámi trader in traditional dress, posing in front of the flag

The Sámi have become aware of the originality of their culture and that a plan to safeguard it is necessary. Proud of an identity often classing them as a primary nation, they are now organised to better defend their interests and those of their land. Even if relations were already possible between Sámi repatriated among Sweden, Norway and Finland, it is only a couple of decades since contact was established with Sámi in Russia, after years of long isolation. The Sámi are legally protected and benefit from an area of administration, which is dedicated to them. However, in Sweden the farmers and the forestry companies call into question the right to reindeer grazing. Only 10% of the population herd reindeer, often contrary to common assumptions.

Politics now

Gagauzia, the *Christian Turks of Europe*

The Gagauz flag is blue upon which is placed the head of a red wolf. The light blue is the traditional colour of the Turks and the Mongols. The head of the wolf recalls the 11th century Cuman Empire, a Turkish-speaking people who originated from the edge of the river Volga and who emigrated to Europe, from whom the Gagauz are descended.

Gagauzia is a Turkish region of Moldova and the Ukraine. It proclaimed itself the Republic of Gagauzia in 1991, following which the Gagauzians quickly obtained the rights to be a part of Moldova, allowing them to use their language in an autonomous region.

A Turkish people of the Oghuz tribes, they distinguish themselves from Turks through their religion. Indeed, Christianised during their settling in Bessarabia during the 19th century, the Gagauzians are Orthodox Christians and speak an Altaic language that is quite different from Turkish. The Gagauz are little publicised. Alternatively under Moldovan and Russian administration, they revolted when the Soviet Empire collapsed in the 1990s. In 1991, an independent leader, Stepan Topal, was elected president of the "Gagauz Republic". After proclaiming its independence, at the same time as the Russians of Transnistria, Moldova was obliged to find a compromise with the Gagauz to retain its sovereignty, while granting a statute of autonomy to the region and making the Gagauz language official. At the time the republic was created, all the towns which were populated with more than 50% of Gagauz were included in the territory. Referenda were held in areas that were more disparately populated.

Today, relations with the central authorities remain very tense. The results of elections are the subject of open conflicts between Moldovans and the Gagauz. Dumitru Croitor, governor from 1999 to 2002, resigned, having been subject to much pressure. Despite their relative distance from Turkey, the Gagauz maintain links with their cousins of Asia Minor. The Turkish government created a Turkish cultural centre and a library in Gagauzia.

Identity card

Names: **Gagauz-Yeri**[1], **Găgăuzia**[2], **Гагаузия/ Gagauziya**[3] (Gagauzia)
Population: **155,700 inhab.** (2005)
Area: **1,832 km²**
Languages: **Gagauz**[1] (Gagauz), **Română**[2] (Romanian/Moldovan), **Русский/Russkiy**[3] (Russian) *(official)*
Number of native speakers: **140,000**[1]
State of guardianship: **Moldova**
Official status: **Autonomous region in Moldova**
Capital: **Komrat**[1], **Comrat**[2], **Комрат/Komrat**[3] (Comrat)
Historic religion: **Russian Orthodox Christian**
Flag: **Kökbayrak** (Blue Flag)
Anthem: **Gagauziya Milli Marşı** (Gagauzian National Anthem)
Motto: **None**

Brief history

Even if the history of the Gagauz is rich, especially in regards to their migration until their settling at the start of the 19th century on the banks of the Black Sea, the most prominent event was the proclamation of independence in 1991. Inspired by their neighbours of Transnistria, the Gagauz proclaimed the Socialist Republic of Gagauzia, essentially to fight a policy of Romanisation forced by the Moldovan authorities. Appointed executive president of the Supreme Soviet, the Gagauz Stepan Topal, became prime minister of the new republic in 1991 for three years. A conflict with the Moldovan authorities ensued who approved the peaceful aspirations of the Gagauz Territorial Autonomy in 1994, recognising the territorial unity of this people. The Gagauz now run their own education system and language policy.

Gagauzia

Geography

With an area of 1,832 km², Gagauzia is situated to the south of Moldova and the south-west of the Ukraine. Comrat, the capital, is situated to the north, while the two enclaves of Copceac and Carbolia, more to the south, are separated by the Gagauz territory. The country is made up of three regions administered by the towns of Comrat, Ciadîr Lunga and Vulcăneşti as well as 29 villages. Estimated at 156,000 inhabitants, the population of Gagauzia is essentially rural. Only 40% of them live in the town. The Gagauz society is multicultural. 82.5% of the population is Gagauz, 5.2% Bulgarian, 4.6% Russian, 4.4% Moldovan, 3.3% Ukranian. These are the political consequences for the Slavic people of the former Soviet Republics.

"Kavalları keskin çaldır,
Duar halkın aydın günü."
(Anthem of the Republic of Gagauzia)
"The shrill playing of the shepherd's flute, the light day of my people is born."

National minorities and new claims

National minorities are often characterised as being communities of an eponymous state. They cannot be qualified as stateless nations, but rather as linguistic minorities. Today, several examples exist in Europe: the Swedish speakers in Finland, especially on the Åland Islands which are the perfect example of peaceful linguistic coexistence, or Hungarian speakers, minorities in many states neighbouring Hungary, who have endured their share of strong linguistic and cultural repression.

Without actually being qualified as minority people, the activists of diverse regions of Europe claim the right to more recognition. Inspired by autonomous regions having great power, they struggle to preserve their original linguistic heritage, as is the case in Asturias and in Aragon, or their cultural and historical heritage, particularly in Moravia, Silesia or in Scania.

Three emblematic national minorities and the regions seeking identity

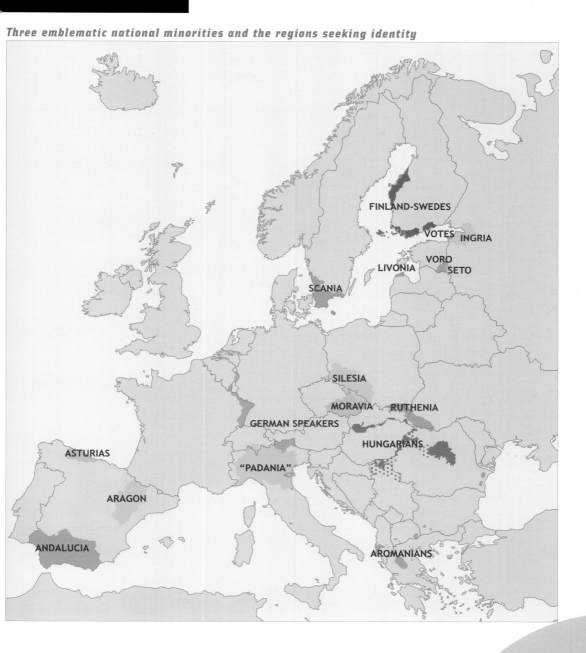

FINLAND-SWEDES

VOTES

INGRIA

VORO

LIVONIA

SETO

SCANIA

SILESIA

MORAVIA

RUTHENIA

GERMAN SPEAKERS

HUNGARIANS

ASTURIAS

"PADANIA"

ARAGON

ANDALUCIA

AROMANIANS

The Swedes of Finland and the Åland Islands

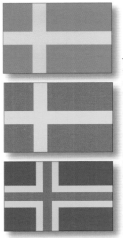

The Swedish flag depicts the colours of the coat of arms of the 14th century, which represents three gold crowns on a blue background. It has the form of a Scandinavian cross dating from the 16th century. It was adopted officially in 1905. The Swedes of Finland simply use their own flag – a yellow cross on a red background, colours of the Finnish coat of arms. The Åland Islands use a flag mixed with the traditional Swedish and Finnish colours.

The Swedes of Finland, more commonly called Swedish speakers of Finland (Finlandssvenska), represent an important part of the population of this country. Well integrated into Finland, they have numerous rights.

Today, the Swedish speakers of Finland represent 5.5% of the population of Finland. Speaking variants of the Swedish spoken in Sweden, they are able to understand each other from one territory to the other. They are one of the best protected minorities in the world.

Due to a legacy of trade between Finns and Swedes, the coastal areas of Finland are almost exclusively inhabited by Swedish speakers. Indeed, since the 16th century, the administrative language in Finland has been Swedish. Made official

in 1863, the Finnish language dominates Finnish society today. This turnaround does not prevent Swedish speakers from keeping and speaking their language of origin.

The legislation on bilingualism is very old. It dates from the middle of the 19th century. Detailing the linguistic relationships between the citizens and the state, it allows, according to certain demographic conditions, a declaration that a city is bilingual or unilingual. Thus, in Finland, the language used is exclusively Finnish or Swedish, or the two equally.

The unilingual Swedish-speaking communities represent 4.4% (principally in the Åland Islands) of Finland, while 10.2% of the population is bilingual.

The Language Act of 2003 regulates the status of both languages. They are both national languages.

Although Swedish speakers of Finland do not claim to be Swedish, as Swedish speakers they ardently defend their linguistic and cultural specificity. A political party represents their interests. It is the Svenska Folkpartiet (Swedish People's Party). It has been associated with different Finnish governments since independence, and this cooperation has enabled it to respond to the aspirations of Swedish speakers and to establish an advantageous linguistic status.

The situation of Åland Islands Swedish is noteworthy. Contrary to other Swedish speakers in the country, they benefit from a growing status of autonomy. Closely related to the history of Sweden, they participated in the war effort of the latter by paying a heavy financial toll in the Middle Ages. Occupied by

Russia in the 18th century, a large part of the inhabitants fled towards Sweden. A strategic archipelago in the middle of the Baltic Sea, the Åland Islands passed through the hands of different powers, including France and Russia during the First World War. Since the declaration of independence of Finland, the Swedish speakers of the Åland Islands demanded their incorporation into Sweden. The League of Nations decided otherwise in 1921, and Finland granted widespread political autonomy to the island. Today, the Ålandians are competent in all domains except foreign affairs, money and justice. Benefitting from a status of neutrality, Åland is a "free associative state" of Finland.

Thus, Åland has used its own flag since 1954, has the right to issue stamps and to speak the Swedish language, which is its only official language. Electing a parliament, and ruled by a government, the Åland Islands can take pride in their very advantageous status.

Åland autonomy stretches very far. Indeed, the political life of the archipelago is marked by a spectrum of different parties in Finland. The Liberals for Åland (Liberalerna på Åland), the Åländ Centre (Äländsk Center), the Non-aligned Coalition (Obunden Samling), the Åland Social Democrats (Ålands Socialdemokrater), the Freeminded Co-operation (Frisinnad Samver-kan) are the most important. However, none seek independence .

Finnish, Swedish, Sami and Karelian minorities

Åland Islands

The Germans of Eastern Europe

The German flag depicts the colours of the *Lützowsches Freikorps* (Lützow Free Corps) who struggled against Napoleonic occupation. It was used by the German revolutionaries in 1848 and became the flag of the German Confederation in this year. German minorities across Europe do not systematically use this flag and sometimes prefer local versions.

Germany, because of its turbulent and sometimes tragic history, has seen its territory evolve due to invasions, defeats and treaties. While the territory of Germany is relatively reduced today, many German people live outside the German borders.

After the collapse of the Nazi regime and the defeat of the German military, Germany's territory was greatly reduced and redistributed to the states it had plundered for many years. These redistributions did not always take the resident populations into account. The radical solution taken at the end of the war was the expulsion of the Eastern Germans of Europe. In all, 12.5 million people who had settled since the Middle Ages were directly affected by these movements.

From 1944 to 1950, Germany welcomed many visitors, now represented by the Federation of Expellees (*Bund der Vertriebenen*).

In certain regions, Germans have nearly all emigrated towards Germany, but others have stayed and these make up a mosaic of Germanic people across Europe.

Thus, the Germanic minorities are numerous at the border of Germany. The latter often don't consider themselves German but Germanic. There are German speakers in the Belgian Eupen region, in the Schleswig region of Denmark and also German-speaking Alsatians and Mosellians.

Besides these Germanic minorities, many Germans are dispersed throughout Europe. The most emblematic case is certainly that of the minorities present in Poland. The people of German origin are estimated to be between 300,000 and 800,000. In reality, only 150,000 claim to be of Germanic origin. Particularly present in Silesia, in Pomerania and Eastern Prussia, their situation since the Second World War has been critical, the weight of history being against them. They sometimes present candidates (*Wahlkomitee Deutsche Minderheit* – Elective Committee of the German Minority) for elections, performing weakly except in Silesia where their number is quite large.

In Carpathia (Slovakia), the Germans (*Karpatendeutschen*) have been present since the 11th century. About 6,000 remain there today.

In Romania, where their number is still quite high, two main communities are to be noted. First, there are the Germans of Banat or Swabs of the Danube (*Donauschwaben*), who colonised this region in the 18th century and who are approximately 70,000 in number today. Secondly, there are the Saxons of Transylvania (*Siebenbürger Sachsen*) who have for their part, been around longer. They defended the Hungarian border against Tartar invasions in the 12th century. Represented by the Democratic Forum of Germans in Romania, they hold several municipalities.

Finally, in the Czech Republic, the Germans of the Sudetenland (*Sudetendeutschen*) are spread throughout the country. They were almost entirely expelled following the Beneš Decree and are now most likely 40,000 in number.

To these communities are added the Germans of Bucovinia, of the Baltics or of the Volga who have almost all disappeared due to deportations under the Stalinist regime.

In the world of minorities, the German situation is certainly the most delicate. Indeed, the consequences of the war and the atrocities conducted by the Nazi regime have tarnished the image of Germans in the eyes of their neighbours. Although the situation has now calmed, the recognition of German minorities recalls Germany's turbulent history.

Moreover, a constant element in the settling of Germans resides in the fact that these populations often occupy an important rank on the social ladder. Aristocrats or bourgeoisie, they were often in charge of the local populations, who today remain marked by this complex situation.

Germanic minorities in Europe and linguistic variants of German

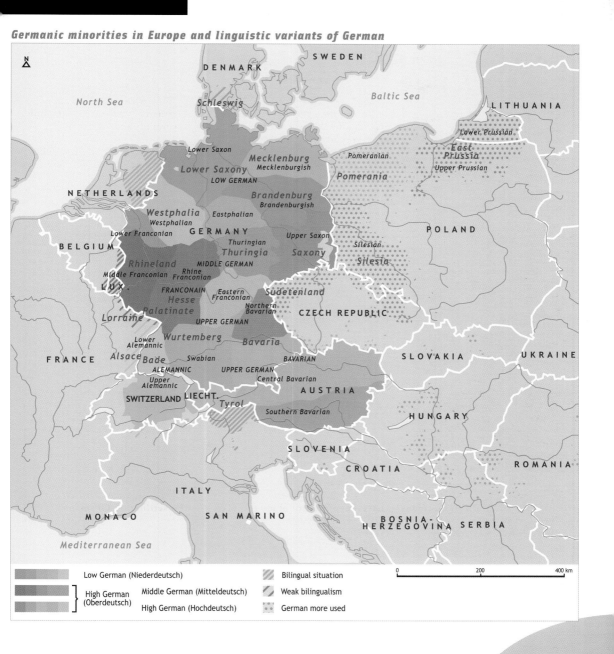

Low German (Niederdeutsch)		Bilingual situation
High German (Oberdeutsch) {	Middle German (Mitteldeutsch)	Weak bilingualism
	High German (Hochdeutsch)	German more used

0   200   400 km

The Hungarians of Romania, Slovakia...

Inspired by the colours of the coat of arms dating from the 12th century, the Hungarian flag was used in this form by the national movement against the Habsburgs in 1848. Adopted by the Republic of Hungary in 1957, it is equally used by the minorities present across borders.

The Hungarians or Magyars occupy a large part of western Europe. Hungary, as it exists today, represents just a core of the Hungarian-speaking territories. Situated between Romania, Slovakia, Austria, the Ukraine, Croatia and Serbia, many Magyar-speaking minorities wish to express their Hungarian culture in complete freedom.

But the question of Hungarian minorities in the neighbouring countries is often sensitive. With a somewhat aggressive past, the Hungarian people did not accept the cuts made in the Treaty of Trianon in 1920. It is estimated that around 2 million Hungarians live in Romania (essentially in the region of Carpathia called Transylvania), 500,000 in Slovakia and 400,000 in Vojvodina in the north of Serbia.

As a champion of minority protection, Hungary wishes to be exemplary in this area. The stated objective is that the same situation should exist for Hungarian minorities in neighbouring countries. However, Hungary's

history must be examined in order to understand this complex situation. Originally occupied alternatively by different peoples of eastern Europe (Celts, Thracia, etc.), Hungary was incorporated into the Roman Empire, then fell into the hands of nomadic people of Turkish origin: the Huns and the Avars. The Hungarians are descended from the tribes of central Asia. Settling on the banks of the Volga, these Finno-Ugric people migrated through Europe towards the Black Sea. It is only in the 9th century that they settled in Carpathia. From the 10th century they adopted a more European way of life (Christianisation and a state constitution), due to the influence of King Stephen I (997–1038).

The Magyar state prospered over many centuries before being incopoarated into the Austrian Empire in 1850. Profiting from the weakness of Austrian power, the state became a confederation made up of Austria and Hungary with equal jurisdictions in matters of internal affairs.

After the First World War, the Austro-Hungarian Empire lost 1,200,000 lives. The defeat of the empire led to the breaking-up of Austro-Hungaria. It was at this time that Austria, Hungary and Czechoslovakia were created. Transylvania was claimed by Romania, the south by Serbia and Upper Hungary by the new state Czechoslovakia.

In June 1920, the Treaty of Trianon, signed in Versailles, reduced Hungary to its present form.

This situation created conflicts. The region was shaken by strong

tensions following Hungarian claims in all the lost territories. Its territory reduced by three quarters and its population by more than half, Hungary became a homogenous state-nation, while more than three million Hungarians became minorities in the neighbouring states.

Since Hungary and certain neighbours joined the European Union, solutions for adequate protection are being sought. Article 6 of the Hungarian Constitution stipulates that "the Republic of Hungary is responsible for Hungarians resident outside of its territory and promotes and maintains their relations with Hungary". In parallel, Hungary wished to maintain its relations with its neighbours by signing two bilateral treaties with Slovakia in 1995 and with Romania in 1996. In 2001, Hungary voted for the "Status Law" amended in 2002, which grants rights to minorities in its territory similar to those granted to Hungarians in neighbouring countries. It allows Hungary to provide assistance in the territory of another state to only part of the population of that state, e.g. in schools, by granting scholarships to learn Hungarian. In fact, Hungary is becoming a deterritorialised state-nation. This law applies to all persons being "related to the Hungarian cultural heritage".

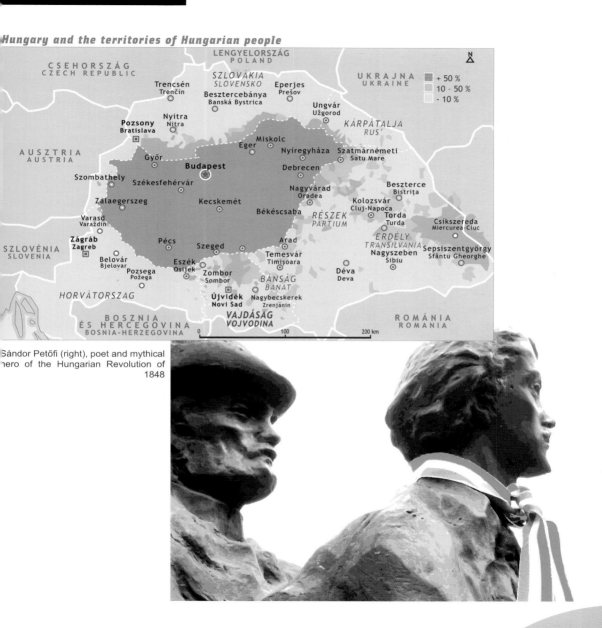

Hungary and the territories of Hungarian people

Map labels:

LENGYELORSZÁG
POLAND

CSEHORSZÁG
CZECH REPUBLIC

SZLOVÁKIA
SLOVENSKO

Trencsén
Trenčín

Eperjes
Prešov

UKRAJNA
UKRAINE

+ 50 %
10 - 50 %
- 10 %

Besztercebánya
Banská Bystrica

Ungvár
Užgorod

KÁRPÁTALJA
RUS'

Nyitra
Nitra

Pozsony
Bratislava

AUSZTRIA
AUSTRIA

Győr

Budapest

Miskolc

Eger

Nyíregyháza

Szatmárnémeti
Satu Mare

Debrecen

Szombathely

Székesfehérvár

Nagyvárad
Oradea

Beszterce
Bistrița

Zalaegerszeg

Kecskemét

Kolozsvár
Cluj-Napoca

Torda
Turda

Csíkszereda
Miercurea-Ciuc

Varasd
Varaždin

Békéscsaba

RÉSZEK
PARTIUM

ERDÉLY
TRANSILVANIA

Zágráb
Zagreb

Pécs

Szeged

Arad

Temesvár
Timișoara

Nagyszeben
Sibiu

Sepsiszentgyörgy
Sfântu Gheorghe

SZLOVÉNIA
SLOVENIA

Belovár
Bjelovar

Eszék
Osijek

Zombor
Sombor

BÁNSÁG
BANAT

Déva
Deva

Pozsega
Požega

HORVÁTORSZÁG

Újvidék
Novi Sad

Nagybecskerek
Zrenjanin

ROMÁNIA
ROMANIA

BOSZNIA
ÉS HERCEGOVINA
BOSNIA-HERZEGOVINA

VAJDÁSÁG
VOJVODINA

0   100   200 km

Sándor Petőfi (right), poet and mythical hero of the Hungarian Revolution of 1848

The Aromanians, *dispersed in the Balkans*

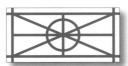

The Aromanian flag is blue and white and depicts the traditional motifs of clothing. It has not really been adopted by the population and little known.

The Aromanians, also called Vlachs and who call themselves "Armâni" are the Romance populations of the Balkans situated to the south of the Danube. Once occupying the whole of the region, with the exception of the south of Greece, today they struggle for survival.

It is a dispersed community that forms a minority population in the north and centre of Greece, Macedonia, Albania, Serbia, Romania and Bulgaria.

Apart from the problem of dispersion, these people are made up of three communities, between which intercomprehension is not always possible. These are the branches of *Fârcherotsees, Grâmouchtenees* and *Pindians.*

Not having any state, nor their own territory, like the Roma, the Aromanians struggle for recognition of their language and for their culture.

Made up of nomadic or semi-nomadic shepherds, they migrate within the whole of the Balkan peninsula. This is not without its problems regarding territories where interethnic conflicts have intensified in the last few years. They also live off trade and traditional crafts. A constantly oppressed people, their principal virtue is resisting the assimilation desired by the states that they inhabit. The emblematic figure of the Aromanian people remains Mother Teresa.

It is principally in Greece that the Aromanians situation is most worrying. An activist vas recently been put on trial for publishing leaflets about the Aromian language. Largely denounced by organisations who defend of minority languages, this situation equally touches the Macedonian minorities of this country.

Timeline

586 • First mention of the Aromanian language.

1186 • Uprising of the Vlachs against the Byzantine Empire.

13th century • Proclamation of the independence of the Great Vlachie and the Small Vlachie to the north of Greece.

15th century • Because of unattackable positions, the Vlachs resist invading Turkey.

1788 • Invasion of the city fortress of Moscopole by the Albanian army, start of Aromanian exodus.

9 May 1905 • By decree, the sultan of Turkey recognises the Aromanian population as forming a distinct ethnic minority of the Greek nation, which leads to the massacre of Aromanian people by the Greeks.

1941 • Fascist Italy occupies the north of Greece and creates an autonomous Aromanian state in the north of the country, called the principality of Pinde.

1947 • Greece dissolves the principality of Pinde.

Identity card

Names: **Armâni[1], Râmâni[1]** (Aromanians)
Population: **2,500,000 inhab.**
Area: **Unavailable** (dispersed people)
Languages: **Armăneshce[1]** (Aromanian) *(without official status except for in Macedonia)* (+ languages in states of guardianship)
Number of native speakers: **300,000 – 2,500,000**
States of guardianship: **Albania, Bulgaria, Greece, Macedonia, Romania, Serbia**
Official status: **None**
Capital: **None**
Historic religion: **Orthodox Christian**
Flag: **Hlambura-a Armânjlor[1]** (Flag of the Aromanians)
Anthem: **Părinteasca dimândare[1]** (The Will of Our Ancestors)
Motto: **Nu te-aspare o Armâne, că nu cheri ni ază, ni mâne[1]** (Aromanians fear nothing, you shall not die today nor tomorrow)

Brief history

In the Middle Ages, many Aromanians were assimilated into the Greek population up until the 18th century. This widely enforced assimilation peaked when the Greek Orthodox Church governed the hundred or so Aromanian schools founded under the Ottoman Empire. Indoctrinated as Greek "patriots", the Aromanian students lost their culture and their language. In response to this situation, the young Romanian state, preoccupied by the plight of its Roma cousins, trained Aromanian professors in 1860, who taught in more than 120 schools, 4 high schools and in dozens of churches in order to educate the populations of Greece, Albania and Macedonia. Because of this alliance, Aromanian literature could be maintained. Until the birth of communism in the Balkans, the Romanians had a policy of assisting their Aromanian brothers for more than eighty years.

Aromanians, area of people in the Balkans

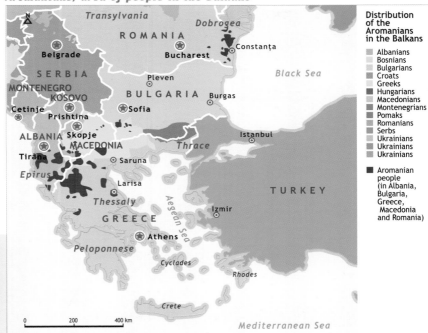

Distribution of the Aromanians in the Balkans

- Albanians
- Bosnians
- Bulgarians
- Croats
- Greeks
- Hungarians
- Macedonians
- Montenegrians
- Pomaks
- Romanians
- Serbs
- Ukrainians
- Ukrainians
- Ukrainians

- Aromanian people (in Albania, Bulgaria, Greece, Macedonia and Romania)

Historically the Aromanian territory is situated in the mountains of Pinde and Epirus, the plateau of Thessaly (Greece) and the south of Albania. Later, oppressed by

omnipresent neighbours, the Aromanians are dispersed. They occupy a wider region but their community is broken up. Particularly present in the north of Greece and in the centre of Macedonia, the majority of their villages are found in the Pinde mountains.

Geography

Towns of Aromanian population
Atena • Athènes (Greece)
Custantsa • Constanța (Roumania)
Larisa • Lárisa (Greece)
Scopia • Skopje (Macedonia)
Saruna • Thessalonicai (Greece)

Geographical names

States and regions (Aromanian)
Albania • Albania
Balcanj • Balkans
Vãryãrie / Vuryârie • Bulgaria
Dobrogea • Dobroudja
Ipiru • Epirus
Gãrtsie • Greece
Macedonia • Macedonia
Romãnia • Romania
Sârbia • Serbia

"Noi nu-avem un tatã, sã ştim iu-i tatãl a nostru, atumţea va nã videţ."
(An Aromanian shepherd)
"We have no king, but if we had one, you would see who we are."

The Iberian Peninsula, a model of autonomy

The flag of Aragon depicts that of the Crown of Aragon. It is similar to that of Catalonia apart from the coat of arms that adorns it. The Andalucian flag was designed by Blas Infante in 1918. The colours are reminiscent of the Caliphate of Cordue and the Almohad Empire. The Asturian flag represents the cross of victory, yellow on a blue background. It dates from 722 when the Asturians won the battle of Cuadonga against the Muslim invaders. King Alfonso III of Asturias adopted it as a symbol of the Asturian state in the 1st century, adding the alpha and omega, which represent eternity.

Many regions of Europe, particularly Spanish, while maintaining some specificities, wish to be recognised as true nations or, eventually, to have greater powers, as is the case for Catalonia, Galicia and the Basque Country. These new claims are emerging everywhere, particularly in Spain and Italy.

The most emblematic case in terms of claims comes from the Iberian Peninsula. In Asturias or Cantaria, Andalucia, Aragon or Castille, the activists are inspired by what happens to their neighbours.

The Asturians speak Balbi and the Aragonians speak Fabla, two Roman languages related to Castilian. The Castilians, for their part, fight to be the heart of the Spanish state. Rich in turbulent history influenced by the Arabs, the Andalucians recently received greater autonomy following popular demand. The Canary Islands have made the same claims. Moreover, the local autonomist parties there are quite powerful. One of the other characteristics of the Iberian Peninsula is the emergence of specific political parties representing local demands. These may or may not indicate a political desire for greater powers.

The only official languages in Spain are Castilian in the whole of the territory, as well as four minority languages:
• Catalan in the Generality of Catalonia, the Valencian community and the Balearic Islands
• Basque in the autonomous communities of Euskadi and in the north of Navarre
• Galician in Galicia
• Occitan (Aranised variant) in the north of the Generality of Catalonia in the Aran Valley.

In addition to these four languages there are two other languages, which do not have official status. These are considered by certain linguists as being variants of Castilian. They are:
• Astur-Leonese, spoken in the Principality of Asturias, Léon, Cantabria and Extremadura
• Aragon, spoken in the north of Aragon.

Most Spanish communities have political parties who have autonomist or even secessionist aspirations, in:
• Andalucia, where the Nación Andaluza and the Asamblea Nacional de Andalucía claim independence
• Aragon, where the Chunta Aragonesista, member of the ALE, polled respectably in parliamentary elections with 4%
• Asturias, where the Partíu Asturianista Asturias is the first to have obtained elected candidates in the different local authorities
• Canary Islands, where the Coalición Canaria comprising nationalists, conservatives and former communists, govern the Cortes Generales today
• Cantabria, where regionalist movements are emerging
• Castille, where some movements fight to represent the Castilian spirit and wish to benefit from an autonomy in relation to the central state
• Léon, where the Unión del Pueblo Leonés is starting to make significant electoral gains (more than 10% of municipal elections from 2007).

Thus, the Spanish political landscape is very diverse today, even if the two big parties won the majority of votes in the last legislative elections.

Iberian Peninsula, historical nationalities

Logo of the political forum Galeuscat, "Galiza, Euskal Herria, Catalunya", allowing Galicians, Basques and Catalans to find common solutions to fight Spanish centralisation.

Northern Italy, union of the Gallo-Italic people

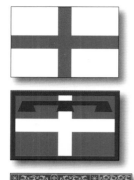

The flag of Lombardy depicts the flag of the city of Milan, the capital, which dates from the 10th century. There is a red cross on a white background, called the St. George. The flag used by the autonomists of Liguria is similar. It is the flag of the Republic of Liguria (1797–1815). The Piedmontese pavillon is a Savoisian flag, completely blue. The Venetian flag represents the lion of St Mark on the ground, symbolising sovereignty.

As seen in the Iberian Peninsula, the Italian boot is experiencing the same claims from minorities. Following the example of the Sardinians, the Friulians and the Tyroleans, some Italian regions are calling for greater recognition. However, there are some ambiguities relating to their claims.

The new autonomist claims, if not separatist, were born in the north of Italy, in the regions considered today as economic motors of the country. Italian reunification, like that of Germany, is recent. It dates from 1861. Born of very different people (Etruscians, Veneti, Ligurians, etc.), the regions that make up the country increasingly demand to govern themselves

without Rome imposing a vision of a country that is not their own. The ambiguity, in relation to these claims, is of two kinds. On the one hand, this Nordic movement is considered by certain people as a will to separate rich Italy from the poor, as well as the south. On the other hand, the most prominent party in this "fight" has been strongly criticised for joining the coalition that governs Italy.

These aspirations are not limited by these two factors. Indeed, the Gallo-Italic regions, i.e. the north of Italy, such as Lombardy, Piedmont, Liguria, Venetia, have a history that distinguishes them from their neighbours in the south.

Indeed, whether one or the other of these regions, they were integral parts of the Germanic Holy Roman Empire in the 13th century. Autonomous for a long time, in the 19th century Venetia and Liguria were finally incorporated into Austria and France respectively.

Venice is certainly the state which left the most important mark on the history of the region, becoming one of the biggest economic powers in Europe. The "Serene Republic" stretched the length of the Adriatic coast. For a thousand years, Venice remained a powerful state, until the Napoleonic campaigns, which put an end to a long historical tradition. Today, Venetian, the most idiosyncratic language of the Gallo-Italic varieties, is very present.

Lombardy was initially populated by Celts, then Germans, from which it gets its name. Little by

little it was romanised. Passing under the yoke of its neighbouring powers, it was eventually integrated with Italy. Today, it is the wealthiest region.

Piedmont, a principality from the 15th century, is not a uniform region, and it remained for a long time under the rule of its Savoyard neighbours. Piedmontese, French, Arpitan, Walser (a variety of German) and Occitan are spoken there. Italian was not introduced until later. Piedmontese, whose literary tradition dates back to the 12th century and whose teaching is not standardised, is spoken by more than half of the population.

Today, the aspirations of these last few northern Italian regions is complicating the political scenario. The Pandanian movement is trying to create an entity – "Padania" –without historical reality. This artificial region in the north of Italy characterises the regions of the Pô Valley, from which it gets its name. The Northern League (Lega Nord) has been fighting since 1991 for the northern regions to have greater autonomy. Polling well, especially in Venetia (27.5% in the general elections in 2008) and Lombardy (21.6%), the League of the North has many ministers in the ultra-conservative government of Silvio Berlusconi.

Thus, the regions of northern Italy are trapped in often ideologically unstable regionalist claims, sometimes abetted by government parties.

Northern Italy, the five Gallo-Italian regions (Emiliano, Liguria, Lombardy, Piedmont, Venetia)

Scania, torn between Danish and Swedish cultures

Created by the historian Mathias Weibull at the very beginning of the 20th century, the Scanian flag is a yellow Scandinavian cross on a red background. It depicts the yellow cross of Sweden and the red background of Denmark. It was used by the region of Scania alongside the coat of arms. Today, it is flown over many public buildings in Scania.

Scania is a region in the south of Sweden, which brings together three provinces of the same state. It is marked by an undemanding historic particularism, which binds it equally to Sweden and Denmark.

In a large sense Scania was bound to the kingdom of Denmark in 800. Made up of the four provinces Halland, Blekinge, Scania and Bornholm, it was ceded by Demark to Sweden in 1658 by the signing of the Treaty of Roskilde, with the exception of the island of Bornholm, which was returned to the Danish crown. The term Skåneland is regularly distinguished from that of Skåne. The first describes the region while the second, used officially, describes the county of Scania as a Swedish administrative entity, created in the 1990s.

The Scanians, rarely considered as a stateless nation, but rather as a Swedish region, refuse this simplistic description. Even if the stated objective of Scanian culture defence movements is not independence, they fight for more decentralisation and for the management of regional affairs.

From the 13th century, the Scanians fought against Danish absolutism. The turbulent history of this country is also characterised by a form of neutrality with regards to the two neighbours, Sweden and Denmark. During conflicts between the two states, Scanians offered asylum to soldiers.

Scania, despite this dual identity, recently saw the appearance of a party with federal tendency, the Federalists of Scania, who obtained some votes in regional elections.

Timeline

11th century • Integration of the region of Scania into Denmark by king Svend Estirdsen.

14th century • Scania is a kingdom, rex Scaniae.

1397–1523 • Sweden, Denmark and Norway unite and create the Union of Kalmar. Demark governs this collectivity.

16th century • Following the independence of Sweden and the opposition of the Swedes against the central power, wars opposing Sweden and Denmark follow.

1658 • Treaty of Roskilde, final incorporation of Scania into Sweden.

1660 • Return of Bornholm to Denmark after the rebellions, the people oppose the Swedishisation of society.

1710 • Attempted recovery of Scania by Denmark.

19th century • Creation of the first Scanian movements.

20th century • Swedish parliament refuses the proposal of elected Scanians teaching the history of Scania in local programmes.

Identity card

Names: **Skauneland[1]**, **Skåneland[2][3]** (Scania)
Population: **1,668,000 inhab.** note 11
Area: **20,010 km²** note 11
Languages: **Skaunska[1]** (Scanian) (without official status), **Svenska[1]** (Swedish), **Dansk[3]** (Danish) (official)
Number of native speakers: **600,000[1]**
States of guardianship: **Sweden, Denmark**
Official status: **Provinces in Sweden, Departement in Denmark**
Capital: **Malmö**
Historic religion: **Protestants and Lutherans**Flag: **Skaunelands flagga[1]** (Scanian Flag)
Anthem: **None**
Motto: **None**

Brief history

The rebellion of Bornholm was one of the major events in the history of Scania. In 1658, sometime after the Swedish general Printzenskiold had been dispatched from the island for marring the process of "Swedishisation", the population rebelled against its new masters. Led by Jens Kofoed and Poul Anker, the rebellion took place in the town of Hasle. Printzenskiold was defeated before the rebellion reached the seat of the Swedish administration in Rønne, located a little further to the south. Although the Swedes fled the island due to confusion and fear among soldiers, Jens Kofoed created a provisional state and sent a message to Frederick III, king of Denmark, who definitively liberated the island. An integral part of Scania, Bornholm was reintegrated into the kingdom of Demark in 1660. Swedes and Danes signed a peace treaty this same year.

Scania, the four provinces and the Isle of Bornholm

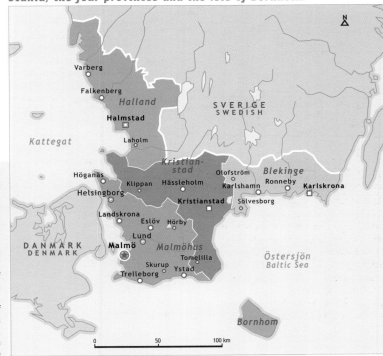

Geography

Scania is a flat land, in contrast to other regions of Sweden. It forms a buffer area between Sweden and eastern Denmark. Copenhagen is only a few kilometres away. Landscapes of plains and towns (90% of the population live in an urban zone) make up the country. This situation is conducive to the development of agriculture on very fertile grounds. The production of cereals is very important.

Scania is made up of four historic regions – Halland, Blekinge, Scania (as a Swedish administrative region made up of Malmöhus and Kristanstad) and Bornholm. The first three are situated officially in Sweden, the last in Denmark. The historic capital of Scania is Malmö.

Silesia, mosaic of central European people

Silesia uses two flags. That of Lower Silesia is made up of two horizontal bands, white and yellow, featuring a black eagle. Meanwhile, the flag of Upper Silesia is made up of two horizontal bands of blue and yellow. A shield with a yellow eagle on a blue background is found in its centre.

A region of central Europe, situated between Germany, Poland and the Czech Republic, Silesia is a model of pacifist multiculturalism.

Traditionally divided into two parts: Lower Silesia and Upper Silesia, Silesia covers an area of 45,000 km². This region of central Europe is a mosaic of people, cultures, languages, traditions and religions due to its turbulent history. Lower Silesia is populated by Silesians although numerous Poles settled there after the Second World War and its resulting wave of population movement. Upper Silesia to the east is largely a

combination of Poles, Germans, Czechs and Silesians who live together. Typically an industrial region, its economy is largely restructured and orientated towards high-tech industry. Anxious to guard its rural character, Lower Silesia traditionally turned towards agriculture and crafts, although today new industries are developing, particularly in Wroclaw/Breslau, the capital.

The Silesians are western Slavs. Over the course of the last few centuries they have maintained privileged relations with the Germans, who have mingled with the local population. While according to the last Polish census, only 173,000 people (of which a third speak Silesian) declared being of Silesian nationality, it is estimated that this should be multiplied by three to attain an accurate figure.

Because Silesian is considered a dialect of Polish, the Silesians have difficulty in asserting themselves as a people. The creation of a Silesian political party recently created a polemic in Poland, which refused to recognise it as a representative party of a minority. The Court of European Justice decided otherwise.

Timeline

10th century • Christianisation of Silesia.

1202 • Division into two entities (Upper and Lower Silesia).

1526 • Period of the Habsburg crown to the Czech crown.

1724 • Period under Prussian control (except for the south of Upper Silesia, which remains joined to Austria).

18th–19th century • Rapid industrialisation of Upper Silesia.

1922 • Division of Silesia between Germany, Poland and Czechoslovakia.

1945 • Silesia returns almost entirely to Poland but has disappeared as an entity.

1989 • Thanks to the fall of the Communist regime in Poland, several political initiatives are born.

1999 • Administrative reform in Poland: Silesia is not always recognised as a territory in its entirety (separation into three regions).

Identity card

Names: **Ślůnsk[1]**, **Śląsk[2]**, **Schlesien[3]**, **Slezsko[4]** (Silesia)
Population: **10,120,000 inhab.** note 15
Area: **48,500 km²** note 15
Languages: **Ślůnski[1]** (Silesian) (without official status), **Polski[2]** (Polish), **Deutsch[3]** (German), **Česky[4]** (Czech) (official)
Number of native speakers: **56,000 to 1,250,000[1]**
States of guardianship: **Poland, Czech Republic, Germany**
Official status: **Regions without particular status in Poland, no recognition in Germany and in the Czech Republic**
Capital: **Wrocław[2], Breslau[3]** (Lower Silesia) / **Opole[3], Oppeln[3]** (Upper Silesia)
Historic religion: **Roman Catholics**
Flag: **Ślónsko Fana** (Silesian Flag)
Anthem: **None**
Motto: **None**

Brief history

Silesian history is full of casualties. A buffer zone between Germany and the Slavic states, Silesia, while never independent, was passed under successive regimes of its neighbours. After the First World War, the referendum of 1921 had the objective to rule on the ownership of Upper Silesia, either to Germany or to Poland. It was at this time that the Silesian independent movements appeared, but they were excluded from debate. Remaining German, Silesia was almost incorporated fully into Poland after the Second World War. Two million Germans in Silesia were excluded. In the years 1970–80, it is estimated that 700,000 people left Silesia voluntarily to settle in Germany. After the fall of the Communist regime, Silesia saw the appearance of regionalist movements and parties representing the German minority.

Silesia, Upper and Lower Silesia, Lusatian and Moravian Silesia

Silesia is a region of central Europe shared between three states: Poland, the Czech Republic and Germany. It is bordered by Saxony and Brandenburg to the west (Germany), Great Poland and Little Poland to the north (historical Polish regions), Bohemia, Moravia and Slovakia to the south. The topography is varied, marked especially by the mountains of the Sudetenland and the Beskids, which stretch the length of the south border. Mount Sniejka (Śnieżka in Polish, Schneekoppe in Germany) peaks at 1,602 m. Upper Silesia is a region of mountains while Lower Silesia is principally made up of plains. Upper Silesia is essentially made up of a collection of large towns. Its capital is Opole. Wroclaw (Breslau in German), capital of Lower Silesia, is populated by more than 600,000 inhabitants and is one of the biggest cities in eastern Europe.

Geography

Principal towns
(Polish / German)
Bielsko • *Bielitz*
Brzeg • *Brieg*
Cieszyn • *Teschen*
Częstochowa • *Tschenstochau*
Gliwice • *Gleiwitz*
Głogów • *Glogau*
Hlučín • *Hultschin*
Jelenia Góra • *Hirschberg*
Katowice • *Kattowitz*
Kłodzko • *Glatz*
Nysa • *Neisse*
Opawa • *Troppau*

Opole • *Oppeln*
Raciborz • *Ratibor*
Wałbrzych • *Waldenburg*
Wrocław • *Breslau*
Żagań • *Sagan*
Zgorzelec • *Görlitz*
Zielona Góra • *Grünberg*

Regions (Polish / German)
Górny Śląsk • *Oberschlesien*
Dolnośląskie • *Niederschlesien*

Geographical names

Moravia, no to assimilation!

The Moravian flag is particularly used by movements for self-determination. The colours of the flag are yellow and red. They are inspired by the colours of the traditional Moravian coat of arms.

Moravia is a region of the Czech Republic, maintaining historic links with its German and Silesian neighbours. It is a region situated to the east of the Czech Republic and its name is derived from the river Morava, which flows to the north-west.

Initially populated by the *Boii*, a Celtic tribe, Moravia is, with Bohemia, one of the cradles of the Celtic civilisation in Europe. At the centre of Europe, the country saw the passage of many people, for example Germans and Slavs (Moravians) from the 6th century. At the beginning of the 9th century, the principality of

Moravia was born under favourable circumstances. It was under the reign of Svatopluk I in 890 that Great Moravia reached its territorial peak. It encompassed Bohemia, Slovakia, Lausitz and northern Hungary. In 906, Moravia was invaded by the Magyars. It was linked on and off with Poland and Bohemia but it was with Bohemia that its fate would be bound eventually, whilst remaining independent. It became a Margraviate fief (created to protect itself from neighbouring countries) within the German-Hungarian Empire. It lost its rights when it passed to the Germanic Holy Roman Empire from the Austro-Hungarian Empire.

After the fall of the Austro-Hungarian Empire in 1918, Moravia was integrated into Czechoslovakia, then the Czech Republic in 1993.

Today, the Moravians are aware of their particular identity and their rich history. Speaking Czech as do their neighbours, centralisation through Prague is no longer welcome. The Democratic Autonomist Union for Moravia and Silesia fights for the recognition of Moravian specificity and for more autonomy.

Timeline

60 BC • The Boii, a Celtic people, occupy present day Moravia.

5th century • The Moravians, a Celtic tribe, are succeeded by different settlements of Germanic people.

833 • Creation of Greater Moravia.

846 • Ratislav, first king of Greater Moravia.

906 • End of Moravian grandeur. The Magyars take power.

1918 • At the Congress of Vienna, Moravia is integrated into Czechoslovakia.

1939 • Moravia is invaded by Germany. Bohemia and Moravia become protectorates.

1989 • Creation of the first Moravian autonomist party.

1993 • After the split of the Czech Republic and Slovakia, Moravia is integrated with the former.

Identity card

Name: **Morava**[1] (Moravia)
Population: **4,100,000 inhab.** note 16
Area: **28,500 km²** note 16
Language: **Česky**[1] *(official)*
Number of native speakers: **4,100,000**[1]
State of guardianship: **Czech Republic**
Official status: **None**
Capital: **Brno**[1] (Brno)
Historic religion: **Roman Catholics**
Flag: **Vlajka Moravy** (Moravian Flag)
Anthem: **None**
Motto: **None**

Brief history

Moravia can be proud of having established the first true state system of the Czech Republic. Great Moravia occupied a territory larger than present-day Moravia. Having struggled against the Frankish Empire mainly to the west, prince Rostislav asked the Byzantine emperor, Michel III, to send him Orthodox priests. Thus, it was in 863 that Cyril (Constantine) and Methodius of Thessaloniki (creator of the Cyrillic alphabet) arrived in this region of Europe. The liturgical language used in place of Latin was Slavonic with the agreement of the Pope. This event marked the history of the Moravian people. It wasn't until the 10th century that the Magyar (Hungarian) invasions put an end to this powerful state of central Europe.

Moravia

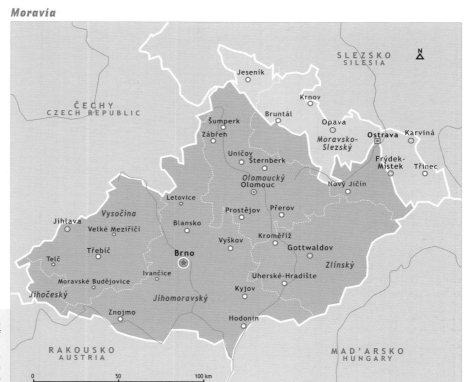

Moravia occupies the eastern part of the Czech Republic. Surrounded to the north by Silesia, to the west by Bohemia, to the east by Hungary and to the south by Austria, Moravia was, for a long time, a buffer territory between the great powers. Made up of plains in the centre, the country also contains many plateaus and mountains for example, to the north-west is the Praděd in the Sudetenland, which peaks at 1,490 m. Between 1782 and 1850, Moravia (known under the name Moravia-Silesa) also included a small part of the former province of Silesia. This part of the territory situated to the north has always been integrated. Two towns there have a privileged place: Brno, its capital, and Olomouc, a little more to the north.

Geography

Ingrians, Votes, Livonians, Võro and Seto

The Livonian flag (green, white and blue) represents the forests, the beaches and the sea beside Courland in the form of the Latvian flag. The Ingrian and Votic flags are Scandinavian crosses. The Ingrian flag depicts the colours of the coat of arms from the period where Ingrians was under Swedish domination. It was made official in 1920. The Votian flag represents the blue of the Swedish flag recalling the historical links with these people.

The Livonians, the Votes and the Ingrians are three indigenous peoples of the Baltic countries. Very few in number, today they rarely protest.

The Livonians live in Livonia, of which a large part became Latvia. Like Estonians and Finns they are a Finno-Ugric people. Today, there is a very low number of people who speak Livonian. In 2000, it decreased to only 177. However, they have populated the banks of the Baltic Sea since 3000 BC. Traditionally fishermen and cattle rearers, this peaceful people has traded for a long time with its Baltic Sea neighbours, such as the Germans, Swedes and the Danes. But in the 13th century, encouraged by the western people converting to Christianity, the Livonians joined the Order of the Knights of Porte-Glave, under Germanic rule. These "crusades" had the effect of destroying almost the whole of the

Livonian territory. Ravaged by wars against the Russians and the Latvians in the 16th century, it was only one century later, under Swedish rule, that the Livonians could express their culture. From the 18th century until 1914, the Livonians were based in Latvia and their language was no longer spoken except at the extreme tip of Courland. This region was known under the name of *Livõd Rānda* (Livonian Coast). Despite a few cultural advances, such as the creation of the Livonian Society in 1923, the teaching of Livonian in school and the creation of a monthly magazine *Livli* (The Livonian), the Germans and the Russians forbade all expressions of identity by this small people during the 20th century. Since Latvia claimed its independence in 1991, the Livonians have been recognised as an indigenous ethnic people, of which the language and the culture can be protected and defended. Also, the Livonian language has been reintroduced into primary schools in villages on the Livonian coast, as an obligatory subject. Today, 2,000 people declare themselves Livonians.

The Ingrians, who call themselves *Iźoralanian*, are indigenous people of Ingria, near St Petersburg. Immigrating from more northerly Karelia in the 14th century, they are populations speaking the Finnish language (Livonian being classed as a variant of the latter) who were under Swedish rule from the 17th to 18th century. They were almost completely expelled between 1929 and 1931 by the Soviets. In the Second World War, during the siege of Leningrad, their territory was destroyed. Numbering 17,800 in 1848, they remain only 327 today (2002). Ingrian is again taught on the Soikino Peninsula.

The Votes live in the same territory as the Ingrians (Russia). Their local name is *Vadjalain* (plural: *Vadjalaizõt*). They are, like the Livonians, a Finno-Ugric people. Exterminated by the Stalinist regime for alleged treason and cowardice during the Second World War, there were only 62 Votes in 1989 (in 1848, there were 5,148).

Ingrians, Votes, Livonians, Võvo, Setos

The flag of the Võros comes from a proposal made in 2004, representing a yellow and blue circle on a blue and green background. It is inspired by the coat of arms of the region. The flag of the Setos depicts a national pattern on a white background. It was chosen in 2003 during the 7th Seto Congress.

The Võros and the Setos are two minorities of Estonia. Like the Estonians, they are Finno-Ugric, but are considered distinct nations.

The Võros live in the official region of Võromaa in the south-east of Estonia. The Setos are found a little more to the east, in the region of Setomaa. These regions are the lowest in the Baltic countries, the highest point being Suur Munamägi (318 m). Võromaa and Setomaa border Latvia to the south and Russia in the east.

The principal basis of Võro and Seto identity is language. A lesser-known people in western Europe, they are more and more active in the promotion of their languages. Very similar to one another, more so than with Estonian for example, the Setos are distinguished by another characteristic trait: their religion. Indeed, they are Orthodox Christian. Moreover, Setos are divided between two states, Estonia and Russia. The Võros have worked largely these last few years on the standardisation of their language. From the 16th to 19th centuries, they used the veil of south Estonia in churches, schools and courts.

Võro and Seto activism is more similar to a cultural movement than to a political one and both now receive support for cultural development from the Estonian authorities.

Each year, the Võros organise a summer school while every three years a Seto Congress is convened. Despite being recognised as minority languages by the European Bureau for Lesser Used Languages (EBLUL), the Estonian authorities refuse to recognise them as being languages that are distinct from Estonian.

Timeline

1686 • Publishing of the New Testament in southern Estonia (predecessor to Võro and Seto).

1885 • Publishing of an ABC book in Võro.

1921 • First Seto Congress.

1989 • First congress of the Võros.

1994 • First day of the Kingdom of Seto.

1995 • Creation of the Võro Institute and the national epic "Peko" in Seto.

2002 • Publishing of the first Võro-Estonian dictionary

2004 • A song in Võro "Tii" (Path) represents Estonia in the Eurovision Song Contest.

Identity card

Names: **Võro[1][2]**, **Võru[3][4]**, **Seto[1][2]**, **Setu[3][4]**
Population: **Võro 70,600, Seto 33,000**
Area: **Võro 4,200 km², Seto 1,582 km²**
Languages: **Võro[1]**, **Seto[2]**, (without official status) **Eesti[3]** (Estonian), **Русский/Russkiy[4]** (Russian) (official)
Number of native speakers: **70,000[1], 10,000[2]**
States of guardianship: **Estonia, Russia**
Official status: **None**
Capital: **Võro[1]**, **Petseri[2][3]**, **Печоры/Pechory[4]**
Historic religion: Võro • **Lutheran**, Seto • **Orthodox Christian**
Flag: **Võro Rõngalipp[1]** (Võro Circle), **Seto Ristilipp[2]** (Seto Cross)
Anthem: Võro • **Linda, vaim[1]** (Flying Spirit), Seto • **Olliq suuróq S'aksa sóaq[2]** (There was a large German war)
Motto: **Võro veri ei väriseq[1]** (Võro blood does not tremble)

Brief history

Võro and Seto are two languages, remnants of an Estonian language spoken in the south of Estonia. These two languages are today in grave danger of disappearing because of their apparent similarity with Estonian. This situation is regrettable for a country that has been under the rule of another state for a long time. Due to the lack of recognition by the Estonian state, the population claim few rights. No application for recognition of the language or for the foundation of schools is likely, in contrast to events occurring elsewhere in Europe. Nevertheless, a Võro Institute carries out research, development and revitalization of these languages. Despite these efforts and a proposal for more recognition in 2004, Estonia refuses to ratify the European Charter for Regional and Minority Languages.

Former minorities, new states

In 1989, Europe was rocked by the collapse of the Soviet system. It was at this moment that many people living as minorities became independent, having been under the rule of totalitarian states. This ripple effect was not challenged by the international community and raised many hopes worldwide, hopes that were dashed a few years later by the conflict in the Balkans. The following examples are interesting due to their relative historical proximity. Indeed, we can analyse the way in which struggles for national liberty and the management of rediscovered liberty can be experienced in addition to the types of relationships with former oppressors. They also serve as an example for ethnic minorities in western Europe who, in the future, will deal with greater devolution of powers and, for some of them, independence.

Former minorities that have become independent since 1989

The Baltic adventure

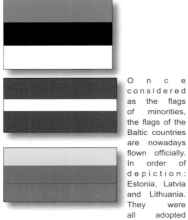

Once considered as the flags of minorities, the flags of the Baltic countries are nowadays flown officially. In order of depiction: Estonia, Latvia and Lithuania. They were all adopted for the first time in 1918 and then banned by the Soviets. The first symbolises the sky, the ground and light. The second and third are the traditional colours of the two states, which date back to the 13th and 14th centuries respectively.

The expression "Baltic countries" is an accident of language. Indeed, in the three countries regularly considered as making up this group, only two are populated with communities of Baltic origin. They are Lithuania and Latvia. The third, Estonia, is closer culturally to Finland. It is culturally and linguisticaly Finno-Ugric.

However, strong links exist between these three countries, because of their history and their cultural unity. They were part of the rise of Hanseatic cities in the Middle Ages and the influence of the three capitals Vilnius, Riga and Tallinn played an important role in the birth of a "Baltic" feeling.
The influence of the Baltic people

and that of the Finno-Ugric has been a historically undeniable fact in the region for millennia.

Prospering in their own lands and warring with their neighbours, the different peoples settled on the banks of the Baltic Sea forging the identity of the three future nations, which would twice become independent.

Incorporated into Russia in 1795, they did not obtain their independence until after the First World War. This independence, supported by the Western states, constituted a "sanitary cordon", protecting them from the Russian giant and thus cutting off its best access to the sea. In the turbulence of the 1930s, the authoritarian fascist regimes were present there.

In 1939, the USSR signed the Treaty of Non-Aggression with Nazi Germany (Ribbentrop-Molotov Treaty), known under the name of the German-Soviet Pact. From this period on, Estonia, Latvia and Lithuania were occupied by their former enemy. In 1944, they were incorporated by force into the USSR. From this date, they obtained the status of Republic of the Union. Russian plans for this part of the territory included depopulation, reinforced by the installation of administrative colonies.

The crumbling of communist authoritarian regimes from 1989 onwards rapidly spread throughout the Soviet republics. A movement for independence began in the same year. On 23 August 1989, a human chain of 560 km in length was organised between the cities of Tallinn, Riga and Vilnius to denounce the German-Soviet Pact signed fifty years earlier.

Independence was underway with the consent of the West. Referenda were organised shortly afterwards, at the beginning of 1991. A "yes" vote was carried by a huge majority: 90% in Lithuania, 77% in Estonia and 73% in Latvia.

The Soviet regime recognised their independence on 6 September 1991, three months before the dissolution of the USSR. The Baltic states would not join the Commonwealth of Independent States (CIS), which consisted of former members of the Soviet Union. Since the proclamation of independence, relations with neighbouring Russia have been complex. The Russian-speaking minorities (dating from the times of Russian colonisation) have to be considered according to the Russians to be 12% in Lithuania, 26% in Latvia and 46% in Estonia). These figures are always contested by the three states concerned.

Two million people linked hands on 23 August 1989 to form a human chain in Estonia, Latvia and Lithuania. This historic day marked the beginning of independence for the Baltic countries. In this manner a quarter of the population of the three countries connected the three capitals: Vilnuis in Lithuania, Riga in Latvia and Tallinn in Estonia. This exceptional action had the objective of denouncing Soviet occupation and the German-Soviet Pact signed fifty years earlier, named after its two signatories Molotov and Ribbentrop.

Baltic countries and minorities

Russians of the Baltic countries: minorities or former colonists?

In 2004, Estonia, Latvia and Lithuania joined the European Union. In fact, Russia has a common border with the European Union. It focused its attention on these three countries during the growth of the union. The grievances of the Baltic states with regards to the Russians essentially concerned the plight of Russian-speaking minorities of Estonia and Latvia. Access to citizenship and the status of the Russian language consolidated the grudges of a country that had difficulty accepting the collapse of the empire created under the Soviet regime. Indeed, the naturalisation of Russian speakers appears to be an obstacle in these two countries. In Latvia, for example, a large part of the population is "non-citizen", and thus deprived of political rights. Candidates for naturalisation must know the language of the country, but a large number never master it.

The Russians want the European Union to protect minorities in its member states. The international bodies believe, for their part, that the difficulties met by the Russian speakers are not as important as elsewhere. For many Estonian, Latvian or Lithuanian citizens, the Russian minorities do not really constitute a minority, in the sense that the Russians would wish to give it: these are not indigenous populations who should benefit from a particular status, as they are former colonists who arrived with the Soviet regime.

Ukraine, the Orange Revolution

Depicting the colours of Kievian Rus, the Ukrainian flag was adopted in 1918 for the first time representing the sky above the fields of wheat.

The Ukraine, formerly called "Rus" from the name "Ruthenia", was a powerful state of which Kyiv was the administrative centre. Situated between Europe and Russia, for a long time it was under the influence and the attacks of Eastern and Mongolian populations.

In the face of internal struggles and the Mongol invasion, it fell into the hands of the Polish and the Lithuanians from the 14th century onwards. Following a popular revolution by the Cossacks, an autonomous Ukrainian state was established during the 17th century, but Russia quickly annexed it. During the 19th century Ukrainian nationalist movements were born but they were defeated by Russia. From 1917 to 1920, after the October Revolution, a brief period of independence allowed Ukraine to emancipate itself from its Russian neighbour. The Ukrainian People's Republic was proclaimed. Ukraine was invaded by the Red Army shortly afterwards. The Russians coveted the agricultural resources of the country. Its nickname of "granary" explains what would be gained by annexation and Stalin took advantage so as to finance the industrial revolution.

The Russian policy with regards to the Ukraine was ferocious. When Stalin proceeded with land collectivisation and harvest requisitions, he caused one of the largest famines in history. Seven million Ukrainians lost their lives at the end of the 1930s. This genocide, called *Holodomor* in Ukrainian (extermination by hunger), left its mark. There were also deportations to Soviet camps. The Second World War was to have a strong impact on the Ukraine, first because of the Nazi invasion of the USSR. Eight million Ukrainians perished in this conflict.

However, the Ukraine gained certain international recognition in 1945. Finally being recognised for the role they played in the fight against Nazism, the Ukraine obtained a seat in the United Nations. From then on, Ukrainian sentiment was reinforced. But it was only in 1989 that Rukh arrived (a national Ukrainian movement that elects the deputies to the *Verkhovna Rada* (Ukrainian parliament). On 16 July of the same year, the parliament adopted a declaration on the sovereignty of the Ukraine and on 24 August 1991 it proclaimed independence, confirmed in December by a favourable referendum of 90%.

Today, the Ukraine is confronted by many crises, in part caused by its Russian neighbour. Recent events have shown another side to the present state of the country. Led until 2004 by Leonid Kuchma, a former communist suspected of corruption, the presidential elections took place in an unwholesome climate.

Popular pressure managed to bring about a second ballot. It is this which is known as the Orange Revolution, after the colour used by the pro-Western activists. The initial victor, the pro-Russian former prime minister Viktor Yanukovych saw his main opponent Viktor Yushchenko take victory. Largely pro-Europe, he benefitted from pro-Ukrainian votes. The charismatic Yulia Tymoshenko became prime minister. Equally gifted in business and in communication, she accused the president of corruption. She was dismissed, the president duly accusing her of corruption. This climate of doubt favoured the return of the pro-Russian camp (the Regional Party), who became the main political force in the Ukraine. Its rivals, the Tymoshenko Bloc and the presidential party, Our Ukraine, polled in second and third place respectively. The latter two did not reach an agreement and the situation in the Ukraine remains unstable. Nowadays, divided alliances are always played out between pro-Russian and pro-Ukrainian parties.

Czechs and Slovakians, the peaceful schism

The flags of the Czech Republic and Slovakia depict the Pan-Slavic colours. The first, used by Czechoslovakia, was kept by the Czech Republic. The red and white are also the colours of Bohemia. Slovakia adopted a flag already in use since the European revolutions of 1848.

The Czech Republic and Slovakia have achieved what others have failed to do: separating without war or conflict. Contrary to the social unrest of Yugoslavia, Czechoslovakia left in place two states that were recognised quickly by the international community and the members of the European Union.

On 9 November 1989 the Berlin Wall fell and with it the authoritarian regime that ruled the German Democratic Republic (GDR). Many eastern Europeans took the opportunity to escape, the Hungarians and Czechoslovakians being first. This historic event had a chain-reaction effect rarely seen in history: the fall of dozens of Communist regimes on their last legs, no longer offering the bright future that they had once promised their citizens. In Czechoslovakia, there was considerable unrest at the end of November 1989. Students gathered to commemorate victory over the Nazis who had closed the University of Prague fifty years earlier. Their celebrations were suppressed. Other demonstrations had been taking place since 1988. This suppression was enough to trigger a wave of protest, and demonstrations and strikes followed. The streets were invaded by protestors. Overtaken by events, the leaders did not have the will to suppress these attacks on their power. Power was abandoned by the leadership classes. Following this, things progressed very quickly.

Free elections led the former opponent Václav Havel to the post of president. However, during these elections, the two movements created by the Czechs and Slovakians, the Civic Forum and Public Opinion against Violence respectively, did not succeed in coming to an agreement. They briefly assembled together in parliament. The Slovakians wished to be more noticed in the name of the country. The name of "Czech and Slovakian Federal Republic" was adopted but only for a short time.

However, this liberation movement did not allow links to be maintained which, until that date, had unified Czechs and Slovakians. In 1993, the split was made official and the two nations had their own governments. After the "Velvet Revolution" came the "Velvet Divorce". However, relations between the Czech Republic and Slovakia had not broken down. In 2004, they both joined the European Union. This shows that the path to independence does not have to pass through violence and bloodshed. The authorities play on fears to create confusion. The division between the Czechs and the Slovakians took place in a peaceful manner. In fact, due to the significant transformation that the country underwent, the Czechs did not really insist on keeping Slovakia in the federation. One could say that it was the Czechs who triggered the process of disintegration. In 1992, the national Slovakian council adopted a constitution. The same year, it was decided not to organize a referendum but to simply abolish the Czech and Slovakian Federal Republic.

The economic situation of the two states was not the same. While the Czech Republic turned towards the West in reasonable economic health, the Slovakians had more serious difficulties: unemployment and weak foreign investment. However, thanks mainly to the return of independence, Slovakia was the first state of the former Warsaw Pact to officially adopt the Euro (the common European monetary unit) on 1 January 2009.

Moldova and Transnistria

The Moldovan flag, adopted in 1990, depicts the colours of the Romanian flag, overlaid with the country's coat of arms, while the flag of Transnistria is the same that was used by the Soviet Socialist Republic of Moldova before independence, often with the hammer and sickle included.

Moldova and Transnistria are linked by history but follow opposite paths. Moldova is a territory of the former USSR. A Romanian-speaking country, it proclaimed its independence after the fall of the Russian Empire in 1991. Immediately, it faced a conflict with the region of Transnistria, mainly populated by Russians and Ukrainians, who seceeded with the newly created republic in December of the same year.

In 1991, following the dissolution of the USSR, the Republic of Moldova proclaimed its independence. Romania, very close culturally on account of speaking the same language, recognised this independence immediately in the hope of incorporating the new state into Romanian territory. This explains the events which rapidly followed in Transnistria.

Indeed, Transnistria, sometimes called Transdniestria or Pridnestrovia (in Russian), is a strip of land barely 20 km wide and 200 km long, which follows the river Dniest between the Ukraine and Moldova, a state whose guardianship it is under. More than 60% of the population of this country, which proclaimed its independence in 1990, are Russian or Ukrainian.

In 1992 a conflict followed between the young Republic of Moldova and this secessionist state, who based its legitimacy on the memory of the Soviet period, despite the refusal of the USSR to recognise it a few years previously. It is estimated that this war, which lasted six months, claimed thousands of victims. The conflict between Moldovans and Russian speakers was essentially focused on the question of language. Until the independence of Moldova, the Russians infiltrated power in this Romanian-speaking republic. Independence claimed, the policy with regards to the Russian speakers was radical and the impact quite brutal. Demonstrations quickly spread and the situation escalated.

Moldova has conserved the integrity of its territory. According to the terms of a ceasefire signed in July 1992 between Boris Yeltsin and his Moldovan counterpart Mircea Druc, ex-leader of the Popular Front, which liberated the country from the Communist yoke, Transnistria broke away from the central power in Chisinau, the capital of Moldova. Since then it benefits from a strong autonomy which provisionally allows it to govern its territory without resolving the underlying problem.

Today, Tiraspol, capital of Transnistria is de facto independent from Chisinau and has a large concentration of the country's wealth. Moreover, present-day Russia based the 14th Army at Tiraspo and, on account of its proximity to Transnistria, aggravates the people so as to destabilise Moldovan power. However, one can currently consider Transnistria to be an independent state without international recognition. This small country of little more than 5,000 km² has all the attributes of a sovereign state: a flag, an anthem, a president, a parliament, an army etc.

Unfortunately, even if the aspirations of the people of Transnistria can be understood, no state, not even Russia or the Ukraine, maintains links with this region, nor recognises it. Since the 2006 referendum, organised with the support of Russia, 97.1% of voters are strongly in favour of being incorporated into Russia. Despite the comments of international observers who believe that the ballot took place under normal democratic conditions, the European Union does not want to recognise the result.

Russia guards many interests in Transnistria. It maintains a certain ambiguity as regards its intentions and uses this in the management of conflicts between it and the international community, such as in Kosovo, Ossetia and Abkhazia.

Transnistria

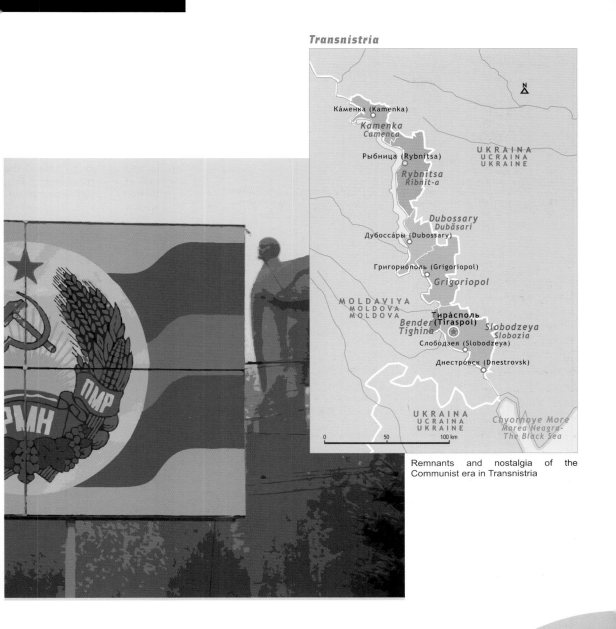

Remnants and nostalgia of the Communist era in Transnistria

Yugoslavia, soul of the Balkans

The reconstitution of Yugoslavia allowed each state to have its own emblem. None of these states re-adopted the Yugoslavian flag, which was made up of three horizontal bands of the colours blue, white and red (Pan-Slavic colours), stamped with a Socialist red star. Serbia uses a flag almost identical to that of Yugoslavia, the bands being in a different order, just like Croatia's, which carries little shields representing the regions of the country above its coat of arms.The history of the flag of Bosnia-Herzegovina is more complicated. To ensure the flag was symbolic of peace, the high commissioner of the United Nations devised a flag comprising the colours of Europe, with the three points of the triangle representing the Bosnian, Croat and Serb communities. Slovenia re-adopted its former flag, replacing the red star with the country's coat of arms. Finally, Macedonia, confronted by Greek intransigence, had to change its flag. In effect, Greece forced it to name itself the "Former Yugoslav Republic of Macedonia" and not Macedonia as it desired. Equally the country had to abandon the red flag overlaid with the star of Vergina (a present-day town in Greece) and replace it with a different version, nevertheless still drawing strong inspiration from it.

The national liberation of the eastern European people, which marked Europe in the 1990s, was not carried out in a peaceful manner in all of the states. The events that marked Yugoslavia aroused passions buried for many decades, recalling the turbulent history of the Balkans.

Occupied by the Austro-Hungarian Empire in the north and the Ottoman Empire in the south, few states in this part of the Balkans can claim to have been truly free at one time. Only in Montenegro, an independent principality in 1815, could they boast of being a sovereign state. It wasn't until 1918, following the dismantling of the Ottoman Empire in Europe, that the kingdom of the Serbs, Slovenians and Croats was created, which in 1945 became Yugoslavia, under the form of a federal state, made up of several nationalities.

A multinational state by definition, Yugoslavia has had to manage the large number of people and languages that comprise it. Although Serb-Croat writing using the Latin and Cyrillic alphabet was the language of communication (a language of the army for example), the other spoken languages of the country benefited from a particular status. These were, among others, Slovenian, Macedonian (a form of Bulgarian dialect) and Hungarian.

Tito, an emblematic figure of Yugoslavia, laid down the foundation of the new state in the struggles that the people of this country led against fascism. Quickly breaking from Stalinist ideology, the Yugoslavian regime was less authoritarian and more open than its Communist cousins of the eastern bloc. Decentralisation, reinforced in 1974, was one of the pillars of this system. Being economically backward due to an archaic system of agriculture, the regional disparities were more and more pronounced. A system of complex redistribution of wealth attempted to overcome this. However, strong tensions led to a crisis that awoke the national consciousness of the people who made up the country. It was in this context that, in 1989, Serbia wished to establish its authority over the other republics while suppressing, for example, the autonomy of Kosovo and Voivodinia. Anxious about Serbia's vague nationalist desires, it didn't take much to push the Croats and Slovenians to declare their unilateral independence.

By definition, the Yugoslavian model was made up of three pillars: Tito, the Communist Party (CP) and the army. With Tito dead in 1980, the CP having created local units and the army being under the supervision of the Serbs, this system was no longer sustainable. The wars that followed the proclamation of independence by Slovenia and Croatia would mark Europe. There were more than 200,000 deaths. Often overlooked, they require some consideration. These were not necessarily wars of independence but lasting conflicts between fringe groups of nationalists from each nation that made up Yugoslavia. In fact, the most important conflict affected Bosnia and Herzegovnia very badly, seeing the Serbs and Croats trying to divide up the country to their own advantage. The end result of the dream of the great Serbia of Milošević or the great Croatia of Tudman would see Bosnia the victim of its neighbours' appetites. Often supported by the international community, the Croatian nationalists, fundamentally anti-communist, also committed abuses.

The International Criminal Tribunal (ICT)

The ICT for the former Yugoslavia (ICTY) was established to try those responsible of crimes committed during the war, which put different communities into conflict with one another. It was established in 1993 by the United Nations to judge war crimes. More than 150 people were accused by the ICTY. Currently, nearly a third of these have been charged. Among the accused was Slobodan Milošević (1941–2006), on the grounds of war crimes, crimes against humanity and genocide. He was tried by Serbia in 2001. Other criminals will be tried, of which there is a group on trial for atrocities committed in Vukovar, which includes Serbian officers such as Radic. Today, as many Bosnians as Croats and Serbs are appearing before the ICT.

Yugoslavia, new states and communities before the war in 1991

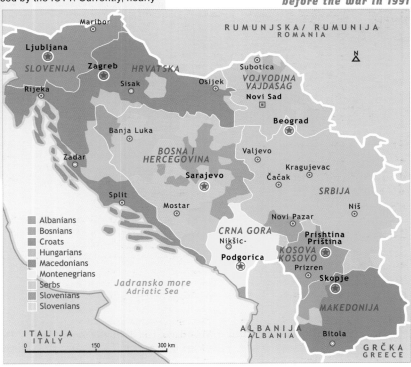

RUMUNJSKA/ RUMUNIJA
ROMANIA

Maribor

Ljubljana

SLOVENIJA   Zagreb   HRVATSKA

Rijeka   Sisak   Osijek   Subotica

VOJVODINA
VAJDASÁG

Novi Sad

Banja Luka   Beograd

BOSNA I
HERCEGOVINA   Valjevo

Zadar   Sarajevo   Kragujevac
Čačak

Split   SRBIJA

Mostar   Niš

Novi Pazar

CRNA GORA   Prishtina
Nikšic-   Prištinа

Podgorica   KOSOVA
KOSOVO

Prizren

Jadransko more   Skopje
Adriatic Sea

MAKEDONIJA

Albanians
Bosnians
Croats
Hungarians
Macedonians
Montenegrins
Serbs
Slovenians
Slovenians

ITALIA
ITALY
0   150   300 km

ALBANIJA
ALBANIA   Bitola

GRČKA
GREECE

Montenegro and Kosovo, and what followed...

Used since 1993 and adopted officially in 2006, the flag of Montenegro is red, featuring a crowned eagle. The design was inspired by the coat of arms of Nicholas I of Montenegro (1910–18).

The flag of Kosovo, close to that of Bosnia-Herzegovina, is inspired by the colours of the European flag. It was adopted in 2008. A yellow map of the country is mounted with six stars representing the six communities present in the country: Albanians, Serbs, Turks, Gorani, Bosnians and Roma

The final act of dismantling Yugoslavia occurred between 2006 and 2008. Two minorities had not been able to decide freely on their fate in the tense geo-political environment. To avoid a war similar to that which occurred in Bosnia and Croatia, the Montenegrins and then the Kosovars chose to stay their hand.

More than 55% of Montenegrin voters voted in May 2006 for independence and to abolish Serbian rule. This breakup was carried out without conflict, contrary to what the international community had feared. Montenegro was completely legitimate in wanting to become independent, although its population was a genuine mixture of people. Already organised into semi-independent duchies, then into an independent kingdom in 1910, it was annexed into the kingdom of Yugoslavia in 1918. Therefore, out of a population of 620,000, 43% are Montenegrins, 32% Serbs, 8% Bosnians and 5% Albanians. The remainder is divided among Romas, Italians and Croats. In fact the former Serbian majority has become a minority.

The outcome of this process is a guarantee of stability for Europe. In fact, the observers of the OSCE described these polls as "fair and transparent". Acknowledged almost immediately by the international community including Russia, this independence took place without any obstacle.

The accession to independence by Montenegro naturally led to an identical process in Kosovo. The Kosovan prime minister, Agim Çeku, declared that before the end of 2006 Kosovo would join Montenegro as a new state. It took until 2008 for Kosovo to eventually declare its independence.

Kosovo, in contrast to Montenegro, is not made up of a mosaic of people. The Albanians live there as a majority (94%), while the Serbs of Mitrovica represent 3% of the population. It was placed under the administration of the United Nations in 1999 following violent inter-ethnic confrontations a few years earlier. The Serbian dictator, Slobodan Milošević, attracted hatred in this part of the Balkans. Abolishing the autonomy of Kosovo in 1989, Kosovo proclaimed its independence in 1991 by an unofficial referendum, which was not recognised by the international community. A few years later the Kosovo Liberation Army (in Albanian: Ushtria Çlirimtare e Kosovës) entered into a rebellion. More than 10,000 Albanians were killed by the Serbian authorities. The terror provoked by this situation led to the exodus of many Kosovans.

This difficult period in the history of Kosovo has left its mark. Especially since the Serbs consider Kosovo as the historic heart of their nation. Indeed, in the 14th century, the Serbian Prince Lazar was victorious against the Ottomans on Kosovan ground. However, today Kosovo is well and truly Albanian. Moreover, the pressing question at the moment is whether it will become a province of Albania in the next few years. The Kosovans are considered in effect more Albanian than Kosovan (the word Kosovo is a word of Serbian origin). Before independence, they used an Albanian flag before adopting a more consensual flag.

Has Pandora's Box been opened? Living mostly in the region of Mitrovica the Serbs of Kosovo in effect demand their incorporation into Serbia. Serbia does not accept a solution that would involve the de facto recognition of Kosovo as an independent state.

In Europe, the question arises of other nationalities. After Kosovo, what will be the next independent state? Will it be in the west? Scotland and the Basque Country are preparing to organise referenda. The question remains open. In any case, it is important that this type of event takes place in conditions that allow citizens to be sovereign and to decide in complete freedom.

The Albanian flag is often used by the Kosovans, more than the new official flag. Red featuring a two-headed black eagle, it depicts the symbol of Skanderbeg, who lead a fierce struggle for independence against the Ottoman Empire in the 15th century. From the time of the first period of Kosovan independence in 2000, the blue flag of Dardania (former name of Kosovo) has been used.

Kosovo, provinces and communities

Joyful demonstration in the streets of Pristina, the Kosovan capital, at the announcement of independence

The new European deal

What is the future for the minority peoples of Europe?

A bloc to the east and a bloc to the west. Such was the world before 1990. It was the result of the Cold War, which pitted the countries allied to the United States against those allied to the Soviet Union. This situation, which lasted from 1947 to 1980, as well as creating extreme tensions and many conflicts, froze the political situation in Europe. The people wedged in this ideological and political straitjacket could only express their identities timidly. In the east, the Soviet dictatorship and its allies appeared to lead an open policy regarding the question of nationalities. Whether in the USSR or Yugoslavia, the Western world is realising rapidly that this was only a front that hid serious latent crises. The wave of declarations of independence after the fall of the Communist regimes in the east is obvious proof.

But the end of the bipolar world has not solved everything. Indeed, after realising the uneasiness that existed in the east, one sees that the conflicts, which endure in the west, have a similar nature, even if they are expressed differently. The extreme tensions in Northern Ireland or in the Basque Country are to be placed in this context. The Catalan, Frisian or Breton claims are of the same nature. The growing autonomy of the Faroe Islands and the wish of the Sámi to have municipal institutions is also an expression of this uneasiness. The minorities in western Europe desire more recognition. The means of expression are different according to each community, as well as the aspirations. Obviously one cannot put the Basque conflict and the Ladin linguistic claims on a par, or equally the future consultation of Scottish people for independence and the desire of Bretons to see their territory reunited.

However, linguistic claims are a constant throughout Europe. Every nation wishes to preserve this heritage and to make it grow. Some people, excessively crushed by centralizing states, have sustained great losses to native speakers. Indeed, in a census of 6,000 languages by UNESCO, many linguists estimate that 50% of them are in danger of disappearing by the end of the 21st century. While the report is alarming, initiatives to safeguard, initiatives to promote and initiatives of linguistic standardisation are more and more important and reveal a desire for cultural emancipation of the people of Europe.

Some people have successfully met the challenge of administrative autonomy and of assuming independence, but not everything has been resolved. A lot remains to be done so that all minority peoples of Europe can feel at ease in this new era. Even if small sections of the population are still hostile to all progress in the domain of minority rights, leaders tend to give in less and less to the ultra-nationalist ideology which prevailed not so long ago.

Europe will grow when it is equipped with institutions that allow each person to find their place. The federalist model that is emerging and gaining more and more supporters will enable stateless nations to be fully integrated into Europe. Whether they are autonomists or separatists, they will be able to decide their future and safeguard their cultural and linguistic heritage.

The European flag in the sunlight on the 50th anniversary of the European Union.
Europafest / Special summit of the European Union, Berlin

Bibliography

ABALAIN Hervé, *Destin des langues celtiques*, Ophrys, 1989

BAÑERES Jordi & STRUBELL Miquel, *Argumentaire sur les langues moins répandues*, EBLUL, 1998

BENOÎT-ROHMER Florence, *Les minorités, quels droits ?*, Éd. du Conseil de l'Europe, 1999

BIJELJAC Ranka & BRETON Roland, *Du langage aux langues*, Gallimard, 1997

BREATHNACH Diarmaid, *Mini-manuel des langues moins répandues de l'Union européenne*, EBLUL, 1998

BRETON Roland, *Peuples et États: l'impossible équation?*, Le Mot et le Reste, 2006

BRETON Roland, *Atlas des langues du monde, Une pluralité fragile*, Autrement, 2003

BREZIGAR Bojan, *Des Alpes à l'Adriatique, les Slovènes dans l'Union européenne*, EBLUL, 1996

BUSEKIST Astrid von, *Nations et nationalismes XIXᵉ-XXᵉ siècle*, Armand Colin, 1998

CALVET Louis-Jean, *La guerre des langues et les politiques linguistiques*, Hachette, 1999

CHALIAND Gérard & RAGEAU Jean-Pierre, *Atlas stratégique, géopolitique des rapports de forces dans le monde*, Complexe, 1991

CHANNON John, *Atlas historique de la Russie*, Autrement, 2003

CHARTIER Erwan & LARVOR Ronan, *La France éclatée? Régionalisme, autonomisme, indépendantisme*, Coop Breizh, 2004

CITRON Suzanne, *Le mythe national, l'histoire de France revisitée*, Éd. de l'Atelier, 2008

DAFTARY Farimah & TROEBST Stefan, *Radical Ethnic Movements in Contemporary Europe*, Berghahn Books, 2004

DENEZ Per, Bretagne, *Une langue en quête d'avenir*, EBLUL, 1998

DIECKHOFF Alain, *La Nation dans tous ses États, Les identités nationales en mouvement*, Champs Flammarion, 2000

DUFFY Sean et al., *Atlas historique de l'Irlande*, Autrement, 2002

GELLNER Ernest, *Nations et nationalisme*, Payot, 1999

GÉRÉ François, *Pourquoi le terrorisme?*, Larousse, 2006

GONEN Amiram, *Diccionario de los pueblos del mundo, de los Abadja a los Zuwawa*, Milhojas, 1996

GUIBERNEAU Montserrat, *Nations Without States, Political Communities in a Global Age*, Polity Press, 1999

HÉRAUD Guy, *L'Europe des ethnies*, Éd. Presses d'Europe, 1963

KERSAUDY Georges, *Langues sans frontières, À la découverte des langues d'Europe*, Autrement, 2001

KOTT Sandrine & MICHONNEAU Stéphane, *Dictionnaire des nations et des nationalismes dans l'Europe contemporaine*, Hatier, 2006

LABASSE Jean, *Quelles régions pour l'Europe?*, Flammarion, 1994

LAMAISON Pierre (Editor), *Histoire de la civilisation occidentale, Généalogie de l'Europe*, Hachette, 1994

LE CALLOC'H Bernard, *Les Csángós de Moldavie*, Armeline, 2006

LE CALLOC'H Bernard, *Les Sicules de Transylvanie*, Armeline, 2006

LUDWIG Klemens, *Ethnische Minderheiten in Europa, Ein Lexikon*, Beck'scheReihe, 1995

LYNCH Peredur, *Minority Nationalism and European Integration*, University of Wales Press, 1996

MACLEOD Iseabail & MACNEACAIL Aonghas, *Langues d'Écosse, une réalité à trois dimensions*, EBLUL, 1995

MALHERBE Michel, *Les langages de l'Humanité, Une encyclopédie des 3 000 langues parlées dans le monde*, Seghers, 1983

MEAUFRONT Marcel, *Le guide multilingue des communautés d'Europe*, Fédération Européenne des Maisons de Pays, 2000

MINAHAN James, *Encyclopedia of the Stateless Nations, Ethnic and National Groups around the World*, Greenwood Press, 2002

Ó MURCHÚ Helen, *L'irlandais face à l'avenir*, EBLUL, 1999

OGWEN WILLIAMS Euryn, *L'Europe du petit écran*, EBLUL, 1995

PEDERSEN Roy N., *One Europe, 100 Nations*, Channel View Books, 1992

PLASSERAUD Yves (Editor), *Atlas des minorités en Europe, De l'Atlantique à l'Oural, diversité culturelle*, Autrement, 2005

PLASSERAUD Yves, *L'identité*, Montchrestien, 2000

PLASSERAUD Yves, *Les minorités*, Montchrestien, 1998

POCHE Bernard, *Les langues minoritaires en Europe*, Presse universitaire de Grenoble, 2000

PRICE Adam, *Les dividendes de la diversité, Langue, culture et économie dans une Europe intégrée*, EBLUL, 1997

RENAN Ernest, *Qu'est-ce qu'une Nation ?*, Mille et une Nuits, 1997

SANJUAN Thierry, *Atlas de la Chine, Les mutations accélérées*, Autrement, 2007

SELLIER André & SELLIER Jean, *Atlas des peuples d'Europe centrale*, La Découverte, 2002

SELLIER André & SELLIER Jean, *Atlas des peuples d'Europe occidentale*, La Découverte, 2000

SEURUJÄRVI-KARI Irja, PEDERSEN Steinar, HIRVONEN Vuokko, *The Sámi, the Indigenous People of Northernmost Europe*, EBLUL, 1997

SEYMOUR Michel (Editor), *États-Nations, Multinations et organisations supranationales*, Liber, 2002

SIBILLE Jean, *Les langues régionales*, Flammarion, 2000

SIENCYN Siân Wyn, *The Sound of Europe*, EBLUL, 1993

TRAVERSA Anna Maria, *The Vallée d'Aoste, a range of resources*, EBLUL, 1994

THUREAU-DANGIN Philippe (Editor), *Atlas des Atlas*, Courrier International, 2005

THUREAU-DANGIN Philippe (Editor), *Cause toujours ! À la découverte des 6 700 langues de la planète*, Courrier International, 2003

VAUTIER Ben, *Atlas des futures nations du monde*, Lo Lugarn, 1998

WALTER Henriette, *L'aventure des langues en Occident, Leur origine, leur histoire, leur géographie*, Robert Laffont, 1994

WEINSTROCK Nathan & SEPHIHA Haïm-Vidal, *Yiddish and Judeo-Spanish, a European Heritage*, EBLUL, 1996

WENDT Heinz F., *Sprachen*, Fischer, 1961

WITTS Ommo & FORT Marron C., *North Frisia and Saterland, Frisian between marsh and moor*, EBLUL, 1996

YACOUB Joseph, *Les minorités dans le monde, faits et analyses*, Desclée de Brouwer, 1998

Co-authors, *Le courrier des pays de l'Est, Minorités à l'est, Variations sur la reconnaissance identitaire*, La documentation française, 2005

Co-authors, *Lesser-used languages in States Applying for EU Membership*, European Parliament, 2001

Co-authors, *The European Union and Lesser-used Languages*, European Parliament, 2002

Internet sites

Portal
eurominority.eu • **Eurominority**, gateway to the stateless nations and minority *(multilingual)*
minorityrights.org/directory • World directory of minorities and indigenous peoples *(in English)*

News
mondivers.cat • **Móndivers**, news of stateless nations *(in Catalan)*
nationalia.cat • **Nationalia**, newspaper of the stateless nations and the world *(in English, Catalan)*
balkans.courriers.info • **Le courrier des Balkans** *(in French)*
contreculture.org • **Contre culture**, Breton investigation into the French myth *(in French)*

Organisations
ciemen.cat • **CIEMEN**, International centre for ethnic minorities and nations *(in Catalan)*
eblul-france.eu • **EBLUL France**, European Bureau for Lesser Used Languages *(in French)*
ecmi.de • **ECMI**, European Centre for Minority Issues *(in English)*
gdminorities.org • **GDM**, Group for the rights of minorities *(in French)*
minorityrights.org • **MRG**, Minority Rights Group International *(in English)*
fuen.org • **UFCE**, Federalist Union of Ethnic European Communities *(in German, English, French, Russian)*
unpo.org • **UNPO**, Unrepresented Nations and Peoples Organisation *(in English)*
yeni.org • **YEN**, Youth of Ethnic European Communities *(in German, English)*

Flags
fotw.net • **FOTW**, Flags of the World *(in English)*
vexilla-mundi.com • **Vexilla Mundi**, flags of the world *(in English)*

Themes
mercator-central.org • **Mercator** (education, legislation, media) *(multilingual)*
worldstatesmen.org • **Worldstatesmen**, the leaders of the world *(in English)*
conventions.coe.int • Conventions and charters of the European Council *(in German, English, French, Russian)*
e-f-a.org • **EFA**, European Free Alliance *(multilingual)*

Languages
ethnologue.com • **Ethnologue**, the languages of the world
tlfq.ulaval.ca/axl • Linguistic conversion in the world

Notes

1/ The whole of the Breton territory, that being the five departments of the Côtes d'Armor, Finistère, Ille-et-Vilaine, Loire-Atlantique and Morbihan.

2/ The whole of the Irish territory, that being the twenty-six counties of the Republic of Ireland and the six counties of Northern Ireland.

3/ The whole of the Galician territory, that being the principality of Galicia and the border communities of the regions of Eo-Navia, Bierzo and Zamora.

4/ The whole of the Catalan territory, that being the generality of Catalonia and the Valencian community, the department of the eastern Pyrénées, the Fringe of Aragon, the Balearic Islands, the community of Alghero.

5/ The whole of the Occitan territory: see Geography.

6/ The whole of the Friulian territory, that being the four provinces of the Friuli-Venetia-Giulia region (Udine, Prodenon, Gorizia, Trieste) and the historical Friulian part of the province of Venice in the Venetia region (Mandamento di Portogruaro) and the community of Sappada in the north of the same region. Without counting the Friuli-Venetia-Giulia (province of Trieste) sometimes considered as non-Friulian, the number of inhabitants is 1,072,446 (2007) and the area is 8326.6 km².

7/ The whole of the Romansh territory, that being the canton of Grisons, historic territory of the Grisons, populated mostly by Germans, Italian speakers and Romansh people.

8/ The whole of the Ladin territory, that being the five towns historically occupied by the Ladins: Val de Fascia (Trentin), Gherdëina, La Gran Ega (South Tyrol), Fodom and Anpezo (Venetia).

9/ The whole of the Arpitan territory, that being the territories of Franco-Provençal language, including Savoy in France, the Aosta Valley in Italy and Valais in Switzerland.

10/ The whole of the Frisian territory (Frisia), that being the provinces of Friesland, Groningen (ex-Ommeland) and the region of Westfriesland in north Holland in the Netherlands and east Frisia (Kreise of Aurich, Emden, Leer, Wittmund), Dithmarschen, Friesland, north Frisia and Saterland in Germany. This does not include the historic Frisian region of Rüstingen and Wursten in Germany.

11/ The whole of the Flemish territory, that being the region of Flanders, Brussels in Belgium and the Flemish part of France (French Flanders, including the region of Westhoek and Gallican Flanders (region of Lille).

12/ The whole of the Scanian territory, that being the three Swedish provinces of Blekinge, Halland and Skåne (Scania) and the Island of Bornholm in Denmark.

13/ The whole of the Kashubian territory, that being all the districts (powiat) of Wejrowò, Pùck, Kartuzë, the Kashubian part of the districts of Bëtowò, Cewice, Chònice, Człëchòw, Kòscérzëna and Lãbórg and the towns of Gduńsk (Gdansk), Gdiniô (Gdynia), Kartuzë (Kartuzy) and Sopòt.

14/ The whole of the Sorbian territory, that being Upper Lusatia and Lower Lusatia.

15/ The whole of the Silesian territory, that being the voivodes of Lower Silesia (Dolnośląskie), Upper Silesia (Śląskie), Opole (Opolskie) in Poland, the region of Moravia-Silesia (Moravskoslezský kraj) in the Czech Republic and the district of Upper Lusatia/Lower Silesia (Niederschlesischer Oberlausitzkreis) in Germany.

16/ The whole of the Moravian territory, that being the regions of southern Moravia (Jihomoravský kraj), Moravia-Silesia (Moravskoslezský kraj), Olomouc (Olomoucký kraj), Zlín (Zlínský kraj) and the part of Moravia of the regions of south Bohemia (Jihočeský kraj) (a part of the department of Jindřichův Hradec), Pardubice (Pardubický kraj) (a part of the department of Svitavy et Ústí nad Orlicí), Vysočina (Kraj Vysočina) (departments of Jihlava, Třebíč et Žďár nad Sázavou).

17/ The whole of the Basque territory, that being the provinces of Araba (Álava), Bizkaia (Vizcaya) and Gipuzkoa (Guipúzcoa) (forming the autonomous community of Euskadi), the province of Navarre (forming the autonomous community of Navarre) in Spain, the historic provinces of Lower Navarre (Nafarroa Beherea), Labourd (Lapurdi) and Soule (Zuberoa) in the department of Pyrénées-Atlantiques in France.

18/ The whole of the Sámi territory, that being in Norway in the provinces of Finnmark, Troms, Northland, North-Tøndelag, Sør-Trøndelag and Hedmark, in Sweden in the provinces of northern Bothnia (Norrbotten), western Bothnia (Västenbotten), Värmland, and partially in Jämtland, Gävleborg and Västernorrland, in Finland in the province of Laponia ((Laponian lääni) and in Russia in the Murmansk Oblast (Мурманская область).

19/ The terms Kashubia and Sorbia describing the territories of the Kashubians and the Sorbs do not exist in English. They are used in this work in a literal translation from the terms Kaszëbë or Kaszëbskô in Kashubian or Serbia or Serby in Sorbian. The term Sápmi is used to describe the territory of the "Laponians", Laponia being perceived in a pejorative manner and actually replaced in Nordic countries by the name "Sameland" (Sámi Country).

20/ Brussels is the official capital of the Flanders region, the Flemish community and the French community in Belgium, while Namur is the capital of the Wallonia region. Surveys in Flanders tend to designate Anvers as the likely capital of Flanders.

Authors / Photo credits

This book was edited by:

Mikael Bodlore-Penlaez *(Brittany)*

with the help of a team of people qualified in the domain of identities and cultures, particularly in Europe. This diverse team consists of working activists, notably lawyers, researchers, linguists and translators.

Constantin Andrusceac *(Moldova)*
Jakez an Touz *(Brittany)*
Kári á Rógvi *(Faroe Islands)*
Grégory Aymé *(Alsace)*
Yannick Bauthière *(Wallonia)*
Estève Castan *(Occitania)*
Ghjuvà di Cirnu *(Corsica)*
José Francisco Figueiro Vicente *(Galicia)*
David Forniès *(Catalonia)*
Øyvind Heitmann *(Norway)*
Philip Hosking *(Cornwall)*
Wolter Jetten *(Frisia)*
Sullõv Jüvä *(Võro)*
Hannes Kell *(Sorbia)*
Mari Kerpuñs *(Brittany)*
Divi Kervella *(Brittany)*
Alban Lavy *(Arpitania)*
Dídac López *(Catalonia)*
Bareld Nijboer *(Frisia)*
Pablo Orduna Portús *(Basque Country)*
Michôł Òstrowsczi *(Kashubia)*
Perdu Perra *(Sardinia)*
Dewi Prysor *(Wales)*
Andrea Rassel *(Romansh)*
Sjúrður Skaale *(Faroe Islands)*
Bartłomiej Świderek *(Silesia)*
Jean-Georges Trouillet *(Alsace)*
Filip van Laenen *(Flanders)*

List of photographs:

p. 8	**Francis Till** *(2008)*
p. 11	**James Gordon** (US Dept of Defense) *(2007)*
p. 39	**Jean Pierre** *(2007)*
p. 43	**George F. Morgan** *(2006)*
p. 46	**John Haslam** *(2006)*
p. 47	**Frans Zwart** *(2006)*
p. 50	**Chris Perrin** *(2007)*
p. 51	**William Murphy** *(2008)*
p. 55	**Leo Reynolds** *(2007)*
p. 61	**Mansmith** *(2007)*
p. 65	**Christophe Ancelin** *(2007)*
p. 68	**Paolo Subioli** *(2006)*
p. 69	**Wieland van Dijk** *(2006)*
p. 73	**Roberto Cadeddu** *(2006)*
p. 88	**Lars Boludvigsen** *(2006)*
p. 89	**Leo Davidson** *(2006)*
p. 93	**Peter Jongeneel** *(2007)*
p. 106	**Jakub Friedl** *(2006)*
p. 107	**Matthias Kunze** *(2007)*
p. 111	**Álvaro Herraiz** *(2007)*
p. 114	**Mats Andersson** *(2005)*
p. 115	**Onno Falkena** *(2007)*
p. 125	**Ckaroli** *(2007)*
p. 147	**Andrew Kerr** *(2007)*
p. 151	**Ian Turton** *(2008)*
p. 153	**Frankinho** *(2007)*

Special thanks to Ciaran Finn and Elisenda Ballesté for their help with the translation into English

By the same author:

Atlas de Bretagne/Atlas Breizh, *Coop Breizh, 2011 (with Divi Kervella)*
5 ans d'actualités des nations sans État et des minorités nationales, *Mondivers/Eurominority, 2010 (with David Forniès)*
Guide des drapeaux bretons et celtes, *Yoran Embanner, 2008 (with Divi Kervella)*